ANTHOLOGY OF
MODERN SWISS LITERATURE

Edited and introduced by
H. M. Waidson

ST. MARTIN'S PRESS NEW YORK

© 1984 Oswald Wolff (Publishers) Ltd., London

St. Martin's Press, Inc., 175 Fifth Avenue, New York, NY 10010
Printed in Great Britain
First published in the United States of America in 1984

ISBN 0-312-04227-2

Library of Congress Cataloging in Publication Data
Main entry under title:

Anthology of modern Swiss literature.

   Bibliography: p.
   1. Swiss literature—20th century—Translations into
English. 2. English literature—Translations from
foreign languages.   I. Waidson, H.M.
PN849.S92A57   1984   808.8'99494   84–40341
ISBN 0-312-04227-2

CONTENTS

Rhaeto-Romansh:

EDITOR'S NOTE

My thanks are due to Mrs Ilse R. Wolff whose support as publisher made this undertaking a reasonable possibility and encouraged me to go ahead with the project. I must also express my gratitude to Mr Benoît Junod, Cultural Counsellor at the Swiss Embassy, London, for his practical assistance, his advice and enthusiasm which have been so encouraging to me. I should further like to put on record my appreciation of the specific guidance and helpful support of Pro Helvetia, in particular of Dr Paul Kamer. Again, thanks should go to Mr Raffael Ganz for his helpful stimulus and also to that of a number of other authors such as Mr Maurice Chappaz, Dr Herbert Meier, Professor Adolf Muschg, Mr Werner Schmidli and Mr Jörg Steiner, who have at various times given their comments and reactions in matters concerning Swiss writing. For her continuing support I am much indebted to Jean Waidson.

Professor Raymond Tschumi, Mr Junod and Professor Yves Bridel have made major contributions by their suggestions and proposals in the context of literature written in French. The verse and prose from Italian-speaking Switzerland has been chosen by Miss Raffaella Ferrari. I am grateful again to Mr Junod and Dr Kamer for their very necessary guidance in the Rhaeto-Romansh items.

Except where otherwise indicated, the translations from the German are mine. Thanks are due to Dr Ian R. Hilton for his rendering of the verse by Herbert Meier. The poetry in the French language has been translated by Professor Roy C. Knight. I am also very grateful to Roy Knight for his revision of my draft translations of the French prose passages and stories. The contributions in Italian have been translated in the main by Miss Ferrari and Dr June Salmons, to whom a debt of gratitude is owed. Of the Rhaeto-Romansh pieces, the translations by Mr John B. Avery have been specially prepared for this anthology. Mrs Gillian Evans is to be thanked for her assistance in the earlier stages of the preparation of the typescript.

The material that follows consists of verse and prose. The prose items are for the most part either short stories or passages from longer narrative works. It was

1

decided not to include excerpts from drama, but to let playwrights be represented by passages either of their poetry or their prose, for the purpose of this volume. It is hoped that the volume may play a constructive part in spreading interest in contemporary Swiss writing among readers of English.

Finally, I should like to acknowledge Mr Junod's invaluable help in the compilation of the Biographical Notes.

H.M. Waidson

The publishers wish to add their own grateful thanks to the *Pro Helvetia* Foundation for their support in the production of this book.

INTRODUCTION

After the outbreak of war in Europe in 1939, Switzerland looked forward to an uncertain future. As time went on neutrality could be precariously maintained, and in 1941 Walter Muschg, the Basle Germanist, wrote two articles expressing his views on the situation of his country. He noted[1] that Switzerland had participated with uncommon vigour in the process of nineteenth century industrialization and that this had brought to the country buoyant economic conditions and to its mechanical engineering firms world repute; the construction of the St. Gotthard railway had guaranteed a key position to Switzerland in the industrial age. 'Today it is a highly industrialized country, many people say, an over-industrialized country. . . Because of this we are, for better or for worse, bound up with the world economic situation.' Writing again a few weeks later,[2] Muschg asked what the perspectives were for the country's future. Now, in 1941, Switzerland was seen as 'a tiny island of freedom lying within a continent that is in the control of the Axis powers'; what was more, Switzerland contained within its borders a group of German language speakers who had not been occupied by German military power. If Germany and Italy were to win the war, the Swiss might have the alternative of becoming incorporated into the intellectual and economic structure of these régimes, or of hoping to be able to continue to resist annexation. If Britain and America were to be victorious, Muschg considered, that would leave Switzerland as the only European country to have been spared the ravages of war. In any of these eventualities, the Swiss people would be in a position that signified the end of their style of life as they had known it hitherto. Muschg described what lay behind them as 'Seldwyla happiness', a largely unmerited, unstable and casually acquired good fortune as portrayed in a number of Gottfried Keller's Seldwyla stories. The provincialism, in a good and a bad sense, of Switzerland in earlier days entailed membership of a larger entity whose centre lay well outside and beyond the local homeland. This relationship to a larger cultural unit, through the languages shared with Germans, French

3

and Italians, had brought with it an incalculable enrichment to Swiss life. The big nations outside could be seen as possessing the superior intellectual and material power, and with this power went a responsibility that the small country did not wish or was not able to take over. Swiss cultural and economic life had up to now taken place in a happy collaboration with the neighbouring states; but 'the naive neighbourly relationship of the past no longer exists'. For Muschg the future offered at this point four possibilities, three of which he would like to reject. One available option would be to capitulate before the big powers and the fate that would imply; a second possibility would be to settle on the Swiss island as European hermits. Another undesirable outcome after the war would be for her powerful neighbours benevolently to leave Switzerland to be preserved as a curiosity, as 'the nature reserve of a dying Europe', as just a tourist attraction. However, there might also be a more positive possibility: no absolutely certain possibility, 'only a hope, indeed rather a miracle: the birth of a new Switzerland', an entity that would have the vitality to be able to maintain itself from its own inner resources.

Already in 1935 Max Frisch, as a visiting Swiss journalist, had expressed himself in critical terms with regard to what he saw of National Socialist Germany.[3] During the Second World War itself, he wrote ten years later,[4] the Swiss people had not experienced the war directly, and in some respects their role had been comparable to that of the chorus in a Greek tragedy. Their destiny appeared as 'the emptiness between war and peace', as a condemnation to not being quite there, 'impotence in apparent good fortune'. If the Swiss were to reprove the Germans for not having been openly critical of Nazi policies before 1945, the Swiss themselves could likewise be blamed for tolerating their own government's censorship measures which, for example, had prevented knowledge of massacres being made available to the Swiss people during the war itself.[5] But the fate of Switzerland is never identical with that of Germany, even though it may be chained to it.[6] In Germany at Easter 1946, Frisch responds, often with some indignation, to comments he has heard there. The Swiss, he points out, were prisoners within their country for seven years and suffered from this constriction. For the whole of the war-time the Swiss had to reckon with the thought that they too might be invaded and overrun. Now, in 1946, Switzerland was a land of plenty, certainly in German eyes, 'with butter and cheese, with Matterhorn and freedom which grows on the Alps, with chocolate, with coffee and bacon'.[7]) A little later Frisch relects on the need for an international outlook; this alone can preserve the world, and its spirit is to be found at its most vigorous among the small peoples, such as the Scandinavians, the Dutch and the Swiss.[8] But all the same, Switzerland cannot exist, at least not in the long run, without Germany – nor without France and Italy.[9]

In an essay of 1954[10] Frisch looked critically at the position of Switzerland, comparing and contrasting its role at that time with the Switzerland of 1939, when the National Exhibition allowed the Swiss people to become more fully aware of their identity and problems as a nation; they could visualize themselves as a democracy that was threatened on many sides by anti-liberal régimes, they could be reminded of their particular situation in a plurilingual state, and of the large measure of autonomy possessed by the local communes. The National Exhibition provided the nation with a mirror in which it could gratefully recognize its identity. Whereas Nazism and Fascism were felt to be the enemy in 1939, now in the 1950's Communism was regarded as the major, indeed erroneously as the only opponent of a Swiss style of life. American anti-communism would offer no protection to Swiss identity; the American hope for protection by means of nuclear weapons was not our hope. Frisch's diagnosis of Switzerland in the 1950's is admonitory. Its business-men have been content to pursue their best advantage, so that they were coming to be known internationally as the 'nouveaux riches'. He denies that there is a Swiss way of life that is both modern and Swiss; American influence has supervened. Swiss politicians are lacking in imaginative leadership; politics have become a matter of business. Frisch persuades himself to be hopeful; Switzerland is not to be a museum or idyllic backwater, but a small and active land that belongs to the world. Let there be the vision to set about creating a new city!

In the years that followed, Frisch expressed himself with added disillusionment about the way he believed his country was going. The Swiss were afraid of anything new; people with original ideas needed to emigrate if they hoped to put them into practice; the financial boom was making people less willing to take risks.[11] The title of another essay is a complaint: 'Switzerland is a country without Utopianism'.[12] In his speech on being awarded the Schiller-Prize of Baden-Württemberg in 1965, he comments that Schiller's *Wilhelm Tell* is a flattering representation, and that 'we, the real Swiss, have never acted in the spirit of German idealism nor ever will'.[13] However, Switzerland may well have never had so many talented writers as today; the young generation do not write about the recent past of their country, and are seen as apolitical in comparison with many of their contemporaries in Germany. It could be contended that Frisch set an example of a type of political commitment which a number of younger authors eagerly followed, especially in the late 1960's and early 1970's. Frisch certainly sympathized with the demonstrations of students and others in Paris and Zürich, as emerges from his *Tagebuch 1966-1971*. At much the same time he looked critically at the way the Swiss people and their authorities treated immigrant workers.[14]

Friedrich Dürrenmatt has probably made somewhat less frequent direct comment on his country and countrymen than Max Frisch. In 1969 he published his extended essay *Monstervertrag über Gerechtigkeit und Recht* which contains reflections on the role of Switzerland in a world dominated by super-powers. 'The ideology of Switzerland consists in her taking up a passive position.'[15] Switzerland, he goes on here, can be seen as a super-wolf which by declaring itself as neutral, takes on a role as super-lamb; it is a super-wolf that proclaims to be without aggressive intentions towards other super-wolves. Switzerland is said to have a bad conscience because she claims to be a lamb and thereby appeals to the humane feelings of the wolves, and endeavours to make herself useful to them (for instance, through the Red Cross organization). But she is also afraid because in reality she is a wolf, though such a little one that she is 'constantly afraid of being torn to pieces by other wolves'. Dürrenmatt asks what particular qualities make Switzerland merit being defended, and replies sceptically to his own question. The big banks and the armament factories can be justified more on grounds of economics than for any intellectual or cultural reasons. The freedom of the Swiss individual is sacrificed to the independence of the state: 'The Swiss has to present himself as a wolf in sheep's clothing if he want to be a good patriot'. He has to be an 'obedient democrat'. Dürrenmatt is critical, but at the same time expresses his feelings of attachment to Switzerland:

> I am not at all embarrassed to be Swiss, just as little as I should find it embarrassing to have to be French, German or Italian, etc. Indeed I am Swiss with a certain passion. I like living in Switzerland. I like speaking Swiss German.[16] I like the Swiss, and like scuffling with them. I find it difficult to imagine myself working anywhere else.
>
> I know that I am bound to Switzerland by emotional ties, but I also know that Switzerland is only a state and nothing more, that its constitution, its social and economic structure and the people who comprise it have their faults; that finally many of the things for which we are admired abroad are not as they seem, for instance the collaborative living together of people of different languages: they do not live co-operatively together, they live separately side by side.[17]

A good thing about Switzerland is that it is a small state, and consequently it is not concerned to win a war, but to survive it.

Dürrenmatt expresses himself in comparable terms in an essay of 1976-77,[18] adding further considerations. Here he does not see himself as suffering from 'discontent with the small state' (a reference to the title of Karl Schmid's book[19] with its thesis that a number of Swiss writers have had problematic relationships with their own country on account of its being a 'small state'); he is glad to be a Swiss, even if Switzerland has become 'too large a small state'; it has become the eighth largest industrial nation in the world, and should set an example to other powers, for all of them are subject to comparable difficulties. Switzerland should abolish her army, since if she remains a neutral country, this army becomes 'damned expensive folklore'. The only genuine political task that is still left to us is the democratization of the state, which is interpreted as taking counter-measures against the increase of the state's power through bureaucracy, which in its turn has become inevitable because of the increase in population and the growing complexity of technology. Dürrenmatt's reflections on Switzerland's role during the Second World War, in *Stoffe I-III* (1981) are for the most part sombre and critical. In predicting the future, he foresees Switzerland as going along with world tendencies. 'The law of the large numbers' will lead to an increase in criminality and aggression, to demands for more vigorous laws in the name of security, to a return to a conservative approach to social customs (for instance with a renewed emphasis on marriage), and to an ever increasing poverty.

> We are moving towards hard times, that is, if we survive. If. But perhaps they will be better, more humane times. . . In the end there is still the threat of the downfall of humanity. . . For us, the worst alternative, but for life and for this planet, perhaps the best. . .
> But wherever we may drift, to a river-bank that saves us or towards the cataract that destroys us, one way or the other, after the course of all history, whether natural or unnatural, man will have been something unique, monstrous and wonderful.[20]

If some Swiss authors have regretted the restricted size of their country, this will also be associated with the material problem of making a living. Anyone who writes in English may hope to find readers in America and the rest of the English-speaking world in addition to a circle within Britain itself. A book that is published in Germany, France or Italy may be expected to appeal to a reasonable proportion of the inhabitants of these sizeable countries and to a fair number of readers elsewhere in the world. But if a Swiss author depends upon his fellow-countrymen alone (as he had to do between 1939 and 1945) for sales of his books, he is inevitably very much more restricted than his colleagues in France, Germany and Italy. Hans Morgenthaler (1890-1928) complained in a poem 'Dichtermisere' ('A poet's wretched condition'):

> I have a dog's life!
> I shall never regain health that way!
> That's what it's like in free Switzerland:
> Wretchedly narrow and no market for books. . .[21]

Kurt Marti quotes these lines in his book on 'Switzerland and her Writers – the

Writers and their Switzerland'.[22] He contends that it was only with the advent of the First World War that German-Swiss authors felt that they needed to differentiate themselves seriously from their colleagues in Germany itself. During the First World War art and literature of a lively, cosmopolitan style flourished, whereas from 1939 to 1945 refugee authors living in Switzerland were forbidden to publish and had to live quietly. Marti maintains that some Swiss authors were afraid of possible competition from refugee writers, and that refugees needed healthy bank-accounts in order to be welcomed in Switzerland. (Walter Matthias Diggelmann's novel *Die Hinterlassenschaft* (1965) centres upon a young man, David Boller, who discovers that the man who was thought to be his father was in fact his grandfather, and that his parents had been refused permission to enter Switzerland from Germany.) After 1945 plays and other works by Frisch and Dürrenmatt were the first literary exports from Switzerland to Germany, and they paved the way for an increasing number of Swiss authors to find publishers outside Switzerland itself, while many Swiss publishers had active links with markets beyond Switzerland. Eugen Gomringer's 'konstellationen' of 1953 marked an international trend in concrete poetry. But one of the most distinguished authors of French Switzerland, C.F. Ramuz, had to appeal for a donation of 2,000 francs to enable him to afford a final operation before his death. Frisch, in drawing attention to this fact, reflects upon what he calls the wretched position of writers, intellectuals and artists in Switzerland unless they happen to be able to be of service to industry; the position is wretched, 'at least in comparison with the average prosperity of our country'.[23] Paul Nizon has investigated the problem of cultural and material narrowness in his *Diskurs in der Enge*, with particular emphasis on the visual arts as well as on literature.[24] Kurt Guggenheim, however, is eloquently prepared to accept life in Switzerland as it is in its everyday limitations, at least as a positive basis of comparison and contrast with the imagined, ideal Switzerland which more discontented critics look to.[25] And E.Y. Meyer, in his address for the 1 August celebrations in Pratteln in 1976,[26] is more accepting of the status quo than had been Frisch on a comparable occasion in 1957. None the less Meyer puts forward his belief that the need in the present was not for any nostalgic celebrations of past highlights in national history, but of courage to face novelty. It is the case, he goes on, that the major indication here is that Switzerland prefers to avoid risks, since being the second richest country in the world, she is therefore the second most fearful country in the world. Banks and insurance companies flourish to an extent hardly equalled elsewhere. Although it would be foolish to take unnecessary risks, it is just as wrong to live with trust only in the army, the civil defence systems, the banks and the insurance firms. Undue avoidance of taking risks will lead to an impoverishment of creative resources. No doubt many, perhaps most, of these Swiss authors' admonitions to their countrymen may be usefully borne in mind by citizens of other lands; these problems are not unknown elsewhere in the world.

For Yves Bridel, writing in 1970, the course of the literature of French Switzerland has been 'the way of an emancipation'.[27] He describes the French-Swiss writer of the nineteenth century as being liable to two temptations: either to become absorbed into French literature or to become a Swiss writer using the French language. There was, however, Bridel continues, no cultural centre or personality that was strong enough to establish a tradition; neither Geneva, Lausanne nor Neuchâtel could be effective focal points, for the significance of Geneva was based on its political and religious traditions, not on a literary one, and the cultural élite directed their attention to Paris. Between 1920 and 1945 a 'real revolution' took place in this respect, with French-Swiss literature being acknowledged as a fact in Paris. 'Our authors write today (1970) above all with the intention of giving expression to their vision of the world, without in most cases caring whether their work is "French-Swiss" or not.' How far do such writers as Jaccottet, Bouvier, Haldas, Borgeaud and others still feel that the question of an inner relationship to French Switzerland is relevant? For most of such writers 'are concerned with the aesthetic quality of their works, with their meaning and style. . .'

'The domination of Paris is permanent, and her arbitration in the matter still impresses those French Swiss who are interested in literature', Jean-Pierre Monnier wrote in 1975.[28] He argued that whereas contemporary French-Swiss authors have established themselves as writers independent of Paris fashions and creators of an art of universal provenance, the majority of readers from French Switzerland only expected of these authors 'the expression of a certain particularism in books portraying the people of the Valais, Vaud and the Jura'. Apart from the sense of separation felt by French Swiss from Paris, Monnier notes that Swiss federalism 'often leads to isolation, local rivalries and evident fragmentation. . .' Edmond Jaloux is quoted as defining the originality of French-Swiss literature as lying in its particular perspective of 'psychological insularity' or of 'moral solitude'. After the end of the war in 1945 Monnier sees French-Swiss writing as conscious of a feeling of inferiority because Switzerland had not been actively involved in the war, and had thus foregone the sense of being in the mainstream of historical events. Having been spared 'in this little hollow among the rocks of devastated Europe', authors needed to look afresh at their heritage, to which they owed their preservation and which, they felt at the same time, had 'dispossessed' them; and to re-examine the concept of neutrality, whose virtues they could no longer accept. But if Paris' traditional priority was confirmed for French-Swiss intellectuals immediately after the war, by 1973 the situation had very much changed, Manfred Gsteiger reports;[29] this was the year of the award of the Goncourt Prize to Jacques Chessex.

9

Etienne Barilier[30] opens his essay on 'Littérature romande' by maintaining that, having not been involved in two world-wars, Switzerland has only known peace and prosperity in the twentieth century, and that this may lead to the feeling that the country is deprived of reality, or at least of the reality of war and wretchedness. He describes Switzerland as undeniably prosperous and economically active, but with a marginal position in contemporary history. This is associated with a problem of identity, which Barilier argues is more acute for French-Swiss authors than for those Swiss writing in German: 'In each sensitive individual, the uncertainty as to his identity and the doubt about his legitimacy arouse a certain power of interrogation. He who is not sure of existing questions existence'.

In his *L'Etat de Poésie. Carnets 1979*[31] Georges Haldas is concerned primarily with fundamental questions of religion and literature, against the background of some everyday, local impressions. French-Swiss identity is not a main theme of these aphorisms and meditations, though he does express his will to independence of a number of phenomena that he considers to be ephemeral or lacking in fundamental significance. On the concept of a native country, he writes (p.83):

> Native country? Unknown to me. Country – in the sense of *our* country – unknown to me. But beings, yes, moments, places. As revealers of the essential, the universal. Not as a particular native country, as 'this is our country'.

And on his relationship as an author to France (p.130):

> I have neither the *brio* nor the wit nor the degree of abstraction that are needed to please the French. Nor this conservatism . . . beneath appearances of perpetual fault-finding . . . I shall not please the French. And shall do without their approbation.

Karl Schmid's *Unbehagen im Kleinstaat* ('Uneasiness in the Small State') analyzes the work of Conrad Ferdinand Meyer and some other Swiss authors in the context of their consciousness of elements of tension in their relationship as Swiss with the rest of the world. He writes of the feeling that the Swiss may have that they are 'outside history', that they form an audience while 'greater' nations enact important political events as if on a stage.[32] Schmid concludes his study by distancing himself from a belief in the necessity or desirability of outward, quantitative 'greatness'. Some French-Swiss authors have presented the relationship of their Swiss identity with France, Germany, Italy and elsewhere as one which may offer difficulties, but which none the less is taken for granted as there; their part of Switzerland forms a central core, but Europe and the rest of the world have their role too, as an extension of the local Swiss environment and at the same time as an exotic counterpart to it. Nicolas Bouvier has written about the Far East, and in his introduction to Louis Gaulis' novel *Zig-Zag Street*, which is set in Cyprus, he writes that this work of Gaulis is '. . . a heart-rending plea for what is small, therefore human, and like ourselves condemned without appeal'.[33] A number of authors are by birth or perhaps early upbringing, or by adult choice or fate, aware of the influence of other cultures as well as Swiss upon themselves. For instance Georges Haldas has links with Greece, Vahé Godel has an Armenian mother, while Anne Cuneo was displaced from Italy to Switzerland as a young girl. The central figure of Roger-Louis Junod's *Les enfants du roi Marc* takes for granted movement in France, Germany and Italy, and while a French-speaking Swiss, has an understanding of German-Swiss and German literary approaches. Georges Borgeaud's protagonist in *Le voyage à l'étranger* is a Swiss young man who spends an uneasy period in the 1930's as tutor in an aristocratic Belgian milieu. Etienne Barilier evokes the mood of Prague in 1968 in his epistolary novel *Prague* which contains letters from correspondents in French Switzerland as well as from some in Prague. Alexandre Voisard has written verse which has acted as a direct stimulus to the separatist movement in the Jura. Monique Laederach's heroine (in *La femme séparée*) is at home in French Switzerland, but revisits the locality in the Emmental where her grandmother grew up in a German-speaking rural setting, and becomes sensitively aware of this part of her family background. Swiss authors writing in German can, of course, often be conscious of the non-Swiss world as an important part of their socio-cultural outlook. For example, Raffael Ganz writes about America and Africa, Hugo Loetscher has been much involved in Latin America, while Urs Widmer's *Die Forschungsreise*, with its fantasy and humour, centres upon a journey between Frankfurt am Main and Switzerland. England furnishes incidental exotic references in Gertrud Wilker's *Nachleben*. Gerhard Meier's *Borodino* conjures up images and associations of Russia while presenting a localized Swiss setting.

In a conference held at Lugano in 1976 Fernando Zappa summed up the current literary situation as he saw it in Ticino and Italian Graubünden.[34] In the first place he was concerned with the position of the author as creator of culturally estimable material, and secondly with the diffusion of the literary work (publishing, bookshops, libraries, schools and study, the mass-media). 92 questionnaires and 45 interviews provided Fernando Zappa with information. It emerged that 64% of Italian-Swiss writers were teachers, and allowing for other types of employment such as in radio and television, probably 74% of all these writers will have had a higher education; it could be claimed that the literary use of the language seemed to be reserved for an intellectual élite. There were as

11

good as no professional writers as such. One consequence was that almost all the writer-teachers complained of the lack of time for writing. The shortage of grants for creative writing could be contrasted with the relative abundance of grants for academic, in particular scientific research. From the point of view of age-range, only 4% of Italian-Swiss authors were under thirty, while 66% of them were between 40 and 65 (the comparable percentage in this age-range in German-speaking Switzerland was 45%, and in French-speaking Switzerland 60%). The economic situation of an author expecting to live from his writing would be very difficult; half of the Swiss authors received in recent years an annual income of less than 1000 francs.

Giovanni Orelli confirms Fernando Zappa's comments on Italian-Swiss literature, as cited above. In an essay on 'the ambiguous position of the writer in Italian-speaking Switzerland' he declares that 'Italian-speaking Switzerland seems to me to be ill from the first sort of provincialism which leads directly to a form of closing in, of cultural autarchy.[35] Critically, he sums up three categories of present-day Italian-Swiss writing. There is the literature of childhood, where the author's earlier years are idyllically revisited, though there is neither bloodshed nor sexuality, neither private passions nor public struggles. Secondly, there is the exaltation of one's own region, of the part of the earth where one was born. But many of our Swiss singers, he maintains, are reactionary in the content of their songs and conformists in language. In general, this writing is a regression into a consoling past. Orelli also declares here that Italian-Swiss authors tend to be more interested in the activities of their German-Swiss colleagues than in those whose first language is French.

Andri Peer, in an essay published in 1970,[36] emphasized that over the previous twenty years a new generation of writers had widened considerably the scope of Rhaeto-Romansh writing by embodying in it themes and approaches (such as expressionism, symbolism and surrealism) that had played an important part internationally during earlier decades. But literary tendencies in the world at large were considerably delayed in their impact on the isolated Rhaeto-Romansh, Peer maintains in his essay on the 'situation and chances of the writer in a linguistic minority'.[37] In the first place small-scale genres were imitated; Peer mentions the lyrical poem in the manner of early nineteenth-century Romanticism, the patriotic ballad, the realistic tale, and the idyll. Rhaeto-Romansh literature, he goes on, began as writing motivated by nostalgia, by loyalty to tradition and monumentally emphasized history. The present has seen massive changes in Graubünden, with industrial-technological developments, and the contemporary poet will take these into account in his imaginative writing. In their reactions to the theme of 'Home, a Swiss problem?' other Rhaeto-Romansh writers have their particular responses.[38] Hendri Spescha asks why cannot literature be a service to the community, and be an approach to readers who wish to become more educated. Cla Biert believes that sympathy, inner commitment, is an important prequisite for a literary work. The creative artist is seen as by nature a sceptic who behaves less securely and less consistently than is often thought. But, Biert says, it seems wrong to demand that the writer should also be a journalist, a politician, an economist and a teacher. Theo Candinas expresses his personal indebtedness, as far as any achievements of his own are concerned, to home in the sense of local community. With the other three national languages of Switzerland (German, French, Italian) there is always an awareness of there being an illustrious culture in the background (writes Peer); Rhaeto-Romansh has to maintain itself without this additional cultural dimension.

The difficulties and professional occupations of writers in Switzerland are no doubt comparable to the position of many authors in Great Britain and many other parts of the world. Loetscher's response to this approach is robustly to query whether there should be particular conditions affecting not simply writers, but Swiss writers: 'If I were a surgeon, I cannot imagine having a problem about the Swiss method of cutting a Swiss appendix'.[39] In discussion on 'home' in a Swiss literary context Peter Bichsel points out[40] that the division of Switzerland into four linguistic and cultural regions does not apply to the realms of economics and politics, and that this has disadvantageous consequences for the effectiveness of culture regarded as a brake upon the willful assertion of economic and political power.

Finally, perhaps some points made by Karl Wagner in an article in an Austrian journal may be cited.[41] This author links Switzerland (German Switzerland) and Austria together as relatively small countries many of whose writers nowadays look regularly to taste in the German Federal Republic and tailor their works to appeal to the German market, bearing in mind that regionalism can be fashionable. Frisch and Dürrenmatt were for a considerable time virtually the only contemporary Swiss authors known in Germany. The early 1970's saw attention being directed to a wider spectrum of a younger generation (with authors such as Adolf Muschg and Diggelmann), often socially and politically involved, while the later 1970's saw the blossoming of a new style of writing where direct political comment is less usual (Wagner discusses, for example, work by Silvio Blatter, Gertrud Leutenegger and E.Y. Meyer, and to these might be added comparable creative writing in French, for instance).

What emerges from the comments and observations quoted above, or what is intended to emerge, is the confidence that Switzerland has at present a lively, varied and often exciting literary landscape.

NOTES

[1] 'Stadt und Land in der Schweiz', *Die Tat*, Zürich, 1 April 1941. Reprinted in: Walter Muschg, *Pamphlet und Bekenntnis* (ed. Peter André Bloch), Olten and Freiburg i. Br., 1968, p.197.

[2] 'Perspektiven', 16 May 1941. *Pamphlet und Bekenntnis*, pp. 203–06.

[3] Max Frisch, 'Kleines Tagebuch einer deutschen Reise', in: *Gesammelte Werke in zeitlicher Folge*, Frankfurt, 1976, vol. I.1, pp. 84–97.

[4] 'Über Zeitereignis und Dichtung'. Ibid., vol. II. 1, pp. 285–89.

[5] 'Verdammen oder verzeihen?' (1945). Ibid., vol. II.1, pp.292–96.

[6] 'Stimmen eines anderen Deutschland?' (1946). Ibid., vol. II.1, p. 311.

[7] 'Das Schlaraffenland, die Schweiz' (1946). Ibid., vol. II.1, p. 312.

[8] 'Aus einem Tagebuch. Für Hermann Hesse' (1947). Ibid., vol. II.1, p. 324.

[9] 'Kultur als Alibi' (1949). Ibid., vol. II.1, p. 343.

[10] 'Achtung: Die Schweiz. Ein Gespräch über unsere Lage und ein Vorschlag zur Tat' (1954). Ibid., vol. III.1, pp. 291-339.

[11] 'Festrede zum Nationalfeiertag am 1. August 1957.' Ibid., vol. IV.1, pp. 220-25.

[12] 'Die Schweiz ist ein Land ohne Utopie' (1960). Ibid., vol. IV.1, pp. 258-59.

[13] 'Schillerpreis-Rede.' Ibid., vol. V.2, p. 363.

[14] 'Überfremdung 1' (1965) and 'Überfremdung 2' (1966). Ibid., vol. V.2, pp. 374–99.

[15] Friedrich Dürrenmatt, *Werkausgabe in dreissig Bänden*, Zürich, 1980, vol. 27, p. 70.

[16] Dieter Fringeli has pointed out that writing in Swiss German dialect is no longer associated with a narrow idealization of traditional folk-culture, but that the decade 1967-1977 saw an enthusiastic revival of interest in a contemporary exploitation of Swiss German; Gomringer and Marti offered considerable stimulus here. Cf. Dieter Fringeli (ed.), *Mach keini Schprüch. Schweizer Mundart des zwanzigsten Jahrhunderts*, Zürich, 1981.

[17] Friedrich Dürrenmatt, Werkausgabe in dreissig Bänden, vol. 27, pp. 77-78.

[18] 'Überlegungen zum Gesetz der grossen Zahl'. Ibid., vol. 27.

[19] Karl Schmid, *Unbehagen im Kleinstaat*, Zürich and Stuttgart, 1963.

[20] 'Überlegungen zum Gesetz der grossen Zahl'. Ibid., vol. 27, pp. 123-24.

[21] See *Lyrik aus der Schweiz* (ed. Frank Geerk), Zürich and Cologne, 1974, p. 18. Or *Schweizer Lyrik des zwanzigsten Jahrhunderts* (ed. Bernd Jentsch), Zürich and Cologne, 1977, pp. 53-54.

[22] Kurt Marti, *Die Schweiz und ihre Schriftsteller – die Schriftsteller und ihre Schweiz*, Zürich, 1966.

[23] Max Frisch, *Tagebuch 1946-1949*, Ed. cit., vol. II.2, p. 562.

[24] Paul Nizon, *Diskurs in der Enge*, Bern, 1970.

[25] Kurt Guggenheim, 'Die Schweiz, Provinz?' In: Dieter Bachmann (ed.), *Fortschreiben. 95 Autoren der deutschen Schweiz*, Zürich and Munich, 1977.

[26] E.Y. Meyer, '1. August oder Von der Freiheit und vom Risiko'. In: Dieter Bachmann, *Fortschreiben*, ed. cit.

[27] Yves Bridel, 'Der Weg einer Emanzipation: Die Literatur der Westschweiz im 20. Jahrhundert'. Schweizer Feuilleton-Dienst, Zürich, 7 July 1970.

[28] Jean-Pierre Monnier, *Contemporary French-Swiss Literature*, translated by Douglas J. Gillam, Pro Helvetia, Zürich, 1975.

[29] Manfred Gsteiger, 'Die französischsprachige Literatur der Schweiz seit 1945', in: *Die zeitgenössischen Literaturen der Schweiz*, Kindler, Zürich and Munich, 1974, p. 414.

[30] Etienne Barilier, 'Littérature romande', *Etudes de Lettres*, Lausanne, 1982, pp. 1–14.

[31] Georges Haldas, *L'Etat de Poésie. Carnets 1979*. L'Age d'Homme, Lausanne, 1981.

[32] Karl Schmid, *Unbehagen im Kleinstaat*, ed. cit. p. 7.

[33] Louis Gaulis, *Zig-Zag Street*, Fontainemore, Journal de Genève, 1979, p. 6.

[34] 'Per una politica culturale nella Svizzera italiana', *Cenobio*, XXVI (i), 1977.

[35] Giovanni Orelli, 'La posizione ambigua dello scrittore nella Svizzera italiana'. In: Egon Ammann and Eugen Faes (editors), *Literatur aus der Schweiz. Texte und Materialien*. Suhrkamp, Zürich, 1978, pp. 478–79.

[36] Andri Peer, 'Rhaeto-Romanic Literature'. In: Alex Natan (editor), *Swiss Men of Letters*, Wolff, London, 1970.

[37] Andri Peer, 'Situation und Chancen des Schriftstellers in einer sprachlichen Minderheit. Beziehungen zwischen dichterischem Ausdruck und heimatlicher Gebundenheit'. In: E. Ammann and E. Faes (editors), op. cit., pp. 462–76.

[38] 'Heimat – ein Schweizer Problem?' In: E. Ammann and E. Faes (editors), op. cit., pp. 494–530.

[39] Hugo Loetscher, *How Many Languages Does Man Need?*, New York, 1982, p. 22.

[40] In: E. Ammann and E. Faes (editors), op. cit., p. 508.

[41] Karl Wagner, 'Dunkelfelder der Ideologien. Anmerkungen zu Schweizer Romanen der Gegenwart', *Literatur und Kritik*, Heft 173-74, 1983, pp. 117-35.

POETRY

Werner Zemp

Landscape before Easter

And so it started: that with every step
which led us from the town, each single step
amid the shadowy net of leafless trees,
between the busy streams and piping birds
we were restored to youth.
To make a start, to start again afresh,
while roundabout, before the flower-blue sky,
the landscape starts anew, with woods that gleam
like rosy marble and hollows hovering in the haze
of the silvery river valley: there's not a single stone
without an angel's wing asleep beneath!

Then secondly, like reading from a book,
we read on tombstones in a cloistered walk
dead names; but all at once we made a stop.
For this was real:
that here, beneath the moistened wreaths,
a woman had been lying dead, some hours,
beside her sisters, just like stone by stone.

When finally we left the dark and graves,
and came, distraught like Lazarus, into
the open air, the day had darkened fast.
The wind descended from the emerald hill
which glowed with green before the tower of cloud,
and with the wind there came along a scent
of youthful buds, and from within a fold
a black horse stormed and stamped and neighed. But this

became the final object which we saw,
and meantime the confused shouts of lovely life
rose up like fanfares:
a pallid face, seen watching through a window –
the final object before, piece by piece,
the convent disappeared behind the hill:
a pallid face beneath a pale-white frontlet,
with gaze fixed on the far, strange, moon-like light.

Snow

When I came to the window, the snow was starting to fall:
out from the window I can see the garden,
can feel the breath of summers that have gone,
the irises will soon bloom blue again,
an ageing man will stand among the flowers.
So much takes place, and no one knows the reason:
I saw on high a hovering like swarms of bees
and then like blossom falling through the trees
and, star by star, extinguished on the ground.
Then nothing further – only thousands of flakes,
a dizzy cosmos of stars of similar shape.
As last year, I was very much afraid.
Whatever was mine was extinguished in my hand.

Perhaps, who knows?, I'd lived too long alone.
Oh stellar grief that is beyond all names!
We go on spanning the void into a frame –
when I came to the window, the snow was starting to fall.

Alexander Xaver Gwerder

Lines for Rheila

Where to at night? I fly to you
in the night along the lawn of your tenderness.
I land
in the scent of the oasis – do not know
where I am, for the moon
drinks from your eyes' velvet.

The sounding caravan of kisses
also lands here late,

comes to a halt
by the well of your mouth.

No one knows of it.

For I am the caravan
in the night
along your tenderness.

★

See too the poppy-field,
the hot savannah of forgetting.
Can you already feel the stubble? Carry
easily the weight of the two of us, fenced round
by eyelashes, to the other bank,
Tiger ferry –

There the seven-eared sun
of the rain-light rises. Once in the moment,
Just once
the blossom is shed
in the cyclone. . .

Come into the river.

★

Now the shadows break
at the foot of the aquamarine – more loudly
your tongue's gazelles take flight
in the jungle fire –
At midday
our hut is in flames.

Before the imminent nightfall
we wish to scatter
the ark in the wind. . .

Farewell.

Urs-Martin Strub

Neptune

ABYSSUS ABYSSUM INVOCAT

Time is consumed,
existence abandoned.

From the anchorages can still be heard
the wild descant,
the voice of mankind.
And from the gardens by the shore
colours, clouds and crafts still seethe up.

But we are sailing out.

A steady breeze will blow us over the surface
as we glide away,
ever moving over the treasure-vault of the sea.
A flock of prophetic birds will go with us.
Their wings record the script of the hereafter.
Their bills sing of eternity.

The mountains, till recently framed in gold,
lie flat, a shadowy shell in the sand,
lapped by the waters.
The mainland's base has sunk.
The buildings have become blurred.
All that is sloping, angular,
edged or projecting
moves towards even quiet,
drowns in the intoxication of eternal level.

Ebb and flow have clasped each other,
Love and hatred have embraced,
the shades of the world below have
kissed the rays of the world above.

Our mouths, goblets of craving,
spill and plunge to quiet.
Our measures fall into the immeasurable.
A light cargo,
our heaviest load
sinks into the sameness.

And at the end of the track,
in the lustrous darkness,
where lightning flashes
illumine the abyss,
where the typhoons' drum roll resounds,
where through the azure chasms
the fish exult
and the seal of the universe breaks,

we ourselves reel,
mystical mariners,
into the unfathomable.
That is our greater grave.
That is our greater death.

The symbols fall apart,
This world and the next,
above and below,
gods and demons
no longer are valid.

The stars have all been dissolved
and have lost their power,
finite infinite
blessed wretched
one within the other.

Eugen Gomringer

cars and cars

cars and cars
cars and elevators
cars and men
elevators and men
men and cars and elevators
men and men

trains and trains
trains and men and elevators
trains and elevators
men and trains
men and men

cars and trains
cars and men and trains
men and men

men and men

americans

americans and apricots
american apricots
apricot americans
apricots and americans

butterfly

mist
mountain
butterfly

mountain
butterfly
missed

butterfly
meets
mountain

ireland

green and
sheep

sheep and
cow

cow and
green

green and
cow

cow and
sheep

sheep and
green

have been
seen

roads 68

SHELL and
ESSO

ESSO and
TEXACO

TEXACO and
BP

BP and
TEXACO

TEXACO and
SHELL

SHELL and
BP

BP and
ESSO

ESSO and
SHELL

SHELL and
TEXACO

TEXACO and
ESSO

ESSO and
BP

BP and
SHELL

the common
smell

Erika Burkart

Family Ballad

I was born in the year
nineteen hundred and twenty-two.
The north-east wind was blowing
and the snow fell in scant dry flakes.

I was afraid of my father.
His eyes were moss-green stones.
When drunk he shot the cat
and nailed up doors after midnight.

He was not keen on paying bills.
He speared them on to the meat-hook
under the frame that was empty
because he had sold the picture
(a skull, hand-painted) to buy spirits.

When he lay dying, mother
peeled chestnuts by his bedside.
He talked about the hunting-grounds,

those here and the others, and that the
Latin-American Indians seldom upset him.
Fine people, he would say cheerfully,
they respected guests and revered the light.
The back of the dead man
displayed, big as a clenched fist,
the wound about which he had never spoken.
At his request the hand remained
armed with the claws concerning which it is said
that they go on growing, even afterwards.
The head of the dead man was small,
like the shrivelled Peruvian head
which, on Sunday mornings,
he had allowed us to see and touch.

★

My mother, from whom I have
inherited the courage to love, called life
a river which carries non-swimmers too.
Her glance, not without a shadow of care
on the eyelids' edge and between the brows,
has stayed bright with forbearance.
While we sleep, she is ironing and baking.
The kitchen window, lit up red
(a square yard's land of the land that we're seeking)
I can see from all sides.

Inexhaustible is her art
of spinning gold out of straw.
– One evening, she had been
repairing fifty shirts for the insane,
she read Bobrowski's 'Reply'–: 'you were living
from what is other.'

About my sister, I believe I know
that she understands me better than she admits.
My sister suffers as I do
from being homesick for the older home.
She knows the instances which make us
accountable for a starving cat,
but she also has pity for the mice.

Beneath the knot her heart
is a nest of tremulous birds.

★

Like everyone else I have dreams
which are repeated from time to time.
Certain illuminations befall me
only in solitude – and if I grow further,
this takes place in cells that are injured.
I learnt to sleep with the knife that heals
while it cuts, before it is too late.

Dealing with sentences is arduous,
at the well of syllables
for certain words
not to be used anymore,
and yet talking,
here, echo sounds of the question from there.
The answer not to be put in words.

They too
handed on further,
with no sort of agreement,
to someone in whom silence
creates a new hearing.

People still keep on encountering me.
On my shoulder the hand
touches where the wing is budding.

Albert Ehrismann

Earth's Children

New Year will soon be here. Before Christmas comes
I would like to see what ordering my affairs has cost.
Count up the unwept tears.
Count up the laughter that has been lost.

Unwritten letters. Broken promises.
For the distress which a lonely heart has known
friendly words would have an effect
that is stronger than bread has shown.

I failed to write the few words,
nor did I invite that man who, lonely and aloof,
said that he would be glad to spend an hour or two
beneath our roof.

And now I am to give my dear ones

25

the presents that I have bought.
Who are these dear ones? Would they give me
a thought,

if I myself were lonely
and wrote with a request to make?
Does one man know what another would do
for his sake?

Do good words that are neither
written nor told
return to their original place
mute and cold?

There is still time, and I make a list
of things to which to refer.
Calculate what is owed or postponed,
and recognize how things were.

And a small scrap of hope can be found:
things might work out after all, they say.
Over the hills above the town
the giant firmament makes its way,

and a tree of lights such as I've never seen
is stretched across the sky.
It's there for the lonely and for us
who have forgotten them, on high.

But the tree would wither, did we not. . .
I won't preach. In the wind the snow
is rustling. That we are all earth's children
is all I know.

But the earth, the earth, the earth. . .

Have you heard the voices from the moon:
'Peace! Peace!'
for all the world?
But my inner ears still always hear
the bomb that's hurled.

Have you seen the men on the moon at work?
Of what hard rock
is the moon's girth,
and how much easier is it to lay
millions of dead people down

in our earth!

Have you heard the lament of Pope Paul
about the hypocrites
who promise peace,
but break their own promises
with hatred and violence
and war's release?

For no violence affects only a few,
since each violent act
hits out at all,
and everyone who kills – even
for the sake of peace –
bears the seed of new death at his call.

Have you seen the man in space,
the man who climbed over
the lunar craft's frame?
But the earth, the earth, the earth,
but the earth moves
all the same.

Shall we conquer the moon and the stars?
Men without forests
and home and mate.
But the earth, the earth, the earth
we shall
obliterate,

unless for us, above and below, to whom the words
'Peace! Peace!'
are more than illusion,
the winds bring not bombs and poison,
but birds, just birds, kites and blossoms
to banish confusion.

Silja Walter

A nun who writes knows
that she is confined
with the rest of society
in an aeroplane that is guaranteed to crash.

To go on discussing at length
its quality, equipment

and personnel,
its seating, fares and menus
she considers to be a waste of time.

It is her mission, inwardly experienced,
to convey to her fellow-passengers
by means of a kind of expansion of consciousness
the moment of the crash,
by noting down
as it were graphically
its extent and consequences.

It can hardly be done any other way,
for it is not a question
of logic alone,
but of a certain light
that is also called faith.

What appears there is landscape
rather than concept.
The attempt must be made to fix it quickly
in contours and diagrams
before the 'show' is extinguished again.

This function,
taken over as inner mission,
requires of the nun
who writes
that she should outstrip
her own crash.

She has to spend a lifetime
in the practice of this overtaking.
This nun's exercise is called monastic
life.
Monastic life means:
he who believes will live,
even when he dies.

She therefore no longer just goes on living –
she dies her life, so to speak,
and lives her death.

She lives it daily
in its smallest units
through monastic asceticism,

and receives therefrom
more and more the essential
experience of LIFE,
the breakthrough into what is existentially other,
into the space of God
where all things are still beginning.

Delighted and full of wonder
she recognizes signs
of this other, coming factor
in the world and society and begins
to love in new fashion
the world and mankind
as signet and track,
as permeable to that new factor
beyond the crash.

From then on in a kind of rapture
she consciously places herself
into the tension between life
before and life after the catastrophe –
to stay with the image of the Jumbo-jet –
and relates what she sees
to all who are willing to hear.

The form of her message,
whether poem or novel,
does not concern her much.
In the total uncertainty
at one with each other and all others
the nun transmits unconcerned
the certainty of her LIFE-experience
from her everyday death,
in the power and in the language
of her hope
and signs what she writes
with her monastic motto
in death and LIFE:
UIOGD:
Ut In Omnibus Glorificetur Deus.

Rainer Brambach

Weariness

I have been trying for a long time now
to give you a name, my antagonist:
you lay upon me the yoke, the dull
sandbag, your blunt hammer,
you make me a labourer.

I carry you from the field home to supper,
I feel your burden
when the moon rises and the bat flies,
at table the others call me a dreamer
while my neck bends before you,
near to defeat.

Caution is indicated

What impels you to write verse?
Why don't you sell salt,
houses, rifles or tobacco?

Caution is indicated, you know this, for soon
the ravens will come again – black preachers
with no oil in their voices – to shout out your poverty
while you are still moving calmly about.

When there is ice hanging from the water-pipes,
the waiting-room remains as your domicile
where, echoing in many languages,
departure and arrival unite.

Men alone in the world

One collects stones.
Another acquires postage-stamps.
A third plays chess at long distance
and one stands lurking of an evening
in the park.
One learns Russian.
One reads Shakespeare.
One writes letter after letter
and one drinks red wine in the evening,
otherwise nothing happens.

They drink, read, lurk, acquire,
the men alone in the evening.
They write, learn, play, collect,
each by himself in leisure time.
One goes to an operetta.
One listens to Bach.
One guards a secret.
Like a watch-dog
he paces the avenues night after night.

Kurt Marti

the lord our god
was not at all pleased
that gustav e. lips
died in a traffic accident

firstly he was too young
secondly a loving husband to his wife
thirdly a jolly father to two children
fourthly a good friend to his friends
fifthly full of many good ideas

what's to happen now that he's gone?
what is his wife without him?
who is to play with the children?
who can replace a friend?
who is to have the new ideas?

the lord our god
was not at all pleased
that some of you thought
that he was pleased at such a thing

in the name of him who awakened the dead
in the name of him who was dead and rose again:
we protest against the death of gustav e. lips

★

she did not make much of a stir
she wasn't in any club
she was born
went to school
had the usual time in French Switzerland
then became a hairdresser

31

later she married
bore him two children
lost him again
and was as they say
a good wife and mother

but who talks
about the gaiety of her eyes
who speaks of
the pleasure it gave us
just to see the grace
with which she pushed back
her hair from her forehead
or who can declare
the magic power
of her simple words
and who can describe
the mobile enchantment
of the small efficient hands
or who praises god
for the gift
of her heartfelt laughter?

she did not make much of a stir
she made two or three men
she made her husband
she made her children
she made herself happy

and that
is more than we think

Herbert Meier

The time of woods that have turned colour

The time of woods that have turned colour
has recently burst forth from the mist

The apples are picked
                fallen ones
still lie in the grass
sown to rot
while many are eaten
in treeless city centres

Meanwhile
many people can be seen gathering
and taking to the streets

In earlier times there were plagues
it is said
Now there are uprisings
that build their nests
in the cities
and break out
before the very eyes
            of the rulers

Obviously
            peace
cannot be conjured forth
in any other way
Only words remain
            painted on boards
            and raised aloft
a silent wood of language
in which a spirit roams
which no powers can destroy by fire

What purpose would be served
by me sacrificing my life
            in war
Where can you still
place yourself before microphones
and put the word sacrifice
in your mouth

No one
has any longer the tongue
for words like this
            after everything
            no one
Most tongues
            have withered
and are covered
            with words
with words words
which are apples long fallen
and rotting there in the late grass

33

On the edge of woods that have turned colour
the false acacias now jangle red

Paths one afternoon

Paths one afternoon
lined by emperors
who had been swallowed up in the mists
of time and tide

their heads are tiles
for the shoes of strangers
and are trodden on
        in honour of those days
        that have sunk from sight
and survive
        in toasts
        for any
who sit from time to time
on the remains of columns
        in the reflected light
from a petrified candelabrum
booty of some emperor perhaps
who razed a temple
and drink in
from microphones
        names from long ago
their feet among the stones
of a via sacra

At the milestone
the glow from the guide's cigarettes
dies down in the grass

Eyes

Eyes
        that ride
ride on light waves
        messengers
that not for one moment
look right through
figures nocturnally erect
        along the bank

where the ants roam
and despatch their birds
carry off larvae on waterways
and battlefields of algae
                    of predatory fish
            It is always possible
that individual words may radiate
                    and illuminate
what the poem rides through on its journey

Poems by Herbert Meier
translated by Ian Hilton

Beat Brechbühl

Simple Mirror

My notebook is my head.
What does not hold is forgotten.

My buyer is my head,
This mouth is insatiable.

My data-bank is my head.
Humanly imprecise, hence the wars
and the famines,
the prayers for peace and freedom.

My slaughter-house is my head.
The animals remain healthy;
and with glazed eyes
the people drown in their blood.

My cemetery is my head.
Without cypress trees or marble,.
without grave, without urn,
without shroud.

My sleep is my head.
All is dead and breathes, many dreams,
everywhere sleep,
sleep till the alarm clock sounds.

My archive is my head.
Aye, aye, how much I have forgotten!
But I hold on to myself.

My house is my head.
Not a word all day;

35

then suddenly cheerful guests.

My future is my head.
Coloured birds,
towns of plans,
and nothing lost.

Being Ill

Then the world becomes so unimportant,
pushed away to a point,
it removes itself
with a loud, empty yawn, without interest,
without myself.

I became this point.
I am the cause of the heat.
I am the weak, damp cloth
I am cut up
into a thousand screaming parts,
the stomach contracts with pain
for kilometres,
I, only
I.
No one can gainsay me.

The demands become easier.
I remember only
that I have already experienced everything.
I talk with no one.

The self-evident becomes round and rolls off.
Perhaps hot tea still,
a handful of coloured pills and then
sleep sleep sleep,
I know nothing about awakening,

Everything else has gone away
very precisely.

Jörg Steiner

At school the children hear a story,
they hear the story of Hiroshima,
Hiroshima is a village in Switzerland.

Hiroshima is a Celtic settlement,

in Hiroshima things are not ideal,
the farmers are discontented.

Hiroshima needs industry,
the children read aloud together,
the teacher writes a word on the blackboard.

When there were still frontiers

I should like to tell about a man
who crossed the frontier illegally,
who was not persecuted by us,
who found work here, a place to live,
and was accepted.

I should like to proclaim the words
that he did not learn from us here:
alien, police, documents –
and that his first word in our language
was the word happiness.

I should like to assert
that his wants were covered,
that he did not need to be pitied,
and that we did not make ourselves smaller
than we should.

But the man is not theré
about whom I can tell,
he's not there,
the man.

Report of a man who was not deported

And then it is none the less
almost as we know it from films:
bursting suitcases
held together with cord,
women quietly weeping,
the dark eyes of the children,
the employer's last testimonial:
Mr Marco Massari was proficient.
The sky is slightly overcast,
the voice in the loudspeaker speaks German,
the lines gleam by the signal-box,

normal gauge, not trans-Siberian,
and someone who spits upon our freedom –
in the hall by the exit is a four-colour print
of the Swiss holiday paradise,
two policemen are leaning against the wall.

Dieter Fringeli

Slight Change

In the morning she went
Past my house
On the way to work
In the evening she came
Past my house
On the way from work
This morning she went
Past my house
On the way to work
And did not come back again
(Past my house)
On the way from work

In the evening.

Fear

Fear does not have a slow tongue
It comes close to you
With a soft voice
Keeps watch in the pillows
On which you are sleeping
Breaks into
Your pulse beat

Fear leaves behind
No tracks in the snow
On the way home:
You take it with you in your footsteps
While your heart beats in your throat
And it turns to laughter
Which makes you choke.

Morning Post 11.7.74

The letters testify:
I'm still available

My address
Is beyond
All doubt

I'm there.

French

Philippe Jaccottet

The night is a great city that is sunk in sleep
where the wind blows. . . It has come from far off to
The shelter of this bed. It is June midnight.
You sleep. I have been drawn onto these infinite shores.
The hazel tosses underneath the wind. Then comes
this call approaching, now retiring, you could swear
a glimmer of light was fleeting across the woods, or else
the shades eddying round, as they say, in the underworld.
(That call across the summer night, how many things
I could say of it, and say of your eyes. . .) But it is only
the bird called screech-owl, calling to us out of the depths
of these suburban woods. And already our odour
is the odour of putrefaction in the early light,
already under our skins so warm you can feel the bone,
while all the stars sink and drown at the street corners.

Interior

I have been trying for a long time to live here,
inside this bedroom that I make believe I like,
the table, and the carefree ornaments, the window
opening after every night a different foliage,
and the blackbird's heart beats in the dark ivy,
everywhere glimmers of light finish off the aged shadow.

I too consent to think the air is mild,
that this is home, that the day will be a good one.
It is just that there is, at the foot of the bed, that spider
(it comes from the garden), I should have been more careful
to stamp on it, I can't help thinking it's still at work
on the trap set to catch my fragile ghost.

The Office of the Poet

The proper work for an eye that weakens hourly
is not to dream, no more than to fashion tears,
it is to keep watch like a shepherd, calling up
whatever may be lost if he falls asleep.

And so I, against the wall lit by summer
(or is it not more likely by its memory),
in the tranquillity of the light I look at you,
as you move ever further and further away, escaping,
I call you, in the dark of the grasses yawning
as once long ago in the garden, you voices or glimmers
(nobody knows) that link the departed with childhood.

(Is she dead, that Lady – you know – under the branches
her lamp gone out, her baggage scattered?
Or else will she come back again from under the ground
and I, I would go out and greet her, saying,
'What have you done with all this time when we could hear
neither your laugh nor your footsteps in the lane?
Should you have stayed away and never told a soul?
Lady, oh now return and be among us. . .')
In today's shade and time, there stands concealed,
not speaking, that shade from yesterday. So with the world.
We do not see it very long, just long enough
to keep of it what sparkles, nearly extinguished,
to call again and yet again, and tremble
that we can no more see. So the impoverished struggle,
like a man on his knees that you might see endeavouring
to rake together against the wind his scanty fire. . .

Letter of June the 26th

Leave it to the birds henceforth to tell you of our life.
A man would make too much fuss about it
and all that you would see behind his words
would be a traveller's bedroom, with a window
on which the mist of tears veils a woodland slashed with rain. . .

Night comes on. You hear the sound of voices under the lime-trees.
The human voice gleams out, as below the earth
Antares which is sometimes red and sometimes green.

Stop listening to the clatter of your cares,
stop thinking of what is happening to us,
forget even our name. Listen how we talk
with the voice of daylight, and simply let
daylight shine. When we are released from all fear,

when death is nothing to us but transparency,
when it is clear as the air of summer nights
and we fly borne up by our own lightness
through all those delusive walls driven by wind,
then you will hear only the sound of the river
flowing behind the forest; then you will see no more
than the glitter of night-time eyes. . .

*

The day we speak with the voice of the nightingale. . .

Poems by Philippe Jaccottet
translated by Roy C. Knight

Anne Perrier

This last song
O my birds my fountains
Will tear out my veins
And my blood

Somewhere else perhaps
A new beginning
Three olive trees
Wreathed in air
And starlings
The long swaying of the seas
The hour
For a king's rising
Arrayed

The flowers
Even lost beneath the snow
And broken
Without the fires the scents
That drive the bee mad
The flowers are brightness

Cheerless flutes
When will the nightingales come back on earth
And the golden wind of the fireflies
The leaves of my tree
Will have fallen

Poems by Anne Perrier
translated by Roy C. Knight

Alexandre Voisard

Ode to the Country that will not Die

Clay, my country of potter's clay,
My country of harvests and agonies,
My country turned in upon itself,
Coiled on its loves, on its dark roots
My country with its cathedrals still in birth,
My country with its past of mildewed seed-corn,
Forged from adventure, forgiveness and shards.

My country of distress and revolt,
My country of suffering and broken gleams,
My country dedicated to oaths, to burning words,
My country shot through with the blood of the lightning,
Red with impatience, white with anger,
My country of burdens and of clanging chains,
My country laid out on the slate of the centuries.

They came, the grasping shepherds came,
The yellow traders in straw and privileges,
The crackpots, tongues all sewn with tinkling bells,
From over the valleys sunk in sleep.
They came by years, they came by smiles
With their bulls trailing in the dust
A tail of venom, a scrotum empty of seed.
They came with their she-goats
Dangling frozen udders in the mud.
They came with their table of wisdom
And their gallows and their laws like threats
Over our roofs, over our children, over our poems.
They came with their cadence and their spittle
To slaver on our books and on our centuries.

My country, O people patiently waiting
In the gardens where songs live on,
My people impatiently waiting in the depths of the branches,
At the foot of the firs where the sap unceasing blazes,
You arise and your cry rings through the cornfields
So suddenly that the night at last draws back
And the forests tremble as on some pristine morning.
O country, the axe is gleaming,
Prayers travel on from vigil to vigil,

From white cottage to inn of gules.[1]

My country of cherry and *russule*,[2]
My country of brandy and legend,
The tide is rising still
And the years like a string of invectives
Bite at your lips, travel on in your open eyes,
The page is blank where you bleed today,
But those who come to terms, the ponderous shepherds,
The makeshift puppeteers under the jackboot,
The jeering burgomasters, the whiskered chefs,
Are already spitting out the lees of their axioms
While with one hand
We have put out the implacable eye of the Great Bear.

My country of clay, country of harvests,
My country forged from adventure and shards,
Shot through with the blood of the lightning,
See how there now gush out from the rock of our fathers
The new honey, the limpid season,
The irrevocable tumult of the unbroken mares.
My country of cherry and of legend,
Red with impatience, white with anger,
The hour is come to pass through the flames
And grow great for evermore
Together on our reawakened hills.
My country of clay, my liberty reborn,
My liberty pouring back, my country uncrushable,
My country uneffaced, ineffaceable,
Drunken with leaps of no return and wild
With your naked liberty.

[1] Or 'full of rowdiness' or 'of gorging'.   Translated by Roy C. Knight
[2] A kind of mushroom.

Tristan Solier

Origin

Like the leaf
of the Saint-John's-wort:
a thousand lights
daughters of
a thousand wounds

44

Trinity

I have three eyes
each wants something different
one the light
the other the shade
the third more demanding
wants what trembles in everything,
I carry it about like a mule-bell,
like a mule-bell that is killing me.

Day of Ashes

Tears of tar. Frenzied wing-cases. Curare violin bows. Bleatings of bevels. Chalk tongues. Red-lead harvests. Quicklime moorings. Flint hair. Iron oaths. Roughcast visions. Transhumance of craquelure. Diamond seism. It is apoplectically dry.

My heart is being cut by the shears of nothingness. Shutters of oblivion slam against the window sockets. Pain takes up quarters in sensitive flesh. A lava harrow sinks into my face. All the crystals shrill in bitterness. Dialogue of faults and fissures. A red ploughshare shoes the bones. Dreams fall in one over the other and fill the suffocating rooms. Charcoal clothes the skin like a black pox. Salvos of rays gouge out new stigmata to truss me to the stake with bonds of glowing embers. My humours, changed to volcanic exhalations, escape towards a sky of farewell which sentenced me long ago to confinement. Suddenly, shrivelled, my line of life breaks loose and joins the upward flow of burning logs. Fiery whips scourge my shade till it swoons. Within my ruin a squirrel falls, from warm branch to hot branch, before it plunges into the refuge of the ash, from which perhaps you may retrieve the grey mummied corpse of my hope.

Poems by Tristan Solier
translated by Roy C. Knight

Vahé Godel

I pass through a forest

I pass through a forest of transparency
the shape of the mountain blurs as I approach

the sun glides level with the soil
I read my death among the branches

kindling at every step a hundred thousand
violet eyes I pass through darkling ploughlands
unending
in the sky dissolve
catfish of pollen and of feather
my memory is a golden hair

I pass over a river

I pass over a river motionless
where burn
where mingle all the writings
a river
of receding banks
– but I can neither swim
nor fly
there is no bridge
the last of the ferrymen has drowned
(what is
this river that passes suddenly through me?)

Where are you?

I have picked up the slightest clues
questioned all the stones
searched the site from top to bottom

I have gone over every floor
in deepest night wailing: where are you?
what do you fear? and why
do you not answer?

I have lost my voice so doing
and now I myself do not know where I am
just what I hope to find
– what I am flying from

As you go up the river

As you go up the river
so red you will pass under an old bridge
of wood: brush your lips against its arch
and let your fingers
run over the maple beams

shut your eyes – forget you are a fugitive

Poems by Vahé Godel
translated by Roy C. Knight

Pierre-Alain Tâche

Sacro Monte

The word has found the quivering vault
and the silence, in us, has thickened
as a hogshead of dust,
after the blast of a great anger,
might fall again soundlessly on the sacred plot.

The cottages of heaven,[1] where we are going,
cannot hold together any longer;
they gave way when the birds
bore, as they wove them, the garlands of the day
and now we can see
their clanking wattles full of seawater still.

Each nacelle has an inmate – and you always find
a man who wants to bow his head:
so long have his eyes been lifted
towards the dome he could not reach
(and the wolf doesn't mean to be wheedled any more,
but makes an excuse of the foam and shakes himself).

In the lap of the shades that have no fire
Saint Francis seems to journey among the trunks,[2]
among the dried flowers and the lilies.
At the bar he takes some refreshment and begins to make out more clearly,
in the mandorla of silence gaping after the manner
of a fleshy fruit of the passion,
the flickering candles, on the top of Sacro Monte,
beacon lights turned on to guide him
as a night-wandering plane is brought safely home.

[1] Or perhaps 'The celestial bedlam . . . it gave way'.
[2] Or 'poor-boxes' with perhaps a play on the two senses.

Île Dieu

A Host. It might be a Host
lifted up at the offertory of recall
in the hour when we stand firm without memory.

47

Releasing, endearing – who shall say? –,
it exults in painted empty palaces,
underneath the low boughs of the sunset.

You seek a messenger, a brush of contact,
in which to contain the pure desire of joining:
it may be drifting within your grasp.
On the grey paten, it is silence
(and that is another song we ought to know).
The unleavened Element has unpicked your hunger.

San Giulio Garden

Between the ivies and the woods
we shall have seen an angel fall
– to cause obstruction in the space for return.
He grazed with a wing our watching eyes
or the snub features of a simpleton girl.

We were working back then up the dusty day,
as a sculler cancels the stream,
towards the eternity of the present,
which is alive, between the dishes and the words
that one says in the end out of hearing
of the birds, of a tree-scent, a strong scent,
and of one part of us that cannot break away.

Poems by Pierre-Alain Tâche
translated by Roy C. Knight

Raymond Tschumi

Them

Ineluctably, they will accuse me of trying to escape; but what proofs could they bring? The elsewhere for my refuge is nowhere to be found. I freely grant them that all thought is as empty as a shadow.

So they leave me for peace only the void of meditation. That is what saves me, they don't know where I am burrowing.

Division of labour: for me the pick, for them the shovel. I provide them with the materials they shift, they leave me the void that replaces their wealth.

Who is it that sweeps the horizon, walks in the valley floors, hovers over the virgin spaces, leaps on the lacework of the hilltops and plunges into the shadows cast over the plain? He who leaves to them the millions and the tons, the gulper of void, the eater of glass.

I have succeeded in drowning them in their indifference: it is to me as transparent as the faintest rustle of the wind, the blackness of nights, the anacolutha of stratus, the presence of absences and the absence of presences. My breath crosses the mountains even when the clouds sweep victoriously over the passes.

Let us leave them to deal with their materials and transact their business; mine be the mathematical mass relative to the weight of the stars abstracted from their varying particularities, mine to overpass race, moment and milieu, mine the impalpable nullity of cobweb dust in my stinking cell, a counterpoise to the universe!

Now see how their millions and their ingots melt like blocks of ice in the transparency of my invisible brightness which they fail to see because it falls impartially on everything and evaporates their tutelary stars.

Though their warders keep guard at the gates with their caps, their rude features, their expressionless faces, their regulation uniforms and rigid poses, their superiority devastates an absence pent up behind their automatic pacing and their pulverized souls. Their cage rings hollow, and even so it is the only hole they have been able to dig for anyone but themselves. They who gather up our refuse, they have needed a great deal of darkness, tunnels, laws, armies, whistles and banks to be able to provide a prison cell for everyone. Their society has made the effort, paid the price, and put a cell with no exit at the disposal of every mother's son.

So reigns the permanent night in which we forget the hour. They keep waking at every moment, they line us up and count us: we lie to them when we answer 'present'. Never has any one of us given his real name. They take our bodies and our voices to fill their cells, but all they have dug is repeating holes, automatic-weapon holes, more digits, more trillions without the slightest trace of anything living. The greatest mathematicians among them have long ceased to understand anything but digits.

They don't look at us: they inspect us. Everything with them, in their gaol, is regulated, checked, ticked off. No exceptions. One pair of socks per week and the same billycan for all meals. Their system is so perfect, their science so accurate, their administration so sound that we almost pity them: for my part, I am tempted to lend them a piece of my flesh or try out a quick-march just to please them, but there is no pleasing them with all the love in the world. They remain alone in their perfection.

Open Barn

If I were totally civilized, protected and insulated by technical devices, installed on a planet to survive, I should be left without feelings, should not know what wood or hay or rain are.

49

Happily, it still rains inside me.

Yes, rain not only wets me, it also penetrates into me and lives in me.

When I climb up to the highest dwelling, my black dog loves to roll on the pads of snow crushed by my heavy shoes.

I take refuge then in my barn, open to all the winds, all the skies. Where I live there is nothing left to desire, nothing to steal: I have swept away the dust of falsehood, and great birds, of a species long extinct, have come to hover over my cleaned-up spaces.

Under my unreal roof, the suffering from every horizon rises up to take refuge for an instant, as if I could offer it an eternal respite. To safeguard its repose, I drive away all inevitable noise, all material bodies, I clear out the obstructions of cut straw or old cupboards and I send the mice to get warm by the cattle.

In my snowy habitation where it reposes, the suffering of the world brings forth the day.

Poems by Raymond Tschumi
translated by Roy C. Knight

Italian

Giorgio Orelli

For a Friend About to Be Married

Tonight I want you to remember Isolde
clinging to Tristram on a scooter
between Tuscany and Emilia
                                (we had left
behind a yelping storm at sea,
and, used as we were to firtrees, the light
from wind-struck olives ravished us),
                                Isolde
gently poised, suspended, the heels
of her tiny feet submissive
as if she were a rung higher than a merry-go-round;
then hail through hazels and beloved locusts,
snow revealing some green along the way.
But the world changed before long,
a new wind blew up and showed us
the sun's passing;
and in the darkening air, in land already Lombard,
on the bridge above us as we arrowed past, we saw
two shadows embraced against the sky.

Translated by Lynne Lawner

In the Family Circle

An extinguished funereal light
frosts once more the firtrees
whose bark survives past death;
and everything is still in this shell
dug sweetly from time,
in the family circle
from which it is senseless to escape.

Within a silence known so well,
the dead are livelier than the living:
they descend from neat rooms smelling
of camphor, through trapdoors into heated
wood-lined cubicles,

adjust their own portraits,
then return to the stables to view again the heads
of a pure dark breed.

                                    But
without a mole's tools or umbrellas
to ensnare swallows, after what carillon
have you boys run through numbed meadows,
neither cautious nor forgetful in your pursuits?

The whetstone is in its horn.
The henroost leans against its eldertree.
The spiders have been entangled
a long time on the church walls.
The fountain keeps itself company with water.
And I am restored
to a more discreet love of life.

Translated by Lynne Lawner

March Strophe

A wicked rain with a backhanded
slap.
(My daughter can say what she likes, but tell me something
that begins with an *r* in the middle.)
A woman (pregnant) who hasn't sunbathed in a month
across from my balcony
(I've seen little more than the tips – nothing to boast about –
of her toes).
The wicked rain stops and starts.

But then it stops, and the sun comes back
as in the *Gerusalemme Liberata*,
and the blackbird gives less of a damn than ever
about our chatter, and even the dung, which sparkles squirting
on the fields in broken swarms from the spreader, and these
children who watch each other eat
candy, and
the boy who whistles without knowing it, in defiance of the *cogito*.

Translated by LV

Second TV Program (or Conflicting Program)

Around ten o'clock
in the sleepy clearing at the top of the palace
the creamy milk rims the ankles
of the National Commission's members,
the Chairman wanders about
(he frequently confuses *blagues* with *bêtises*),
but the three women who sit about my heart
given a little encouragement: 'What does he want?,'
says one, very gentle, blonde, 'My boss
is a school teacher, a colonel, he's a stickler for commas,
he doesn't know that it's not always the same, that not even the
      comma
always resembles itself.' And the other, the tawny one:
'I can't complain about mine, he's a good man from the south,
                if I'm late
he doesn't yell at me too much.'
The third, dark, huge, when she wasn't smiling
prematrimonially
stood like a cloud at night, like a mother
in orbit, waiting.

                               Translated by LV

Sinopie

There's one of them, I think his name is Marzio,
every two or three years he stops me as I go by
slowly, on my bicycle, and asks me from the pavement
whether Dante was married and what was his wife's name.
'Gemma,' I say, 'Gemma Donati.' 'Ah yes yes, Gemma,'
he says with his smile, 'thanks, excuse me.'
                          Another man,
still older, whom I meet more often, it's always I who say hello
first, and I think: maybe he doesn't remember
that rainy windy night when I went out for medicine
and he helped me with his tools (at that hour!)
to fix a wheel mangled by my umbrella.
A third, almost a hundred, deaf,
usually shouts as soon as he sees me: 'Hey, young man,' and by
                    his gesture you can tell

that, if he could, he'd give me a fatherly slap on the shoulder,
but sometimes he limits himself to smiling at me, or, suddenly
                                        excited,
he exclaims: 'You see! the camelia is always the first to bloom,'
or something else, depending on the season.
                                I'd like
to talk too about some of the others who are already mere sinopie
(without the fine derision of peach and apple trees)
crossed by century-old cracks.

                                        Translated by LV

Angelo Casè

The Same Cause

The faint glimmer, mere thread in the shadow, disquieting
the room – so reason, if it unties the snare
of days ever more absurd: a slant of light
seeping between door jambs, between edges of cupboards. The fine mesh
of love is woven of failed quests,
of impulses suddenly halted by the pitiless smile, the ambitious
silence. The same cause disturbs the day, the foolish
rule perpetuating fear. Life's accounts are settled with too much
silence, too many smiles. I note the address on the back
of an envelope, before the factory siren lets loose the blandishments
of Saturday afternoon. The opening widens, hope persists.

                                Translated by Raffaella Ferrari
                                      and June Salmons

Remo Fasani

Ode

Firs,
impassive trees,
you do not flower in the sun
and do not lose your green in the frost;
alpine firs,
you bend not under the weight of snow,
only lightning
can bring you utter death:
you who keep watch in the sky and among the ravines,
I marvel to hail you now

nameless companions of my childhood
and maybe still of today.

We are not alike you and I. . .
and yet I feel that something, a seed
of that life of yours
has taken root and grown within me.

Giovanni Giacometti

Bregaglia, a valley, almost a prison
in the rocks of the Alps. . .
And you had left, had gone away when young
to see the world. And you had seen it.
But then? Something lingered in you
obscure, unanswered.
It was another world, the first, which called to you
wanting to say
or hear its own word. Going away, in fact,
is right when you have left with those who stay behind
no questions, nothing unsaid
or when you come back bringing an answer.

You did come back, and brought one. This same valley
which you rediscovered, old and yet new, was no longer
a prison. It was part
of the world, the world itself, contained,
condensed in the circle of mountains and granite.
For these, this circle, its harsh peaks,
sharpened by the winds of the high lands
and primaeval like few others on this earth,
you hardly heeded them. You left them
to another, who climbed up from the plains and perhaps climbed too high,
to where, imperceptibly, stealthily, the void begins.
You, however, came down from the peaks to the lands of men.

Painting, for the other, meant choosing. For you
breathing, feeling alive, part of life.
You would move now from meadow to tree, from tree
to bridge, from the bridge (your symbol) to people, and at the same time
                                                                from light
to shade, from sun to storm, from face
to hands: not rapid journeys these, but pilgrimages
in which things and people found themselves, returned to themselves
and to others: this is where they were. They found their identities anew,

and had a history: 'Evening, 27th May 1910,
at half past eleven' (the child sleeps, time has stopped),
they had a meaning: 'May love's sunshine forever keep you warm'
(and in the autumn garden children play 'Flowers in flower, dead dead leaves').

You mixed your colours: essential if you were to do justice
to the richness and truth of the world:
but the more you mixed the more they came out intact,
in miracles of flame and ice.
Flames the grass and flowers in the meadow,
molten flames the bridge under the sun;
and ice the river and the footsteps in the snow.
But flame, ice, alternate and commingle. And now look
the young girl strides out untouched
into the square, in the blaze of noon where only
the horse twisting upon itself can seemingly endure.
Look, the trees and houses are not consumed by the shudder of the
                                        coming storm.

The last word was perhaps what you said to your fellows,
a man to men . . . in the evening to the card players
taking up, after work, religious talk;
to the women, after the toil of the day, drawing water
from the fountain, humbly, as one draws on God's grace;
to the young girl who crosses, as in an invisible trial
by fire, the noon time void, and has no fear;
to the two peasants, sitting by the Alpine hut in a pentecost of light
and a hand reaching through the air is the last word utterable. . .
To all these people, so like the Apostles,
if not like Christ (is not your face an icon?),
seen by Masaccio as into a new world he moved.

Poems by Remo Fasani
translated by Raffaella Ferrari
and June Salmons

Grytzko Mascioni

The Spring of Life

The spring of life seemed to you perhaps
only a cunning rape, a delightful
gentle whirr of insect wings

over the meadows?
                          Today however like a dragonfly
you desflower
other plains in joyful reckless flights
of love, on the blurred boundaries
of stealthily
approaching sunset
to the ancient melody of vain laments:
a murmuring swarm
of distant words.
                          And in the dim light
of the evening air you stand, your mauved cheeks
a silent witness that the spring of life
becomes a wind
which ravages
the flower beds of the sun.

Whitsun in Lugano

All is a misted glow: and white sails,
dappled sails, are flames in the wind,
almost dream balances (and scales poised here)
wing and flight on the lake (is it a flickering
which distorts all things, or the vision
which guides us to wisdom?), in the pale light
sails racing this morning in grey festivity:
Because today it's the Regatta, as you told me. . .
Call it rather a day of anguish, in this light
(the spring rain stops, rainbows
arch over tired cornflowers),
just as you can take or make of me
what you will to suit your story,
your world-pattern or a will-o'-the wisp
or frenzy of an inviolate
hour. (And I stay watching:
clusters of multi-coloured parachutes
have fallen from the sky, humming bi-planes
have darted past, and I follow the gentle
swirling of brightly coloured and silver confetti
lit or quenched by some will bewitched.
I look from the room where you record

by imperceptible signs the unsteady heart
missing beats or losing blood
and time beats away
on a dial beneath the surface). *And you spoke softly*
of future plans, of joys and of the work
that still remained for us to do. . .
But I am only aware of a seething, of the chill
of the wind bursting in from the lake, or is my breathing
keeping pace with the wind, with the fear,
night frost plunging into darkness,
nocturnal lamp, into which sink silently
those craven hearts of ours that search and question,
the only escape from time is to squander it,
the absolute mercy
of a godless peace.

Poems by Grytzko Mascioni
translated by Raffaella Ferrari
and June Salmons

Alberto Nessi

It's a Blessing

It's a blessing to stroll among the chestnut trees
you say to me one morning in November
while the broken stalks of Indian corn
lie glistening under the windows and the village women
open their shop doors. It's a blessing
to play truant from a life not ours
to listen to a crackling of the leaves
that is our own: words fall blithe
as the red berries of the cornel tree.
It's a blessing not to miss the path
towards the hill from which the hermit
centuries ago looked over Lombardy

and where among the stubble we embrace.

Translated by Raffaella Ferrari
and June Salmons

Rhaeto-Romansh

Andri Peer

The Föhn-wind

Last night
the wind played the organ
in the woods
all around.
Thrashing rain-squalls,
broken branches
on the ground,
blackened bones.

Between one gust and the next
I heard your voice.

On looking at paintings by Paul Klee

Your pen carves a furrow
into the paper.
And the paint is
your outspilled blood,
congealed by the light.

Here's man
with his 'pins'
in the air.

Down from the branch
where he's nice and safe,
the bird sings
mockingly.

The night
is aglow.
Kisses
fly
through the air,
as light as
balloons.

A landscape in the making.
The banks are crumbling,

and the lake is all poured out.

The face of a countryside,
its eye nearly hidden,
and midsummer's corn-flails
will not leave you in peace.

Combs with teeth which yield.
The two iron blades,
twins of haste,
twist
instead of forming a knot.

Onward!
The arrow flies.
The banner rallies to itself
the planets.

A gesture is born.
Lines of love
show the way to the wind.
Fire devours the mask.

Rope after rope
snakes
through space
and seeks to bind you.

Steeples full of menace
rage with hunger.
Ropework dragons
held in check
but how against their will.

Poems by Andri Peer
translated by John B. Avery

Flurin Darms

Peak

Staggering in the air
under the glancing knife-thrusts
of a midday sun
the peak trembles
and shudders,
crumbles over on its back
onto its own shoulders

and lives on the earth
dead,
its feet upwards,
the piercing blue steel slivers
in its paunch and ribs,
eyes closed,
only a yellow and green chin
which stretches high
from the brown and red snout on the ridge,
a murdered victim
sprawled in the coagulation of its own blood.

To the climbing wanderer
a blinding vision,
a sight which pains his eyes
and grieves.

And just at evening
when the shadows come in,
it rises then again
and comes alive,
grows high and swells large
again terrifying,
a giant
that curses and threatens in the darkness,
intent of purpose
immune
severe
it shows its face.

The murderers have fled,
dispersed by your threats,
and you grow,
you swell large terrifying,
my dark guardian
mountain,
lap of fears and dreams,
of old and new loves,
of anguishes trembling in deep ravines,
guardian
whom the poets and storytellers seek in order to live
and the world's fugitives and exiles in order not to die.

Translated by W. W. Kibler

All I have is my mother-tongue,
this heirloom of speech . . .
Let me take it up in my hand, like a harp,
Like a costly
and precious instrument
and let me run my fingers over the strings,
calling forth their sounds,
listening to their harmonies,
my ear attentive
to the way these surge
and unite
into one great hymn,
into the song
of my land and my people,
of harvesting and scythes
of love and death amid the reapers' bright blades
one summer's day,
and how they sing
of countless hidden
joys
which fill my dreams and my hopes
for you, my darling girl . . .

All I have is my mother-tongue . . .

Translated by John B. Avery

Theo Candinas

Vision of Childhood

Your childish laughter has sunk
into the mossy soil of the woods.
The rain has washed out your footprints
and the colour of your blue eyes
The Rhine has buried deep in his bed.

The wind from the heights has parted us
but the yearning has lingered on
and we fly now like butterflies
on tender wings through the night
of longing and love

62

I – half of you
You – half of me.

Cold

The fox that howls
and scents the bait
the wind that wails
about the cabins.
The cold that creaks
under the shoes
of a traveller
who is lost.

The heart that sighs
and is afraid
of becoming the prey
of the fox that howls
of the cold that creaks
under the shoes.

Poems by Theo Candinas
translated by H.M. Barnes

Hendri Spescha

Two Sonnets

I

The weary day, with broken wings
falls like ripe fruit
into the arcane troughs of dark
and clouds go like a thousand lambs

through the silence of the brown pathway
towards the gates of rest.
The scythes lie weary in the windrows
and through the sand-reeds runs a pent-up whimper.

Soft light fumbles through heavy curtains
and a voice sings
and closes the eyes of a child.

Dreams come through a curtain
of silver and gently take the child
aloft with them on light wings.

II

Through dark chamber and cold hall,
through pains of day you gently glide,
O Sister Night, great temptress,
and through my hands and my last musing.

You lay your pallid wool
upon my weary shoulder and my name.
You lose yourself within the folds of brain
and wrap my senses in your leaden veils.

You come with me as with an evildoer
to the edge of the silvery sea, of the brown dream,
of the unsatisfied black desire.

And your weight falls unceasingly
into the depth of the nascent dark
that tempts me with a melancholy smile.

Translated by H.M. Barnes

PROSE

German

Max Frisch

Sketch   Translated by Geoffrey Skelton
              From *Sketchbook 1966-1971*

There is nothing to be said . . . But he doesn't even say that. His wife does all she can to make him speak, in recent times even by picking a quarrel – which ends in tears, because he won't argue. He stands at the window, hands in pockets, as if considering a reply. Silent. Then, when he at last turns around, he asks if the dog has been fed.

. . .

As the years go on, things get worse.

. . .

All the guests keep on talking and don't notice that he, busy with his duties as a host, is not talking. Their usual conclusion: a nice time. Only his wife is unhappy. Afterward she says, 'You used to have ideas of your own.' He doesn't deny it. 'Haven't you anything at all to say?' Of course, if he makes the effort, he can say something; it's just that he has the feeling he has already said it all before. Who could be interested, except at most the other people?

. . .

He is in his middle forties, thus not old.

. . .

His wife at first puts it down to their marriage. There are couples who no longer have anything to say to each other. She goes on trips, etc., in order to revitalize their marriage. When she returns after two or three weeks, there he is at the station or the airport, waving. He takes her bags, kisses her – but there is nothing to be said.

. . .

There are words he never utters: he knows what they mean when others say them; if he says them himself they mean nothing, the same words.

. . .

He is a lawyer, head of a trust company, president of the House-owners' Association. He has a lot to do, much of it boring, but he never complains, even

65

about that. He meets plenty of people every day, all sorts of things happen. 'Why do you never tell me anything?' Then he turns on the television. 'You and your football!'

Taken to the zoo in his childhood, he thought that fish couldn't speak because they were under water; otherwise they surely would. . .

People like him. His quiet ways. There are always enough people around with something to say; it's usually sufficient just to listen. As a guest he comes in the category of those who stay seated, who never realize it is time to go, but just silently remain seated. Nothing occurs to him even when he is alone.

· · ·

When she says to him, 'You must be thinking something!' he gets up as if a conversation has just ended, goes out and feeds the dog, which simply wags its tail and eats and has no desire to make him talk.

· · ·

His clients respect his habit of not saying what he thinks; all they want him to do is look after their interests.

· · ·

His hobby: chess. No opponent would ever dream of asking: What are you thinking about now? All he needs to do is in his own good time make a move; silent as the chessmen themselves. His patience as his opponent now reflects, his air of relaxation, etc., he does not feel bothered when his opponent suddenly calls, 'Check.' What is there to say to that? He is grateful for every game, even when he loses after two hours – hours free from conversation.

· · ·

He turns on the radio the moment he gets into his car.

· · ·

Views on Nasser and Israel, on heart transplants, Ulbricht, Franz Josef Strauss, on the Common Market, *Der Spiegel*, on women's rights in Switzerland, on the statute of limitation for war crimes – everybody has views of some kind, naturally. Which is why his wife says, 'That's what Heiner thinks, too', as he is uncorking a bottle.

· · ·

The dog becomes more and more important. He spends hours walking with the dog. His wife can't stand walking for hours beside, in front of, or behind a man who has to exert himself even to say, 'There's a hare!' If she starts talking, he listens until an answer is called for; then he suddenly stops and looks at something: Nature as an excuse for not talking. . . When he goes out alone with the dog, he doesn't notice that for hours he hasn't spoken his thoughts, and, if he has none, the dog doesn't notice.

· · ·

What he likes: films. But he always avoids films that excite controversy. He prefers Westerns.

· · ·

Only people who don't know him ask the usual question: What is your opinion? Then he says something or other, but he could just as well have said the opposite; he is confused, as he used to be in school when the teacher said, 'Quite right!'

. . .

When he has drunk too much he does talk, without asking himself whether he has anything to say. Next morning he can't remember, and that bothers him: what could he have found to talk about from nine in the evening till four in the morning?.

. . .

His daughter has also noticed now that he never speaks. He is just fatherly. He can usually tell what she wants to know, but he doesn't elaborate: he just knows what 'idiosyncrasy' means (according to the dictionary), and then he pretends to be busy. Mowing the lawn. If his daughter shows signs of being bored at home he wonders what the trouble is; he asks her. He permits her almost everything. He reads Mao in order to understand her – then plays ping-pong with her.

. . .

The doctor has forbidden him to smoke. But he can't stop – not with people around waiting for him to say something.

. . .

He has to go to the hospital for an operation. An enjoyable three weeks: all he needs say is that he has hardly any pain, then leave it to the visitor to talk about the weather outside, the heat in the city, a divorce among their acquaintances, etc.

. . .

Eventually he loses contact even with the dog. The dog stops running after the fir cones he throws. The dog stops coming when he calls. The dog finds its own amusement.

. . .

Once, at some public ceremony, he has to speak on behalf of the management. He acquits himself excellently, not without humour, in front of two cameras. When he sees himself on TV he admits he did it well. No difficulty there – as long as he doesn't have to say what he thinks.

. . .

When he has the house to himself he may suddenly start frying a couple of eggs, though he is not hungry. The minute one has nothing to do there is a danger that one might think something.

. . .

It's true that he used to have opinions. He can remember that. For example, he (more than Doris) was of the opinion they should get married. Now he has no opinion even about that.

. . .

Sometimes in his dreams he has something to say, but then the fact that he wanted to say it wakes him.

. . .

It has nothing to do with Doris.

· · ·

How odd it is that people can hardly be in a room together before they know what to talk about – the same on the telephone or in the street! They greet one another and then at once know what to talk about.

· · ·

He now avoids any situation in which he can hear his own silence. He stops at building sites: the noise of drills, etc. But every noise ends some time.

· · ·

For a time, earlier on, he possibly used to speak to himself when silent: he still knew – in words – what he was keeping to himself.

· · ·

From the outside he seems quite normal.

· · ·

A suicide plan goes astray because in the letter he feels he would owe his wife he has nothing to say . . .

· · ·

Funerals never upset him, even when he was fond of the dead person. Everyone in black, some grieving, all admitting they don't know what to say, a consoling hand: there is simply nothing to be said.

· · ·

Later he does it without a letter.

Friedrich Dürrenmatt

From *Stoffe I-III*

For my father came from another age. He was already forty when I appeared on the scene, while in the year of his birth, 1881, Bismarck was still Imperial Chancellor, the Czar Alexander II was assassinated and the Russian secret police Ochtana was established, Dostoievsky died and Böcklin painted 'The Island of the Dead'. In return, as if some poetic justice ruled in the history of art, Picasso was born in the same year. The generations come thick and fast like waves, are carried away by time, and their traces are for later generations often enigmatic, often moving, seldom grandiose, and sometimes not without a sense of elevated comedy, like the two students walking in full regalia through a wintry, snow-covered cemetery towards an open grave, behind a coffin which contained a dead man whom they did not know and who had not known them, and whom I too – which became ever clearer to me as I walked towards his grave behind the two students – had not known.

It was only rarely that my father had talked about his youth and about his father who had been a well-known politician, but had already died in 1908. A strange, solitary and obstinate rebel: small, bent, bearded, wearing glasses, with sharp eyes, a man from Bern who brought out a newspaper of his own; who hated liberal-mindedness, socialism and the Jews; for whom there was no fitting political cliché and who fought for a Christian, federalistic, rural Switzerland at a time when it was on the point of becoming a modern industrial state, politically a unique figure, whose title-poems were famous and of a sharpness that few people venture to show nowadays.

I never heard my father talk about his mother either, likewise he kept silent about his student days which had taken him to Berlin and Marbach. It was his world which did not concern us children, which he tried to preserve for himself, I can imagine, particularly with regard to myself as I grew older and began to question everything.

My father was pious in a childlike manner, yet he was afraid of death. When I told him that I could not understand how the thought of no longer being 'anything' after death could be terrible – which in fact can only be thought and not imagined – he always contradicted me hastily, indeed with agitation, as if this thought were even more terrible than the thought of hell.

Although he was a scholar, he preached with simplicity and care, he wrote out his sermons in shorthand, this too in a minute script, but he gave the sermons without notes, for he was unable to read his shorthand script. It was in itself illegible, he explained, because he could not actually do shorthand, the illegible notes were only a memory-training exercise. He also recounted that in his youth he had learnt Volapük, which had been superseded by Esperanto, he was perhaps the only living person, he would then say with a smile, who could still understand Volapük.

Above all my father was good at pastoral care, and he continued to visit the sick right up to his old age. He had a concealed sense of humour and was a good listener, a gift which I have not inherited. He was never able to understand that I was a bad pupil, but only on one occasion did he lose his self-control: in the presence of my mother, he declared to me abruptly, so to speak officially, that I was not intelligent enough for the grammar school, nor for being a painter, as I imagined, I should lower my expectations.

When I then became an author, he kept silent about my scribbling, he still came to the first premieres, though not later on, but he was interested in what I wrote, without discussing it with me, was pleased too about successes, but literature was alien to him – apart from the fact that he had an immense regard for Theodor Körner. To make up for this he was one of the first to read Kierkegaard, when this thinker was not yet known among the pastors of the neighbouring villages, and Barth's 'Epistle to the Romans'. He kept Nietzsche's *Thus Spoke Zarathustra* hidden in his library. He did not like it when I routed the book out, but he allowed me to read it.

Only once did he try to persuade me to become a clergyman. On a Sunday evening in the town, shortly after I had passed my school leaving-examination. We were sitting together on a seat in the English Garden, the river was gleaming through the trees down below. My father did not speak in the first place of faith or of Christianity, he did not wish to arouse my opposition. He recommended to me the study of theology as the most interesting discipline intellectually, as he put it, and one that also included philosophy. He spoke of the clarity of the classical languages that he was so fond of; only now, after passing my school leaving-examination, during the study of theology, would their beauty be revealed to me. Not until then did he come to speak about faith: this was something that could not be confirmed without zealous study of Holy Scripture, my doubts derived from the way I exaggerated the conflict between faith and intellect; on the contrary, only an intellect that was placed in the service of what was higher, of faith, as servant and not as enemy, would be able to be of further help to me.

I listened to him in silence, the conversation was embarrassing to me, I no longer recall what answer I gave. My father could not convince me, but he did not display any disappointment. We went home peacefully. He never referred to our conversation again.

My mother must have been particularly disappointed. While my father was in the background, my mother ruled the family, in the village and later in the town. She was the immediate authority. We never experienced an argument between Father and Mother. At the most, in chess. My mother was an excellent chess-player. In the village the doctor and the dental technician came regularly to play chess with my mother; if she was once beaten by the dental technician, the latter refused for weeks on end to play again with my mother, for fear of losing. My father too was annoyed when he lost, even if he laughed about it, and he would then throw the chessmen into disarray.

My mother came from a village that was closer to the mountains than ours was, at the foot of the Stockhorn. In contrast to my father, my mother loved to talk about her father. This man, who like my other grandfather had died before I was born, became a legendary figure for me. My mother was a child of his second wife, I thought of him as a kind of Abraham, as a patriarch. My mother praised his beautiful, carefully brushed, long beard, and at the same time she assured us that he kept the hair 'on his head' closely cropped. He was a farmer who had let out his farms on lease, he still kept an army horse and was president of the district council and nothing else. He was the president of the district council. He ruled his village omnipotently, like a prince. What he liked best was to go out with his army horse at a smart trot, my mother sat behind on the cart, on one occasion her seat came unfastened, my mother was sitting in the road and my grandfather went off with horse and cart and did not notice the loss until he reached home.

70

In other respects too my mother's village must have been full of eccentrics; for instance there was a village schoolmaster who, as she related, used to sit fat and immobile by the side of his desk and to throw now his left clog and now his right one at the pupils who sat crowded together in the schoolroom which brought together all the classes, from the first to the ninth. Once a clog hit my mother on the forehead, but then my grandfather 'spoke very severely to the schoolmaster'.

Then my mother's memory was further haunted by a secret vagrant, whom she often spoke about. Among other things – after many adventures with federal councillors, the Emperor and the Czar – he is said to have almost become Rothschild's son-in-law in Paris, only he noticed at the last moment, as he was already sitting in the coach on the way to the synagogue, that his wife did not have a human head, but that of a pig, whereupon he took flight, renounced his millions and found his way back to Christianity.

A story which has remained with me because I learnt from it for the first time that Jews still existed, about whom we in the village had no idea, for otherwise they only appeared in the Bible. Only once, I obscurely recall, there was great excitement in the village: the Wandering Jew had come; what lay behind this vague recollection, I no longer remember.

Most of all, my mother was full of praises for her father's piety. She lived in a world of triumphant faith, her Christianity had a militant quality, but she was more realistic than my father and less prejudiced against socialism as well. As she was in charge of the house, my father always sent her in advance when he had complaints about my achievements at school. When she once noticed that I never did my arithmetical problems, she ran after me full of rage with a beanpole, my sister gave a horrified scream. Otherwise she punished us by being 'sad' for several days; we then lived as if under a shadow.

For many people she was an important woman who organized conferences of clergymen's wives and evening meetings for mothers in the district, and on such occasions she could give impromptu renderings of Gotthelf stories which were almost as good as the ones he himself had written. But there was always a wall between her and me, a wall which I had erected and which I could not pull down. There were too many peculiarities that disturbed me about her: she affected modesty without needing to do so; she was extremely inquisitive about what I earned, I never gave her the information; however, she had no inhibitions about borrowing money from me, for which I thought highly of her, but she never asked me on her own account, always for others'. I still feel sorry that I was not a more forebearing son to her. Whereas my father, for as far back as I can remember, proclaimed to us every Christmas that this one would be his last – which at first made us sad and later amused us, indeed, we waited impatiently for him to say it – my mother declared on her birthdays that her only wish was not to grow old. When she repeated this wish to me on her 87th. birthday, I did not summon up the necessary sense of humour, and I remarked that at eighty-seven she had after all grown a little old; offended, she kept silent for a long time, and finally answered that she had as yet never worn slippers. When she then became eighty-eight, she confessed to me that Pastor Hutzli had become a hundred and that this 'had been very, very good for him'. I realized that she was striving for a new purpose.

But what disturbed me most were her answers to prayers, they made me furious as long as she lived; for me they were something indecent that I could not accept, for my mother was a passionate prayer, and everything that happened around her took place as fulfilment to her prayers. There was something triumphant about her, everything happened through God's grace; even later, every one of my literary successes had been arranged by God, a conception which annoyed me extremely, all the more so as she suffered my annoyance with a smile. In general there was nothing she liked so much as to talk about her prayer-fulfilments, but I never let myself get involved with her in such discussions, I cut her short. Even during the last evening that I was with her, with my sister; an evening which anyway took its course in an unfortunate manner. But what was most strange was that, in spite of the sponsorship of my comedies by the Good Lord, she could not bear many of the scenes and turned to my wife in tears, saying that I would have to cut these scenes, for instance the three clergymen in *Mississippi* or the scene with the pastor in *The Visit of the Old Lady*, which my father on the other hand found amusing.

She died three months before her 89th. birthday, without having been really ill. To our surprise she wished to be cremated; evidently a book that had gone round the village was still having its effect on her; a pastor who supported cremation described in this book in a horrific manner what happens to corpses in graves. At the time my father had been annoyed about this book, he was in favour of burial.

After my mother's cremation we assembled in the same café as after my father's burial. Relatives from my mother's village were present; I no longer knew them. Some people from my village were there too, for example the teacher with only one thumb.

I grew up in a Christian world which did not let go of me, even later: my son has become a clergyman. The people with whom my parents associated were god-fearing, everywhere I came up against Christianity like a wall of faith, whether I was staying in the Christian Seminary at Bern during the holidays, or whether I was looking after cattle or helping with the haymaking while staying with a farmer with whom my parents were on friendly terms.

Walter Matthias Diggelmann

The Self-Induced Accident

On the sloping stretch between Possens and Sottens he had gone off the edge of the road in a sharp bend to the right. His Datsun 2400 GT overturned two or three times and hit a tree. He died where the accident took place, he died before a farmer from Possens who was going past on a tractor discovered him. The road isn't in itself dangerous, Hugo said. He had come from Lucerne to Echallens for the funeral. He had done that stretch a thousand times. Echallens-Moudon-Bern, said Ruth. In August, said Hugo, after three weeks of fine weather. A light north-easterly wind. Not oppressive then, only hot at midday. He had set out at six. He must have been dead twenty minutes later.

The experts from the police and the insurance companies (he had insured himself against accidental death and had taken out a comprehensive policy for the car) could find no explanation. The car was mechanically in good order. Eleven thousand kilometres, said Ruth, he had taken it to the garage four days ago. Full service. He was always meticulously exact about everything. He would rather have done without a car than have failed to look after it. He changed the tyres when other people would have gone another twenty thousand kilometres with them. Only he didn't wash it much. Serge washed it occasionally. He gave the boy ten francs each time for it.

Had he been drinking the previous evening? Not more than he was used to, Ruth said. A bottle of Salvagnin between the two of them. We were in bed at ten. We went to sleep at once. That is to say, I did. What about him? In the morning he had said that he too had gone to sleep at once. I woke at five because he was getting up. He brought me a cup of coffee in bed. He would be back again in the late afternoon.

The cause of death was clear, he had cut open his head against the left-hand door of the car, a fracture of the base of the skull, not common, but it can happen. The seat-belt was rather too loosely done up. If he had fixed it more tightly . . . Usually he fastened it so tightly that he could not work the radio, Ruth said.

Ruth and he had been married for six years, Ruth had brought a six-year old son into the marriage. He had been the father of two daughters. Eighteen and sixteen years old. When his first marriage had been dissolved, they were ten and eight. He had left the parental rights to his first wife. I shan't marry again, he had said. She, his first wife, had fallen in love with another man. She had run away from him. And later she had said, leave the children with me, they can come to you when you like.

All the same, Ruth said, it wasn't suicide. He never got over the fact that his family had been broken up. A year after the divorce at the latest he had never made any reproaches to his first wife and to her new husband (his successor). It is my problem, he had said. Nobody can understand it. And I don't want to explain it to anybody. I can't explain it to myself. If I knew why Leo (that was what he called his first wife) had left me, she wouldn't have left me.

He found this argument pertinent.

So it wasn't suicide, said Hugo. But perhaps he had tried it once more.

How?

Accident. Severe injuries, said Hugo.

I don't understand, said Ruth.

He had had the experience.

Everyone paid attention to him when he had the first bad accident. Leo fell in love with him for the time being again.

Two months ago he had a thorough examination: stomach, bronchia, kidneys, blood . . . He had been drinking for a time. Did you know that? Why had he been drinking? He had said he had got into a crisis situation. Suddenly he developed a fear of getting old. He had problems of circulation. But it wasn't suicide, Ruth suddenly said. But you did think so, surely? Me? On the telephone . . . when you called me up . . . Really? You said, he's done it now after all. Did I say that? Yes.

He often used to talk about it, he often said, when things really no longer worked out, he would put an end to it. He said you could use a rubber tube to direct the exhaust fumes into the interior of the car. He would never shoot himself. He had always hated firearms. There was also no question of strangling or hanging himself. Poison? Sleeping tablets? No. He had always only talked about the car. Once he had discovered an infrequently used road between Cossonay and Orbe. There he could get the car up to 180 kilometres an hour without difficulty. Then head-on against a tree. On this stretch there are trees at the side of the road. Two hundred kilometres an hour against a bridge pier. But that was dangerous for other people, he used to say.

What did he want in Bern in fact? I don't know. He did not talk much about his work. Not even when he was having trouble with it. Perhaps he had a rendezvous with his first wife. Hardly, Hugo said. He had met her on a number of occasions. In matters concerning the children, she didn't want to decide anything without his advice and consent. He often used to say that the divorce had been senseless, that nothing had changed, he in particular had not changed. The divorce was a catastrophe for him. The divorce had seriously injured him. The wounds had never healed. No, he had not clung to his first wife, not at all, he had loved her too sincerely not to forgive her. He was pleased that she was happy. But that his family had been destroyed . . . That was it. I can believe it, said Ruth.

74

He had already taken on too much as a boy. He was the tenth child of a small farmer in the Sankt Gallen area of the Rhine valley. It had not been possible to put him to an apprenticeship. He had gone to Zürich, and had started as a temporary worker at the Oerlikon engineering works. He had gone to evening-school.

He never told me why he left Zürich and settled in French Switzerland, Hugo said. It was on my account, Ruth said. He had said, you decide where we want to live. On no account in Zürich. That was his only condition. My family has been living for generations at Echallens. We had after all lived for some time in Zürich, for some months in Paris, and later for three years in the Ticino. It was all the same to him.

After six years at evening-school he obtained the diploma as a mechanical engineer. By the time he was thirty he was the chief representative of an American concern in Switzerland. He built his own house in Geroldswil, near Zürich. He had his offices in the town. Twenty co-workers. He not only sold machine-tools, he designed and set up factories, small-scale, medium-sized and large ones. He earned a lot of money. After his first marriage had failed, he sold his office and later only worked on his own. He could do that. He was known in his field and was in demand as an adviser and expert. He still made a lot of money.

I had decided on Echallens, Ruth said. But chance played a large part in it. That is to say, this house came on the market one day. He bought it at once. What is more, my son was living there with my mother. And I wanted my son to be with us, Ruth said.

Was there a good relationship between your son and him? He was often afraid. Of your son? Afraid of behaving in the wrong way to the boy. Was your son jealous of him? At times. Was he unjust to the boy? You can't say that. He never struck him. For instance. He tended rather to spoil the boy. And as has been said already, he was often afraid. Actually he was fond of the boy. But it seldom happened that he really showed it. For instance, that he caressed him or gave him a kiss or something.

Why have you two no children? He didn't want any more children. He was too old now, he used to say. What about you? I have always wanted to have a child of his. But I understood his point of view too.

Why did he marry a second time? He couldn't live alone. He would not have had to live alone. Ruth had not insisted on marriage. If something should happen to me, he had said at that time.

He often said that he felt lonely, Ruth said. He spoke French almost fluently, but he had no friends here, only acquaintances. Although he was exceptionally adaptable.

He was the most wonderful man I have ever met, said Ruth. We made love twice a day, she said. I believe I shall never be able to sleep with a man again. I don't know why he did it.

She said it again now. Once more. He hadn't fastened the seat-belt, she said. I didn't want to tell you.

They had come in their hundreds to his funeral. Although he had been a stranger to them. He often used to say, Ruth said, that he was a stranger here. Whenever we had a big family celebration, he had some appointment or other which could not be put off. My family loved him. They all cared for him. My brother, for example, looked after the garden for him. He is an *agriculteur*, he knows something about gardening. He often used to say that it was his garden and that he did not want anyone to be concerned about his garden. But he was so clumsy about practical matters. He was incapable of fixing on a new water-tap. When we sold the house and the sale had to be legally attested, the discussions with the banks and so on, I had to do all that. That is to say, I didn't understand anything about it either, but my second brother understands it all. In the end, all he had to do was to sign. And before he signed, he asked me whether it was right for him to sign.

I am only tolerated here, he said sometimes. He often suffered from depressions. The change of life. Crisis. And meanwhile everything was running smoothly. His clients trusted him.

No, he scarcely had any relationship with his brothers and sisters. They only wrote to him when they needed money. His parents were already dead when we got married. He liked books, pictures, the theatre and opera, and films too. We often drove to Geneva to the opera. We frequently flew to Munich to see a play. We were often in Paris too. It was only Zürich that he did not want to see again.

Actually he was only looking for love. I have had success instead, he often said. Smiling. But we loved him. I loved him, said Ruth, my family loved him. But he was too suspicious.

It is more blessed to give than to receive, Hugo said. That was something of a maxim, as far as he was concerned. Yes, said Ruth, he was glad to give. He gave himself away. But he . . . Well? He could spend hundreds, indeed thousands of francs without more ado, if he believed he could make somebody happy by so doing, Ruth said. And at the same time he would make terrible scenes if I spent money on things which he considered as unnecessary. He could become furious if we had a meal in a restaurant and Serge asked, May I have a dessert? He said we are here to get nourishment, it's not a festive occasion.

He had not bought a watch for twenty years. He found watches too dear. He bought his first watch when he had bought a second car, for his first wife, Hugo said.

He told me once that he would have to leave me, that is, us, said Ruth. He could not cope with Serge, he said. At times he hated Serge. Because Serge is a bad pupil at school, wants to spend all his time watching television, even when he doesn't understand anything about the programme, because Serge boasts every other day about his fights in the school playground . . . Serge really could not know how he was to win the love and affection of his stepfather. He was a medicine-man as far as Serge was concerned. Once he promised Serge fifty francs if Serge would at least read the *Diary* of Anne Frank. Naturally Serge did not look at the *Diary* for months on end. One day Serge came and said he could buy a small collection of Formula One models for fifty francs. He retired early to his room and in the morning he told us the story of Anne Frank. He got the fifty francs. I believe he hated Serge at that time. He drove off during the following night. For four days I did not know where he was. I rang up all his friends, you remember, I rang you up as well. He came back after a week. I told him that Serge had not left my side the whole time. Apart from when he had to go to school. The next day he bought him a horse for five hundred francs.

He often said he had been a good pupil at school only because he hated violence. He had never got into fights. He did not beat his children either. After the divorce, when we were already living together, friends told him that he ought to have shown his first wife more often who was boss. Women needed a knock or two occasionally. He thought this over seriously. And one day he hit me. He had to be sick afterwards, and was ill for three days.

What had happened before the fatal journey? A quarrel? No. Nothing at all. The day before he had received a letter from his first wife. She wrote to him that she was going to spend the holidays this year with the two children in Tunisia. So the children weren't coming to us in the holidays.

I don't know whether that could be a reason, said Ruth. He'd not had an accident driving for fifteen years. Every two or three years he went to a driving course. He could control the car in all situations.

But what happened about his first car accident? asked Ruth. Oh, that was fifteen years ago. His first marriage was going through a dull patch. A painful calm on the lake. Moonless nights. And in the daytime deep blue cloudless skies. In Valais, apricot harvest. It happened on the long, straight stretch between Martigny and Saxon. He was on the way to Brig, Simplon, Domodossola. A Dutch car overtook him, though he was already doing 180 kilometres an hour in his Alfa. The Dutchman grazed him, he was at the same time trying to take evasive action and drove at the same speed into the apricot plantations. His car was a write-off, he himself had severe internal injuries, though not gravely dangerous ones . . .

I only wanted to say that when he was discharged from hospital, Leo came to collect him, and Leo looked after him at home as if he were a child. Until one day Leo said, that's enough, the doctor has said that you are capable of going back to work . . .

I know, said Ruth, he was always looking for affection, he always wanted to be caressed. Even in bed. He wanted to be seduced. I had to take the initiative. He wanted to be loved, and when we loved him, he became suspicious. His mother had never made a proper recovery after his birth. Some sort of abdominal complaints. The family doctor had never brought in a specialist. They couldn't afford hospital treatment. His mother had no strength left for him, and no time. He was a burden to his mother. And to his brothers and sisters. The father said that it was his fault that the mother . . .

He had not learned how to be loved. Perhaps that's it, said Hugo.

Raffael Ganz

If You Don't Shout, You'll Leave Empty-Handed
translated by Don S. Stephens

My brother has been lying in the hospital for more than a week now; every day I bring him newspapers, magazines, and whatever else he needs. Karlheinz says it's not easy to get used to being sick. But whatever else you experience in a hospital, you are quickly inured to it after just a few days. You just overlook the people in wheelchairs and those on crutches, the ashen-grey figures in the corridor, and those who are rolled inconspicuously to the bath beneath sheets. And if someone cries out in a ward, it sounds like they're doing something to someone in a film on TV. Only among the old women who sit on the benches in the waiting-room and whose hands tremble, who stare at you so long that you can feel their glances on your back, there you sometimes get the shivers. Well, also with the one in the next bed. The old man has already been lying here in the sickroom longer than all the others, a critical case. Stomach operation, kidney failure, something the matter everywhere, even with his larynx, can scarcely whisper any longer. His vacant stare fixed stubbornly on the ceiling. He always starts moving his lips when someone happens to look at him. All his life the old man has been a farmhand. Won't last much longer; it's hard to know what keeps such a sick man alive. Karlheinz reported all that to me when they had rolled the old man away once for an X-ray.

Then it struck me: No one seems particularly to care about the old farmhand. The nurse goes hastily to the old man's bed, sticks a thermometer in his mouth or claps the respirator on his face, takes his emaciated wrist between her fingers, counts his pulse, and opens the clamp on a plastic tube under a bag that hangs on a gallows above his head and from which a glass-clear liquid trickles down into his thin arm. Underneath on the bedframe hangs another plastic bag half-full of a liquid that looks like motor oil. My brother says that the old man's life is running from one bag into the other. A pathetic old fellow, if you think about it.

Only his alarm clock, a massive old monstrosity with two bells sticking out like ears, still reminds him of his home, of the low-ceilinged unfinished room in the attic or next to the hayloft; it stands next to his toothbrush glass on the nightstand but doesn't work. They wouldn't allow the old man to wind up the clock any longer because it ticked so loudly. The old man was terribly angry because of that; afterwards he sulked and was rebellious for days on end. Now he is too weak to wind up the alarm clock again.

The old man breathes with difficulty, as if he can't catch his breath. His head lies in the middle of his pillow, a few scratches dabbed with iodine on his forehead and down over his cheekbones. 'He pants like that all the time; I can't get to sleep at night', my brother says between his teeth, so that the old man can't hear him. Last night he had fallen out of bed and had torn out all his tubes, even the catheter. My brother said he rang right away, but ten minutes or more passed before the night nurse came; he had not been able to help – how could he? Tonight would probably be another bad one for the old man. So my brother asks me to get him some Oropax.

Since there is a drugstore not far from the hospital, I start to run down right away. As I go by the old man's bed, he looks at me with his water-clear eyes, seeks my glance just as he would like to catch the glances of all who come into the sickroom or who sit at the patients' beds. Just as Karlheinz said, he always moves his lips if you look at him; the old man moves his lips now, too; I think that he, in his own way, is saying, 'See you later,' – perhaps. Already at the door, I wave to him, and I have the feeling as if the old man were breaking down in utter despair.

On the way to the drugstore I can't get the old farmhand out of my mind: Once in the afternoon, a clergyman was sitting at the old man's bedside and reading from the Bible. As if hypnotized, the old man hung on the pastor's every word; at the same time his hand groped again and again across the bedcovers into the emptiness between the edge of the bed and the clergyman, whom he wanted to touch. He sat too far away, however. Unceasingly, the old man's lips moved, as if he were repeating the Biblical words. The spiritual comforter spoke the Lord's Prayer, clapped the book closed, stood up. Then the old man tried to raise himself, struggled like crazy to say something; he reached out his hand – the clergyman took it paternally in both of his hands, patted it lightly, and said, 'Yes indeed, I'll come again, soon'. Exhausted, the old man fell back onto his pillow, turned his head to the side.

Understandably, when a person is so sick, everyone looks away. A patient doesn't like it and visitors make themselves scarce then for sure. No one wants to give a thought to the life of this unshaven, trembling, pale grey face on the pillow; no one wants to picture how the old man lived. His whole life worked away, worn out like a bonded servant, perhaps shunted off from farm to farm

79

because in ice-cold servants' quarters he had already caught something in his lungs or had a twisted back, arthritis in his joints, and rheumatism before he was forty. Was able to talk only with animals, and now and then a few words with the farmer about the weather, about a cow down sick. If he wanted to say something else, to talk about his schooldays, about his first boss, about his father, or about a church celebration years ago, no one listened to him. Now he is more pitiable than ever, a poor devil who can't be helped any longer.

The big day: My brother is discharged but still has, as he puts it, a row of ants on his belly. We start to go straight through the revolving door in the hall to the outside; then Karlheinz asks: Did you pack my razor? He had placed it on a cupboard shelf behind a ledge, so that it wouldn't fall down; I had overlooked it. So, I had to go back up again.

The old man now lies alone in the sickroom. At his bed there prevails, as usual, the oppressive, 'clinical' chaos around a person who is on his last legs. I find this atmosphere unpleasant, and now I find the old man even stranger than before. Besides, his eyes pursue me unflinchingly; they remain on me while I step to the cupboard, find the razor, close the cupboard, go to the door.

Now the old man raises his head, as well as he can, from the pillow, reaches out his hand, trembles, lets it fall back on the covers, raises it again; his lips, his chin, his tongue, his eyes, his entire face speak to me, without words, only a croaking. I say: 'Get well soon'; but I think: You poor bastard! I can't wait to pull the door shut behind me.

In the corridor I involuntarily remain standing as if struck with a case of bad conscience, with a feeling of not doing something that is demanded of me. I recognize this feeling: An event that had been seared into my memory. Before his death, my father also lay in a sickroom. One afternoon, while freed from pain and fear for a few hours, and in a mood that recalled happy times, he said to me, 'You know, I'd like to drink a little glass of white wine once again.'

The next day I brought along to the hospital a small bottle of white wine in a paper bag. But I asked the doctor, stupid as I was, whether wine could hurt my father. The resident spoke of house rules; they didn't take to such things; my father would only have to throw it up again anyway; besides he already was causing enough trouble for the nurses; so better not. I didn't take the bottle out of the paper bag; once, twice my father's eyes rested on it, but he asked nothing. I still regret it today: It would have been enough for two, three small glasses: a prosit once again like at the table; I would have been rewarded for ever with the smacking of my father's lips after his first sip, with his contented laugh if the wine was good. Yet: I did not fulfill his last wish. Every time I think about it, I am depressed and enraged. For that reason, the bottle is still standing in the cabinet today. Even if the wine becomes vinegar or evaporates, it will serve as a reminder for me: If you decide to do the correct thing, the so-called right thing, or what others consider right, then you end up doing wrong.

So, I stand in the corridor, the doorknob still in my hand; I think it over: Did the old man really want to say something? Did he perhaps also long for . . . I am already standing in the room next to his bed; I bend over; I don't really know why; put my ear to his mouth, hear: . . . 'I'. He coughs in my ear, then again, scarcely audible: '. . . I – would like to see.' Slowly, between puffs of breath, the words come out of him.

And I don't understand them.

See? What does the old man want to see? I look into his eyes. What can it be that he wants to see? At a loss, I shake my head; he stretches out his hand points to the window the width of a night-table away from his bed.

Now something comes to me that I had noticed only incidentally up until now: All the time I visited Karlheinz, the window next to the old man's bed, a narrow window, which goes from the window sill at bed-height to the ceiling of the room, has been as if walled up by venetian blinds. There is no outside view in the sickroom, for framed in the large picture window that extends over the entire length of one wall of the room there is only another wall, the gigantic façade of the other wing of the hospital, geometrically rigid with rows of windows, supports, window sills. Now I ask myself: Has the old man really been trying desperately for days, weeks to say to anyone, to everyone who came in or went out, that he would like to have an unobstructed view of the outside, that he would like to see the sky, a bird flying, just once more, before. . .

I turn the handle. The sections of the blinds shift: The old man's face becomes brighter and more pallid; the stubble of his beard seem to be transparent as glass. He turns his head to the side, sees the venetian blinds soar quickly upwards and the sky enter. On the grounds in front of the hospital stands an old oak tree with mighty branches; the highest forks reach far out over the flat roof, and one branch comes near the window, so near that you could count the leaves. Below, a squirrel is just now running across the lawn, and the wind is blowing the jet of water from the fountain diagonally across the surface of the water. But the old man can't see that, from his bed; he sees only the sky, the new green in the treetop, and behind that the range of Alpine foothills, on which lie the last snowy remnants of a long winter.

I speak loudly to the old farmhand, say that I have to go now. The sick man looks at me; his lips move; I don't know what he is saying. Again he turns his face toward the window. I'd never seen his face like that before; it's impossible for me to describe it.

Gerhard Meier

As If They Were Asked to Judge

After All Souls' Day the trees are for the first time real trees. (And children of four or five bring in flowers from the fields.) Old people sometimes have days when they would rather not be alive, simply rather not be alive. However, after All Souls' Day the trees are for the first time real trees. The delivery vans for customer service from the departmental stores (Nordmann, Neckermann, etc.) return to the towns. The town puts on a sky which people claiming to have taste declare to be tawdry (as if they were asked to judge). The trees are barer, barer than ever.

At the Time of the Gentle Lights

Edges of snow turn black as they melt asphalt in front of the hospitals and the lamps flower, gentle lights. Two or three times a year the moon stands red at the entrance to the village, and those who see it stop, not rightly knowing what they should think, whether: Soon the violets will be in bloom! or: How shall we live tomorrow? Young men skate and as they are skating think of their girls and in the summer still only know the shapes they made in the ice. Many are waiting and looking forward to laughter now, to liberating laughter, now, at the time of the gentle lights.

It Is Raining in My Village

The elephant stands by the garden fence, the toy elephant. It is night, by the swampy meadow, the low lying pasture-land which is transformed at given times, when the snow melts or when there is heavy rain, into a shallow stretch of water, in winter also into an ice-field, traversed by the embankment of the Langenthal-Jura railway. The coffin maker lived here and here he had his workshop. The distiller lived here and here he had his distiller's cart (if it were not standing in front of one of the farms of the neighbourhood). How transparent the leaves are, the albinotic ones, at the base of the variegated sycamore. Occasionally there have been accidents at the level crossing, which is unmanned. When the farmer close-by was dead the rambler roses were in bloom in front of the house, and the wind coming from the fields roamed in subdued manner through the house, through the darkened rooms.

Since then the corn keeps on thriving; above the corn the larks keep on singing every year. Children try to gain colour from the autumn by treating tree foliage with water, in the meantime late thunderstorms move across the country, at night, over historic places. From time immemorial thickets of oak line the same section of the forest.

In the evening, at exactly the right time, the crows came back, always by the same route. The white fretsaw ornaments on top of the posts of the barn roof by the furrier's house became even whiter. The remaining façades acted out simplicity. Over the hills the sky was often red. Tumours grew in hearts. Sufferers from silicosis had trouble with breathing now. Pollen hung over the pine forest at that time. Spiders span webs. Squalls howled in barns when the lady-smock was in flower. Children recited: ' . . . Now everything must change'. At the same time, according to statistics, the suicide figures increased and attained their peak level in May, as they still do today.

One night the Vietcong flag was hoisted up on the Bern minster. Three authors who wrote in German admitted to an interviewer that they had only heard of the restlessness among young people through the revolt.

Somebody remembers observing marble-quarries in the sky; as if there were such a thing as marble-quarries in the sky. In the cowsheds the cows are now munching over what they were chewing a little while previously. Old people dismiss memories. Young people play about with scraps of experience to make collages of the world. Many people are afraid of the coming day.

I have always picked a bouquet for my wife in the early summer, a meadow nosegay of sage, daisies, grasses and clover. It is important to gather bouquets in the early summer.

It is raining in my village. The elephant stands by the garden fence, the toy elephant. It is night, by the swampy meadow, the low lying pasture-land which is transformed at given times, when the snow melts or when there is heavy rain, into a shallow stretch of water, in winter also into an ice-field, traversed by the embankment of the Langenthal-Jura railway.

Often, not in this context, it sounds across the country, the inland country, as if a ship were wailing.

Walter Vogt

The Final Story

The obstetric clinics and the infants' wards were the first to be affected by it. At first there was relief – the strict, busy activity was adapted to a more comfortable pace, the employees had their holidays, the ward sisters sighed and went away to recuperate, the medical superintendents devoted themselves to research. In the country the midwives complained about the loss of earnings. The sacristans began to miss the tips they used to get at christenings, and ageing clergymen regretted that they could no longer introduce their young curates to the lovely rite. Firstly in the middle-class press, then also in the socialist press loud voices were raised against the amorality of a population that was unwilling to accept any responsibility any longer. Oblique, and then point-blank reproaches were made against the manufacturers of the best known pill. But the representatives of the board of directors could demonstrate that sales were, if anything, receding.

Statisticians calculated that in eighty years' time the population would have as good as died out. People laughed. Statisticians had also previously maintained the contrary opinion.

In the meantime similar reports were coming in from the whole world. Here and there was still an occasional miscarriage. In Paris the 123,000 registered medical students came together in the winter sports palace in order to be present at a birth which had already been announced the previous day and which was being relayed there by television and on large screens. There was rioting because the winter sports palace was not able to hold everybody; but the police remained in control of the situation, and at the last moment the President of the Republic arranged for the birth to be transmitted on Eurovision. The United States took over the programme by the satellite 'Ostrich'.

'Mesdames, mesdemoiselles, messieurs, vous allez assister à la naissance d'un *homme*, donc à un évènement éminemment français –'

The Marseillaise, the Arc de Triomphe, the labour-pains – the birth promised to take a normal course. There were 1873 professors of obstetrics in the big hall, they were shown close-up on television. The professors smiled or looked serious. The cardiac murmurs of the unborn infant were recorded. It was a moving scene. At last a brainless monster with a frog's head came into the world. Three minutes and twenty-seven seconds after birth it was dead. A life for television.

A baby's napkin firm in Sweden offered a prize of a thousand million U.S.-dollars for the best piece of work on the fall in the birth-rate. Nestlé and other manufacturers of baby cereal held back for the time being from offering such big awards because after all their products could also be supplied to schoolchildren, sportsmen and soldiers. They resorted to economies.

In the children's hospitals there was a glut of nurses.

Of course the blame was put on atomic tests. There was a wave of suicides in the war ministries of the nuclear powers. Nobody was willing to be X-rayed any more, and people no longer trusted even the harmless little pieces of X-ray equipment to be found in shoe-shops. All at once every layman could see what had so far escaped the attention of the competent authorities: that in this equipment the beam is directed straight on to the reproductive organs. Baby-sitters inserted half-page advertisements in the most expensive newspapers, conciliation agencies folded up, professors of children's diseases were given early retirement.

A zoologist, a shining light in his subject, discovered that the rest of the mammals were continuing to breed in a completely normal manner; so it could not really be the atomic tests – for they affected the just and the unjust and all the animals. Never-ending arguments arose among academics about the possible reason – foodstuffs? But what sorts? Additives to foodstuffs? Medicines? Nobody knew.

Whole research-teams tried to find out at least whether the cause was attributable to women or to men. Whenever they had discovered a deviation from the norm, they stated sadly that they had long been lacking in normal material for comparison.

Questionnaires were constantly being sent out, and they came back with the same result: yes, people amused themselves as always, no, there had been no change in their habits.

Animal experiments were useless.

In the meantime it had become usual to describe the year which had the last births to record as the Year Zero – *Paris Match* showed the picture of a little Javanese boy who could be seen as the last human being by virtue of the exact time of his birth, *Life* presented a charming little Eskimo girl in the same capacity, to say nothing of the *Domenica del Corriere*. It also became usual to describe the children of the final age-group as 'the Last Ones'. The Last Ones were pampered and spoilt.

A professor at an important university wrote a standard monograph on the Last Ones – but unfortunately he illustrated it with numerous X-ray photographs. The populace became hysterical and lynched the respected man together with his three head-physicians. Afterwards people were ashamed, and the funeral took place in a dignified manner, with great expressions of sympathy. At the burial service the clergyman stated that it might possibly be God who was striking human beings with sterility.

Those who were present listened to him attentively.

Spare me from describing all the measures that were thought up and carried out by progressive societies, medical faculties and the ministries, with a view to reactivating parturition. Eskimo women made pilgrimages to the Zulus, a thousand young Papuans were triumphantly received in Paris, Americans mated desperately with Chinese women – in vain. In the end voices were even raised which ascribed the persistence, indeed the origin of the sterility to the very same unlimited promiscuity. A suggestion was made to bring women and animals together – not that anything was hoped for as a direct outcome of this mating; it was intended rather as a stimulus to setting something going – on the other hand the world society for the prevention of cruelty to animals complained against this type of cruelty to animals, and as the relevant laws were completely valid, judgment was given in favour of the animal welfare society.

In Year Seven for the last time children went to school in the first class in a regular way. Throughout the world efforts were made to keep back as many as possible of them for a year. But a year later the end was definitely there. As a consequence public life was seriously affected for the first time. Schoolmistresses were pensioned off, kindergarten teachers had been already, nursery-schools went bankrupt – the further transmission of broadcasts such as children's hour, bedtime story, and children and animals became more and more of a problem – what should be put in their place?

Light music.

In Year Twelve there appeared a kind of mythical hope that the Last Ones woud be chosen to procreate a new and better race. The hopes of mankind were concentrated upon them. As something of a contrast to this, people in countries like Mexico and Guatemala came to form the opinion that it was precisely these Last Ones who would have to be sacrificed to the gods – no one knew any longer to which gods exactly – all the same, it happened . . .

Both eventualities were revealed as equally senseless and stupid. When the Last Ones attained the years of puberty, they were put into the hands of public enterprise which wished to encourage breeding. Obligatory instruction in mating was given in schools, the boys trembled, the girls cried; there was strict control of the enforcement of the process. When the Last Ones became sixteen, seventeen and eighteen without anything else happening apart from a discharge of blood here and there – a terrible disillusionment befell everyone. People had to realize that procreation was definitely finished and that this was very likely through their own fault, because of the crazy coercive measures. Searches were carried out in the Andes, in the Mato Grosso and in Central Asia for hitherto unknown groups of people. Finally a new race of pygmies was discovered in the Mato Grosso; they could neither read nor write nor speak – the little folk had only a highly developed numerical system – and this much could be worked out: their last children had been born in the Year Zero, and since then the gods had been angry with them.

Teenage fashions ceased to exist. The manufacturers went in for old people's fashions, very shortsightedly, for would there possibly be an increase in the absolute number of old people? After an initial boom caused by speculation, property became cheap. The first skyscraper districts were advertised as available as free gifts. Nobody wanted them. There were no longer any food problems. At the time of Year Twenty-Three to Twenty-Four the lower ranks of military instructors became unemployed. This passed unnoticed.

Sculptors went in for objective sculptures of youths and maidens – from memory! – and fanatically enthusiastic crowds would spend days breathing on and praying and shouting to these idols.

Armies disappeared except for generals who were entitled to pensions. Nobody bothered about this.

About Year Forty a movement started in the U.S.A. with the purpose of organizing carefully the decline which obviously could not be stopped, in order to make the most of the last grain of hope. Everything was automatized: the news, weather reports, research, the hospitals – in the big cities there was unmanned traffic – there was unmanned politics and diplomacy . . .

General admiration was aroused by a model of East-West relationships that functioned without friction and which could be switched on to HOT or COLD – the most important airlines flew of their own accord, with the necessary intermediate stops.

Laws were passed to guarantee the maximum possible concentration of population – for all fragmentation signified decline. But when a smallpox epidemic in one of the largest of such centres carried off thirty percent of the population, individual misgivings could also be heard about the principle of concentration.

In Year Sixty-Four a final quarrel flared up between San Francisco and New York; the question was, in which of the two cities mankind should be settled – San Francisco threw into the scale its magnificent climate, New York its greater internationality. New York won. It was asserted subsequently that it was not until this decision was taken that collapse became inevitable; an 'Off to 'Frisco' movement in the grand manner got started – but although the flight connections functioned smoothly of their own accord and in San Francisco the automatic traffic pulsed rhythmically without intermission in the streets, although the city was consumed in a sea of light every evening, radio music resounded from every house and the green of the television screens flickered, in spite of all this and although the climate was still excellent, the city in an undefinable way gave the impression of being uninhabited.

Three members of the Off-to-Frisco committee remained lying unburied on the airfield, the others flew horrified back to New York.

In Year Seventy it was already being demonstrated that it was impossible to go on enforcing the necessary concentration in New York. Most people had long been too weak and fearful to be able to continue to move about in the automatic street traffic, and nobody cared to entrust themselves to the last taxi-drivers, the youngest of whom were in any case seventy.

The ever scarcer human beings stayed hopelessly scattered over the busily humming giant city. They lived rather wretchedly on the automatically distributed dairy products and some tinned goods. At the very last moment, when there was still a handfull of men who were capable of working, at the least a fully automatized canning factory had been transferred from Chicago to New York. The cattle were electrocuted while grazing, then transported on conveyor belts.

In the harbour the sirens of the ships that looked after transatlantic traffic were wailing, and there was an increase in collisions in the airports. Nobody paid attention to the fact that for some time rockets had been setting off into outer space at hourly intervals – and when finally a little chimpanzee landed on the rear side of Sirius and flashed most valuable information to the earth – no one even laughed any more . . .

In December of Year Eighty-Nine one of the Last Ones was sitting in the twenty-third storey of a skyscraper and was dialling telephone numbers at random.

At the beginning of Year Ninety, in January, he suddenly received a reply.

'Lovely weather . . . '

'Fine, but rather cold.'

'Rather cold, indeed.'

'But dry.'

'Pleasantly dry, indeed.'

'Do you like New York?'

'Do I like New York?'

'Rather noisy, isn't it . . . '

'Rather noisy, indeed.'

When next day the Last One wanted to ring up his friendly partner again, he could no longer recall the number.

Werner Schmidli

I Know How Things Have to Look in a Home

1

The room in which Rolf, the son, has to sleep, play, do homework, and live also has to be the drawing-room in which family festivals can be celebrated and visitors be received, so far as visitors come, and friends of Father.

What would people think, says Mother, if they were to pay a visit unexpectedly and everything was in disorder. I'm not used to that. The room which is a drawing-room has to be a living-room, heatable in cold weather, but it is only heated on holidays and for family occasions which occur in the cold time of year. The heating is already off at Easter. During the other days of the cold season the room which is supposed to be a living-room is slightly warmed. The chill is taken off, says Mother, and that is amply sufficient. Otherwise, she says, you won't have any resistance, neither you nor your father, none at all, when you go outside into the cold.

She says: I know what's good and what isn't. I've had my experiences. I know what's what. Let's leave the kitchen door open. And she leaves the kitchen door and the drawing-room door open – the kitchen is always heated except at midsummer. The food that she has cooked on the gas-stove Mother keeps warm on the hot stove-plate.

In this way it is just pleasant in the drawing-room, Mother considers. But all the same we mostly sit in the kitchen.

In the kitchen, in this kitchen, half our life and more takes place. In the kitchen, in this kitchen, everything has its place, nothing superfluous is tolerated by Mother in her kitchen, which is ours too, Father says, which belongs to all of us, where we all live. Everything is practical here, easy to reach, here everything has its proper place and is easy to find. One notices everywhere here Mother's hand, everywhere here one notices her practical side, her experience.

Order rules here.

Just how do you manage it? visitors and friends often ask.

I'm not accustomed to anything else, is all Mother then says.

2

It stays like that when the son, older now, uses the living-room for working, reading, sleeping, living, and receiving friends, girl-friends too. Be careful, Mother says, you know what you have to do, Mother says.

It isn't necessary for me to say anything more to you, says Father, Mother has already told you everything, I believe.

And if the son wishes to smoke in the drawing-room in the evening, Mother says to the son, and also to Father, Do go into the kitchen. People don't smoke in the same room where they have to sleep. You really ought to know that by now.

When visitors and friends have been there, and after family occasions, the drawing-room is cleared and ventilated, and the order to which Mother has accustomed Father and Son is restored.

Mother knows exactly where everything has been placed and does not tolerate anything new; she does not let herself be hoodwinked. Mother knows what belongs in a drawing-room and what does not. And the son knows and Father knows: Mother has said so often enough. Mother has rarely permitted Father or Son to put pleasing objects, gifts, finds, purchases, souvenirs and so on on the furniture that Father has made himself. She has always decided and has then chosen a place. Now and again Mother has allowed Father to put a dainty plastic statuette, the present of a colleague or friend, on the sideboard.

In earlier days Mother used to work as a maid, in a better-class family, as she always says, she also lived in and had her life there.

They taught me early on what order is, she relates. Nothing was left lying about there, everything had its place. And so it has to be. I liked being with this family. I learnt what it means to keep a home clean, to cook and to polish. To take care. They took care about their home there. I know what a lot of work that means. My work was appreciated there. You don't have to tell me anything. I've had my experiences. I know how things have to look in a home. Why do people have to leave unnecessary things lying around? You can make things simpler, surely?

89

Mother goes on talking.

Mother knows what everyone needs.

Mother knows what is good for breakfast and what is not, tea or coffee or chocolate or Ovomaltine. Mother knows what food is appetizing and nourishing, what is good for your health and what is not. After all, one doesn't drink beer in the morning, on an empty stomach! With my family, she said, I've never seen anything like that.

Mother knows what clothes are best for every season of the year. Mother knows what you have to do and not to do, when you are to be silent and when to speak, indeed when you have to speak in order to get on. Mother knows how one is able and intended to remain decent. Mother knows what career is best for the son, and she also knows where, in industry. There you will have a safe future, Rolf, she says.

Mother is anxious. Father has to be anxious too, and he repeats what Mother says.

I've had the experience, she says, I've worked for years with a better-class family. I've seen how they achieved something. She tells about it in the evening in the kitchen, while drinking coffee, and Father tells about it, he often fills in when Mother forgets something, and for a long time now he has fitted in to the order of this home as Mother has learnt and taught it, and likewise Rolf, the son, an only child, has to fit in, for his own good: Order is as Mother says, I have experienced it, says Father, but then he becomes silent and lets Mother talk about what is said at school, again and again, for half a lifetime. And longer.

Someone who has not learnt to be orderly at home won't learn at a later stage.

If you take something away, Mother says, put it back where you have taken it from when you no longer need it.

There is a place for everything.

It saves time and trouble, Father says.

Life will be your teacher.

Then it will be too late.

It can never be soon enough.

There is a place for everything.

We know what we have to do, Mother says, and I don't pay attention to other people. What business of mine are the other people, we have enough to do paying attention to ourselves.

In earlier days Rolf often used to accompany his father to the recreational workshop where Father pursued his hobby, making chairs, benches, chests of drawers, stools, corner seats, tables and so on; Father liked it when his son helped him with the work and did not just stand around; they did not need to do much talking.

On his carpenter's bench, at the glueing table and in his locker Father was orderly, as he was used to being when at home.

Rolf helped Father to carry the finished piece of furniture out of the workshop into the yard and to lift them on to the cycle trailer; he helped Father to tidy up the glueing table and the bench, to make them orderly, Father said, and to hang up the tools in the locker, there is a place for everything, as in Mother's kitchen, in the drawing-room and the bedroom; Rolf helped us to push the cycle trailer home, and when the blanket that was supposed to protect the piece of furniture slipped down, Father and Son looked at each other, kept silent and left the blanket as it was . . .

That is perhaps how it started, perhaps like that, perhaps.

At every piece of furniture that was intended to replace another, older one that had been made two or three years earlier, Mother shook her head, clapped her hands and said that Father was filling up every room full of furniture, including the kitchen and the balcony.

And you, she said to the son, you are already starting. You help your father into the bargain. You are still helping him. You stick together. What do you want in fact? And at the same time she cast her eyes round the room.

We've got everything we need! she said. Do we need to make things so difficult for ourselves then?

Mother suddenly sorted things out, as she said, souvenirs to which Father, Rolf and she herself were attached. That's no use any more, she said, nor that, it has been standing around long enough now, and that, and that also, and that as well, and that also. What do you still want them for?

Then Father said, In my opinion it all fits quite well together. No one thing has done harm to another. Or don't you think so? After all, they bring some life into the flat! They haven't been standing around without reason.

A quiet struggle.

In this way stones which Rolf brought back from a walking-tour with friends in the Jura came to be lying by the side of a wooden candlestick which a friend carved for Father, and nearby, a little way away, a porcelain dish in the classical style, a present from the family where Mother had been in service for many years, and behind it the hand-painted Ticino vase which Father and Son, and Mother too, had at once taken a liking to, that time in Sanacaro.

But Father and Son were scarcely out of the house when Mother removed the stones and the candlestick, she did not throw them away, when she was asked about them, she was only removing them and bringing back the old order that they had been used to for years.

In this way Father and Son kept on setting up new things, perhaps in defiance: things discovered, gifts, souvenirs and so on. These things do all go together, Father said, and the son said. It doesn't do anyone any harm, they both said.

Mother only spared the son's drawer, but now and again, mostly in springtime, she put things in order there.

You can't get through anywhere, you are always bumping into things,

Mother said. In cleaning and polishing you mustn't make more work for yourself than is necessary, Mother said. Is this not so? We have a home, not a museum or a second-hand shop!

So act accordingly.

Mother fought for her order, often to the point of tears, until Father himself removed the things that he had brought home, for the sake of peace, and the son did likewise.

Father had removed the new pieces of furniture made in his free time and the old ones – they are by no means all that old, Mother said: he had sold them or given them away; and he only continued making furniture for friends and acquaintances.

Commissions, said Father.

At the most Mother expressly asked for a larger shoe-cupboard, a new kitchen table, one that pulls out, with a surface of synthetic material and so on.

It's more practical, it would be more practical, she said, a table with a surface of synthetic material would be easier to look after, is easier to look after!

As Mother was opposed to his replacing the old pieces of furniture with the new, more useful ones, Father made new furniture in ever quicker succession, as in earlier days he had made a shop and a doll's house for the son, and then, when shop and doll's house had been fitted out, had made shops and doll's houses for the sons of other fathers, in ever quicker succession.

Father now fitted out other people's homes.

He was pleased when he was later invited into a house that he had fitted out.

In her home Mother tolerated presents which he brought home only for a few days.

You are not married to me, Mother said, you are married to your recreational workshop. You forget that you've got a family. Your son forgets it as well. He's like you. He takes after you. Soon he won't be at home a single evening. Where is your home really? Where do both of you have your home? Isn't this a home? I take trouble, I do everything for you. What thanks do I get for it? Go on then, the two of you! I'm used to it.

Now what are you bringing home this time? she could ask when Father and Son behaved secretively as soon as they entered the kitchen. Now and again, but not often, she took a fancy to a pretty object, on the chest of drawers, on the sideboard or in the kitchen, above the new table that Father had made for her.

The table is really handy, she said.

3

Sometimes, when they are all three sitting over coffee in the drawing-room, Mother will say, after a glance at the vase from Sanacaro: It really was a shame that we could only stay for three weeks in Ticino. I could have stayed longer. Do you remember when we were all in the rowing boat . . . How can I help it, Father says, if I only have three weeks holiday. I too could have stayed longer. I liked the village. And the house. And the large rooms . . .

I was only thinking, Mother says.

Father never had a room of his own as a boy. I didn't have a home, he says, when he is telling about it. He talks about it when he has had a few glasses of wine or three *Schnaps* with his coffee.

You shouldn't drink so much, Mother says then, it isn't good for you. You should at least have something to eat with it. I didn't even have three weeks holiday, Father says. When Mother goes on talking about holidays they have had together, Father says that when he was a child he never had holidays.

Father grew up as an orphan who had been boarded out.

When he tells about it, which is not all that often, he becomes bitter and the veins swell on his brow. He had to go into factory work in spite of his intelligence and the possibilities – I could have become a joiner! Under compulsion, direct from school, because earning money was the first priority.

His foster-parents gave him to understand clearly enough how deeply indebted he was to them.

When Father tells about it, which is not all that often, his face turns red with anger.

I don't know what a home is! I've never known, he adds further.

Well, now you have a home, your own home, Mother then says. When you hear other people . . . things are nice for us, we really don't realize how nice things are for us. We've got somewhere.

I was brought up in a most orderly way! Father then says.

You children, Mother has said, Father has said, other people have said, everybody has said, ought to have a better time one day, later, would have to have a better time!

And grow up and live in an orderly fashion, Mother says, and this is half of life, and more.

Peter Bichsel

The Earth Is Round   Translated by Michael Hamburger

A man who had nothing else to do, was no longer married, no longer had any children or a job, spent his time thinking over once more all the things that he knew.

He was not content to have a name, but wanted to know exactly why and how he had got it. Day after day he leaved through old books until he found his name in one of them.

Then he made a summary of everything he knew, and what he knew was the same as what we know.

He knew that one has to brush one's teeth. He knew that bulls charge red rags and that in Spain there are bullfighters.

He knew that the moon goes round the earth and that the moon has no face, that what looks like eyes and a nose is craters and mountains.

He knew that there are wood, string and percussion instruments.

He knew that one has to stick stamps on letters, that one has to keep to one side of the road when driving, that one has to use pedestrians' crossings for safety, that one mustn't be cruel to animals. He knew that people shake hands when they meet, that one takes off one's hat to people if one has a hat to take off.

He knew that his own hat was made of felt and that the felt was made of camel hair, that there are camels with one hump and with two, that the one-humped are called dromedaries, that there are camels in the Sahara and that in the Sahara there is sand.

That much he knew.

He had read it, someone had told him, he had seen it in the cinema. He knew, in the Sahara there is sand. True, he had never been there, but he'd read about it, and he also knew that Columbus discovered America because he believed that the earth is round.

The earth is round. That much he knew.

Ever since people have known that, the earth has been a sphere, and if one keeps on walking straight ahead one returns to the place one started from.

Only, one can't see that it's round, and that's why for a long time people wouldn't believe it, because if one looks at it the earth looks flat, or else it goes up and down, it's covered with trees or built up with houses, and nowhere does it curve into a sphere; where it could do so, on the ocean, the ocean simply ends, and it ends in a straight line, so that one can't see how the sea and the land curve.

It looks as though in the morning the sun rises from the sea and goes down again in the sea in the evening.

Yet we know that it isn't so, for the sun remains in its place, and only the earth revolves, the round earth, once in the course of each day.

We all know that, and the man knew it too.

He knew that if one keeps on going straight ahead, after days, weeks, months or years one returns to the same place; if he were now to get up from his table and go out, later he would get back to his table, from the other side.

That's how it is, and we know it.

'I know', said the man, 'if I keep on going straight ahead I shall get back to this table.'

'I know it', he said, 'but I don't believe it, and that's why I must try it out.'

'I shall keep on going straight ahead,' exclaimed the man who had nothing

94

else to do, for a man who has nothing to do may just as well keep on going straight ahead.

Yet the simplest things are also the most difficult. Perhaps the man knew that, but he didn't show that he knew it and bought himself a globe. On it he drew a line from here, all around the globe and back here.

Then he got up from the table, went out by the front door, looked in the direction he wanted to take, and saw another house there.

His way led directly across this house, and he could not by-pass it, because that way he might have lost his direction.

For that reason he couldn't yet set out.

He went back to his table, took a sheet of paper and wrote on it: 'I need a tall ladder.' Then he remembered that behind the house the wood begins, and a number of trees grew in the middle of his straight course, those would have to be climbed over, so he wrote on his sheet: 'I need a rope, I need climbing irons for my feet.'

In climbing one can injure oneself.

'I need a first aid outfit', the man wrote. 'I need a raincoat, climbing boots and walking shoes, rubber boots and winter clothes and summer clothes. I need a cart for the ladder, the rope and the irons, for the first aid outfit, climbing boots, walking shoes, winter clothes, summer clothes.'

Now he really had everything; but behind the wood was the river, with a bridge over it, true, but the bridge was not on his way.

'I need a boat', he wrote, 'and I need a cart for the boat and a second boat for the two carts and a third cart for the second boat.'

But because the man could pull only one cart along, he also needed two more men to pull the other carts, and those two men also needed shoes and clothes and a cart to move them and someone to pull the cart. And all those carts would first have to be lifted over the house; for that you need a crane and a man to work the crane, and a boat for the crane and a cart for the boat and a man to pull the cart for the boat for the crane, and this man needed a cart for his clothes and someone to pull that cart.

'Now at last we have everything', said the man, 'now we can get going', and he was glad, because now he needed no ladder at all and no rope and climbing irons, because he didn't have a crane.

He needed far fewer things: only a first aid outfit, a raincoat, climbing boots, walking shoes, rubber boots and clothes, a cart, a boat, a cart for the boat and a boat for the carts and a cart for the boat with the carts on it. Two men and a cart for the men's clothes and a man to pull the cart, a crane, a man for the crane and a boat for the crane and a cart for the boat and a man to pull the cart for the boat with the crane on it, and a cart for that man's clothes and a man to pull the cart, and that man can put his clothes on the same cart, as well as the crane-driver's clothes: for the man wanted to take as few carts as possible on his trip.

All he needed now was a crane to lift the crane over the houses, a larger crane, in fact, and a crane-driver for that and a crane boat and a crane-boat-cart, a crane-boat-cartpuller-clothes-cart and a crane-boat-cartpuller-clothes-cartpuller, who could then load his own clothes and the crane-driver's clothes on to the cart, so that not too many carts would be needed.

All he needed, then, was two cranes, eight carts, four boats and nine men. The first boat takes the small crane. The second boat takes the large crane, the third boat takes the first and second carts, the fourth boat takes the third and fourth carts. So he also needed a boat for the fifth and sixth carts and a boat for the seventh and eighth carts.

And two carts for those boats.

And a boat for those carts.

And a cart for that boat.

And three cart-pullers.

And a cart for the clothes of the cart-pullers.

And a cart-puller for the clothes-cart.

And the clothes-cart can then be put on the boat that has only one cart on it.

That for the second, large crane he needs a third, even larger one and for the third a fourth, a fifth, a sixth – this didn't occur to the man at all.

But it did occur to him that after the river there are the mountains and that one can't get the carts over the mountains, let alone the boats.

But the boats must be got over the mountains, because after the mountains one comes to a lake, and he needed men to carry the boats and boats to take the men across the lake, and men to carry those boats, and carts for the clothes of those men and boats for the carts for the clothes of those men.

And now he needed a second sheet of paper.

On this he wrote figures.

A first aid outfit costs fifteen shillings, a raincoat five pounds ten shillings, climbing boots eight pounds nineteen shillings, walking shoes eighty-five shillings, rubber boots cost something and so do clothes.

A cart costs more than all the rest put together, and a boat costs a great deal, and a crane costs more than a house, and the boat for the crane has to be a large one, and large boats cost more than small ones, and a cart for a large boat has to be an enormous cart, and enormous carts are very expensive indeed. And men expect to be paid for their work, and one has to look for them, and they're difficult to find.

All this made the man very sad, for meanwhile he had reached the age of eighty, and he would have to hurry if he was to get back home before he died.

96

So after all he bought no more than a tall ladder, put it over his shoulder and slowly walked away. He went up to the other house, leant the ladder against it, made sure that it stood firm and slowly climbed up the ladder. Only then I guessed that he was serious about his trip, and I called after him: 'Stop, come back, you're wasting your time.'

But he could no longer hear me. He was already up on the roof and drew the ladder up, dragged it across the roof with a great effort and lowered it on the other side. He didn't even look back when he climbed over the ledge and vanished.

I never saw him again. It happened ten years ago, and at that time he was eighty.

Now he must be ninety. Perhaps he thought again and gave up his trip, even before reaching China. Perhaps he is dead.

But from time to time I step out of the house and look westward, and I should be glad if one day he were to come out of the wood, weary and slow, but smiling when he came up to me and said:

'Now I believe it, the earth is round.'

Gertrud Wilker

From *Nachleben*

In the course of the evening, while I was reading from my texts sitting at a special table to a dozen or so women listeners, yet more women came into the café. They sat down at the remaining tables, smoked, conversed, drank and ate.

Emmy turned towards them and listened attentively. Although they were not speaking particularly loudly, I could not concentrate at all well and made a pause. This evening, I was told, a women's gathering was taking place where men were not admitted.

'What is the reason for that?' I asked.

'Men get in the way. We don't need them', a girl with close-cropped hair replied, 'we prefer to stay on our own for once'.

Emmy's astonishment at the self-confidence of these women. The most she had ventured was to observe in her diary that she felt most at ease in the company of women, even though she had been compelled to undergo unpleasant experiences in this respect during her residential life. Without further ado she would have gone along with the festively dressed women and would have danced with them.

After the reading was over there was a vigorous discussion.

'Are you in favour of women forming a political party?'

In spite of Emmy's vigorous nodding of her head I experienced reservations; I said that indeed I understood the necessity of women working together in the political field.

'Are you with us in solidarity or not?'

I did not want to align myself according to pre-ordained rules of behaviour, I answered. All that I could see coming out of a feminist party programme was a segregation of women.

Emmy found herself unreservedly in agreement with the single-minded feminists.

'We women should help each other much more to bear our solitude by supporting one another quite consciously.'

'Will you as an author commit yourself to the women's cause?' the girl with close-cropped hair asked again.

'As a writer I present slices of life, but don't go in for making recommendations.'

One woman who up to that point had been smiling and nodding her head suddenly opened her mouth. She wanted to know, she said, whether I would depict men just as being as aggressive and brutal as they really were.

Emmy's relief that the shy one had brought herself to speak. She too was shy and kept silent during discussions, although she would have gladly joined in.

'I have met sensitive and reserved men as well as aggressive and brutal ones', I answered. 'There's nothing I fear more than the consequences of hostile images projected from a feminist viewpoint. They will have a destructive effect on the women themselves, of that I am convinced.'

To Emmy's regret the shy woman did not venture to say anything in answer to that. That is how she too felt at times: when now for once she had brought herself to open her mouth, her courage was already at an end; she had not been able even to listen properly any longer to the way the others carried on the discussion.

What was the use of writing that was concerned to describe without taking sides, a girl in white dungarees asked me impatiently.

Again and again the same question. However one tackles it, one is on the defensive.

The girl in the dungarees looked at me with eager expectation. She would be disappointed, for she was expecting from me some form of illumination. One could guess this from her attentive smile.

'There are various answers to your question', I replied.

Her smile became more pronounced.

'You will probably not be satisfied with any of them', I added.

The girl leant forward.

'For instance, I can say that literature is able to stimulate your imagination and involve you in thoughts, feelings and experiences that would not otherwise be accessible to you.'

The girl pulled a face, her smile disappeared.

'Or I can try to prove that literature is a form of memory and an attempt to overcome death.' She looked into space.

'Sometimes', I supplemented, 'Sometimes there arises in the mirror-image of a story the implication of one's own life, so that one can observe it from outside and perhaps understand it.'

But the girl would have liked to hear something different. A declaration of principle?

Emmy was completely in sympathy with just this expectaion. She too had expected to find illumination in literature.

'Art just leaves us empty, whereas the Bible fulfils our daily expectaion, it makes life clear for us.'

This young woman was not going to be helped by literature or by the Bible. She could not be held back from the demand for practical justice either by the reference to the next world or by the 'temptations of art' (as Emmy had put it).

Emmy showed exultant confidence in the verve with which the young women were attempting to bring about the realization of this demand. My reaction was guarded.

'Sceptic!' she reproached me. 'If you had had my excperience, you would not be so superior and reserved.'

'It is not easy to live alone, in our Canton in particular the men believe that a woman without the support of a man may be trampled on.'

I could take this diary entry without more ado as a confirmation of Emmy's solidarity with the young women who were present. For Emmy had hoped to live in the same way as they were trying to live.

'When girls become more independent they will be better able to express themselves and freer. We women must give up false modesty, it is our weakness, to conquer it is part of our civilizing mission. When this modesty has been overcome, we can talk more easily in front of other people.'

Emmy nodded with particular cordiality to the girl in dungarees and took leave of the young women only with reluctance. Outside the door of the women's café she suddenly went off. I made my way alone in the pouring rain through a number of suburban streets to the car-park. In the darkness I heard horse-chestnuts split open on the ground, and I gave a start. It sounded like pistol-shots. I felt a particular spot between my shoulder-blades turn cold, as if the barrel of a pistol were being held against me there.

Adolf Muschg

Distant Acquaintances

For a while I lay alone in the room. I had not yet unpacked my things. They were leaning against the end of the bed, a suitcase and a plastic bag full of clothes. I looked at your things; they were placed tidily, but in a cramped manner, around, as if somebody had pushed them together in a haste, without any feeling for their usual place. The yellow stretch of floor on to which the nurse had wheeled my bed had also seemed to me like a breach; as if here emptiness had struck into a fragile, but perceptible order. I was now filling this position. – On the table in the corner by the window I saw a bundle of newspapers and magazines, a thermos flask, Böll's *Group Portrait with a Lady*, a cardboard container with bottles of beer, a bag of apples, a packet of cigarettes that had been torn open, and no flowers. Your jacket, dark rose-coloured with a waffle pattern, was draped from the chair. On the bedside table between the beds stood some cassette equipment, a telephone without a dial, a row of small containers with brightly coloured pills, and a basin full of ampoules; the syringes that belonged with them were covered with gauze. Your dressing-gown was hanging from the green plastic armchair in the corner by the window. Your bedcover, across which I looked out towards the window, had been loosely spread out. The room was on the ground floor; outside some grounds that recalled the front gardens of newly rich people: a sumac, a cluster of pampas grass, some larches, boulders and a dried-up artificial stream. The exotic plants had lost their leaves and in their transparency showed a leaden and overcast sky. – While I was being moved some blood had extravasated into the catheter tube. I tried not to be afraid.

Then I heard a sound. It was like a throat being cleared and merged into something like words, subdued cursing, incomprehensible and turned away. I observed the cover on the other bed. It rose and sank. Later I tried to breathe in the same rhythm, but the cover moved in an irregular way for which I was not prepared. Sometimes it appeared to be quite motionless again. In the corridor the nurse had told me that you were good-natured, only occasionally rather brusque. I could not imagine how there could be room for a human being under this cover.

The nurse brought me a mobile stand for the infusion bottle. Now I could stand up and put my things in order. I thought that you might have been pleased to be occupying a room on your own, and that that was now a matter of the past. I made up my mind that I would take up little space and would often walk up and down in the corridor, even if I were inhibited by the hospital shirt and could not slip into the dressing-gown properly on account of the catheter. I had to *hop* as soon as possible; a kidney stone is not dangerous, only painful, the patient can help with the emission of the stone by hopping. – The cupboard did not hold all my things, I had to put out books and papers on my bedside table. As I bent down and I was dancing around with the bottle gallows arrangement, which could not be properly steered, I could feel a scratching below the collar bone, though the catheter could not surely be as high up as that. The little column of blood in the tube had grown further.

When I wanted to lie down again and transferred the bottle from one hook to another, you were sitting on the edge of your bed, with your back to me. You were dressed and were wearing a brightly coloured shirt and the trousers that went with the jacket on the chair. You were less than middle size, your hair was combed in tapering fashion. I saw that you were the type of person with whom I scarcely come in contact otherwise. – You turned your head slightly in my direction, I saw your eye in the corner of my eye; it remained there for a long time. I adjusted my head on the pillow, greeted you and gave my name. It was then that you first turned right round, as if you had not hitherto been sure that someone was there. You slid off the bed, placed your hands on the edge of the bed and took them away again. You glanced in my direction; then you went a few paces further, stood still at the edge of the bed, looked at the things on your table and said: 'Excuse me, I've been asleep'. When you said 'asleep', I felt a pain inside my shoulder, and then you gave me your name which I had already read on the slanting piece of paper in the metal frame when the nurse had had to turn my bed in the door; the nurse had only spoken of 'your neighbour'. You spoke clearly and deliberately, your speech gave the impression of being that of an older person than you were, for (this too I had learnt from the nurse) you were just twenty-two. But you stood like a rather old man in front of your table, upon which you put one thing or another into their place without a perceptible purpose, and I understood that I did not need to introduce myself with my illness, because you no longer wished to say anything more about your own. – You had an obstinate expression on your face which did not disappear when you started to read, holding the newspaper near to your face and obliquely against the window. Reading was no longer easy for you, which made me feel ashamed.

In the evening I learnt directly that you could be brusque. You were explaining to the nurse that the removal of blood the next morning would be senseless and would not produce any conclusive results. It was evident that you understood something about your illness and that you were impatient with measures that had no precise purpose and were at most well-intentioned. – In the evening the doctor paid us a visit; we had not spoken much before. You had never started speaking; whenever I did, my answers were given to me with such care that I was afraid of tiring you; with your heavy voice the thoughts acquired a corporeal quality. – As far as the blood removal was concerned, the doctor agreed with you and advised other measures which you agreed to from one instance to another, always after a pause. While so doing, you sat on the edge of the bed without looking at your partner. I gained the impression that the possible things that could be done for you were clearly defined and had often been discussed. You made your choice among them all the more

101

conscientiously. It was not a case of your wanting to be in the right, but in the last resort it was your illness. – After he had outlined my state of health with a few touches and promised me freedom from the catheter, the doctor could also talk about other things. He was concerned about a play just then, he was interested in my opinion, once he opened a book on my bedside table. Then came the early hospital evening-meal, and he said that he did not wish to disturb us any longer.

Later during that long evening I walked up and down in the corridor, carrying my supportive equipment. Suddenly you appeared far away in the doorway and waved. I took fright, but it was only a telephone call, for me. – I told somebody how I was, and you left the room, fully dressed. – Somewhat later I wanted to call you back, that was not easy, you did not seem to hear well. You were all right here, you then said emphatically. I was already almost back in the room when I heard you say further outside that you still wished to keep moving for a bit. You could not count on my still hearing this, at first too I did not understand and you repeated it. You were standing there in this long yellow corridor where night was already falling; then I went back to the room, closed the door, and the thought pursued me that you were now perhaps going on talking.

About eight o'clock I found you in the day-room. You were playing cards with three old men. One likewise had a drip apparatus standing by his side, another who was about my age was only skin and bone. After greeting them through the thick smoke, I watched the news which was turned on very loud. I would have gladly turned it down, but the men were listening while they were playing. Later on further patients came, all men, and stared at the commercials which offered all kinds of fresh and dazzling things until the entertainment programme started. The card players finished one further hand before they turned round to the screen; you did not change your position, even without cards you sat bent down. On one occasion, while the Showman on the box was singing, you told us how a little Scots girl was exploited by the entertainment industry. You pursued your comment to a conclusion, even after the Showman had begun to chatter again. Two men nodded, and one said 'Yes, indeed'; so here you had friends. – I had the feeling that I had put the group off with my concentration on the news; so I sat through two further items of the entertainment programme before withdrawing to the room. – I could not write a letter, for the table was your table; I clambered under my tubing into bed and began reading. – You came after ten o'clock; I indicated to you that you did not need to talk, just because the two of us were on our own. You undressed, put on pyjamas with bright-blue shorts and cleaned your teeth. On the way into bed you said you hoped that you did not snore, and I apologized in case I should have to get up a few times. Then you unexpectedly said that you were waiting for a transplant, the suitable organ for you still had to be found. If the doctor thought

102

that a transplant ought to be tried, then you just had confidence in this view; it was the most sensible thing that you could do, to have confidence in this view. – The illness was not your topic; you started talking about it so that the subject could be got rid of between us, you did not want me to preoccupy myself with it just because you did not speak about it. Before the lights were put out you went on to say that I should make use of the table, you were seldom here, after all, tomorrow, for example, you had dialysis. I said that tomorrow I had gymnastics, indeed I had to hop, as soon as the catheter had been removed, I had to hop. Kidney stones were unpleasant, you said, you had heard about this, and a catheter was unpleasant too.

In the night I awoke from an anxiety dream that the blood which had flowed back into my arm was forming a clot which was about to dissolve and to move towards my heart. You were breathing heavily, it was an intense, moaning sound, you were taking in air as a thirsty man drinks water. I lay there shivering with fear and guilty resistance. Then I held on to a story from a scouts' camp decades ago, when my boyhood friend had fallen over a precipice and had come back with his head bandaged, to spend the night in the tent. You slept beside me, breathing against my ear, and as the breathing became deeper, it began to loosen something that was resisting in your head, a remainder of blood, I thought, and to drag it along with every breath taken, a noise like some terrible whispering which was not so much as twenty centimetres away from me. I said to myself that you were my best friend, that you had been through more than I had, that I should be pleased about your being alive, about your sleeping. But this was of no help at all, I could not help knocking against you, then pushing and turning you away, you sobbed without waking up, then at last you breathed away from me, and I found my own sleep. – So this was your language which you had concealed from me in the daytime. I tried again to breathe in time with you. In doing so I felt something like quiet, almost like agreement with the uncontrollable element in your body, this became stronger than the suspicion in my arm, I felt it as a happiness that I had grown older, and the next time I awoke at the thought that my bottle on its hook might be empty, and that air might be pressing into my vein, I listened to you and went off to sleep again.

In the morning I watched you as you gave yourself an injection in the thigh, with a calmness as if the yellow flesh was no longer yours. The nurse dismantled my arm and tore with short, jerky movements one plaster after another off my skin; I then felt a movement in my vein, the catheter was creeping away; whatever happened, it should not tear, the nurse said and told about a case where an end had got stuck, with serious consequences. Not until she said 'That's it!' did I turn my head back, and I took fright; the catheter, a kind of catgut with slight traces of blood, was as long as I had feared, and its proximity to my heart had not been a delusion on my part. I was terrified because my anxieties while in

103

hospital always seemed to be well founded. – You were sitting in your corner and were pressing the cup to your mouth, no, you were pressing your face against the cup, that's how it was. Your 'values' were bad today, I had heard, and I held it against you because I was afraid on my own account. – I could now slip my arm into the sleeve again, I went across to the kiosk and bought two newspapers and two pieces of cake. – You accepted the newspaper with surprise, you couldn't accept the cake because you had been a diabetic since you were seven months old. I thought about this figure, put both pieces of cake away into the cupboard and forgot them. When I was discharged from hospital they were inedible, but I took them with me and threw them away at home.

When I came back from a walk in the corridor I found some small change on the bedside table, by the side of the carefully folded newspaper. You were already in dialysis, I had the next few hours to myself and the now empty room as well, for your bed had gone too, only your suit was still draped on the plastic chair. The window was open and was letting in the November air; it stayed fresh in the room for a long while. I dealt with my telephone calls. I hoped that because of this the telephone would no longer ring frequently when you were back, for as yet you had not had a single phone call nor any visitor. Whenever I was on the phone you left the room, and I did not know how I could prevent you doing this.

You never joined in laughter with me. Light-hearted remarks you answered with a sound resembling: 'Yes, that's the way things are!' I heard you join in laughter two or three times, belatedly, while you were playing cards; you seemed to be more in your element when you were expressing misgivings. These misgivings concerned administrative questions in society, an impropriety in aviation, or the advantages and disadvantages of a particular therapy. – Careful consideration seemed to be a mode of thought that appealed to you; I heard you say 'on the other hand' a number of times.

In the afternoon, when you were back again, I had visitors; there were three of them at once; you wanted to go, for there were not enough chairs in our room. But I insisted on conversing with my visitors outside; a vacant corner where one could sit was often available in one of the corridors. When I came back two hours later (I had forgotten you for that length of time) you had disappeared; all at once this small room seemed to be too much for both of us, it had almost become superfluous space. The flowers which my visitors had brought had not been unfastened. I put them in a glass on the cupboard, the only free space; all that could be seen there was the tops of the flowers. I hoped that I had not forgotten to thank somebody for their flowers. I did not put any flowers on your table.

Later I saw the artificial fistula in your arm.

On Friday morning you received a telephone call. I had taken the call, as a matter of habit; I just had time to call you back in the doorway. It was a man's voice, so I did not leave the room, not immediately; perhaps you would also no longer leave the room on my account another time. – You took the receiver as if there was something queer about it and transferred it from one hand to the other before holding it up to your ear; later you held it at one time against your left ear, at another against your right ear. You spoke into the mouthpiece without nodding or turning round. From what you were saying I concluded that it was a matter of meeting the caller in the town and that that was causing difficulties; you did not know the place where he wanted to arrange to meet you. It was a well-known café, all young people are familiar with it, even tourists; you were hearing about it for the first time. – I called to you by your name and declared that I would describe the way to you. You turned your head towards me, said 'Wait a moment, please!' into the receiver and put it down while someone was continuing to talk inside it. I repeated my offer and went to the door. There I heard you say: 'Are you still there?' and: 'The Doctor gentleman wishes to explain to me where it is'. The fact that I had visitors, flowers and telephone-calls, did not play cards, and only watched the news had had the effect of inducing you to address me with a title. I was standing by the door to the corridor, and now I would have gladly gone hopping, but I no longer believed that it was a kidney stone. – I could not talk to you about the book by Böll.

In the afternoon I sketched for you the position of the café on a sheet from my writing-pad, with the tram connections. While doing this I learnt that you had worked in an old people's home and were still working there, and that you did not consider it demanding work. Your family lived in the neighbouring Baden area. Some brothers and sisters too, most of them older than yourself. You had not seen your father for a long time, after all it was a fair distance here. You had already been working in this town for four years, that was why you spoke our dialect to all intents and purposes. It would not be good to be always seeing one another. You did not say anything about a mother. You happened not to know that well-known café, but you emphasized that you had already been a number of times in the city centre. – I heard from our doctor, when you were not in the room, that when he had given a talk in the old people's home about complaints, including serious ones, one of the inmates had made reference to you. The cook often complained of the symptoms described by the doctor, she said, otherwise he was a very alert and handy boy, though occasionally somewhat obstinate. It was in this way that you had come to a doctor. When asked, you had said that you had known about it, but that you did not want to be thinking about it all the time yet. – On this particular Friday the doctor informed me that I could go home for the weekend, if I wanted, he would give me medicines to take with me and his telephone number.

After the evening meal I saw you standing in the corridor underneath one of these yellow lights. You were studying the plan which I had drawn for you. I had also got leave, I said, and so it would be simplest if I were to take you along to that café, it was on my way, and I had my car. You made the objection that that was very kind, but first of all you would have to go home to collect something and to get changed. I offered firstly to drive you home and from there to take you on to the café; but that was a roundabout way, you thought, and I replied that I had time, at which you nodded several times.

When we were sitting side by side in my car, you seemed to me to be unusually small in the upholstered seat; later on the word 'resigned' occurred to me, it wasn't the right word. I suppressed the urge to explain the places and squares which we drove past. You had placed your hands, swollen hands, together on your lap. I was pleased when you said, 'Here it is, just a moment'. Up on the hilly undulation stood the old people's home which you spoke of as your 'home'. The wind pressed against the parked car. I saw you fasten your coat and make your way up the winding track, bent forward and probably moving too quickly. I did not want to see you disappear and turned my head the other way. In the garden to the left a collection of withered golden rod; my glance became blurred in the rigid and uneven to-and-fro movements of the bushes in the wind. The piece of land had not been tidied up, hydrangeas and raspberry canes were shrivelling up uncut as they waited for the cold weather to come. Dahlia remnants were turning brown in the places, still recognizable, where they had bloomed; the owner had not thought of digging out the tubers to keep them for another year. A long way beyond, half concealed by the green of fir-trees, there stood the house, a grey, weather-beaten little block with a pointed roof. The shutters had been recently painted blue, and the garden gate gleamed with this blue too. Cold crept against one's feet.

I turned on the radio; an instructive talk was going on about measures, recommended discretion, anti-cyclic procedure, the illness, or whatever it was. – Then you crept in, breathing loudly and holding a small package in your hand. I should not turn off the lecture, you said, if it interested me. We drove to that café which everybody in this town knows. We talked about your colleague, and about the possibility of having colleagues in the old people's home. The home was arranged to meet the needs of older people, none the less there were lectures occasionally, not only about health, but also about black-headed gulls and the realm of the Incas, sometimes also a song recital, Schubert. Work there was not actually very demanding, only one had to *think* a little. The old people, you said, had after all to live dietetically. One almost always had to be close by. Furthermore, it was a good thing that wider sections of the public were beginning to take the problems of older people seriously and were taking steps to make possible for them a whole, rounded life and not such a stunted one. On the other hand, it was no longer so easy for older people to make use of this

106

opportunity. Perhaps therefore a certain amount of psychology was needed as well, if one wished to tackle them properly and remove their fears.–

It was not until Monday morning that I saw you again. I had been sleeping when you had come back, and I awakened now to the feeling of haste, disturbance and voices that were scarcely muffled. A nurse concealed the sight of your bed, soon after the doctor came, then a second doctor and some more nurses; I tried to read a book. – The room was your room again. – Then you called my name. I saw your face behind the back of the nurse who was bending over you, you called my name as if we were alone and asked me softly and clearly if I had had a pleasant Sunday; I confirmed that I had. And what about you? – You too! And you related, while the personnel were dealing with your body, that it had become late on Saturday. Firstly a drink in that café, then another in a second place, and then you had been in a third pub, one that I probably did not know at all, there things had been lively, yes, something had really been going on, there were people there and music, and so they had stayed. You bit your lips a number of times, but through the pain you went on talking, not hastily, but in a controlled manner. The evening had not been wasted, it had been worth the trouble, you thought so indeed. No one had got home before three o'clock in the morning.

I nodded, joined in with laughter about all the unknown people of whom you had been one and by no means the last one; you were no case of bad conscience, you could prove that to me. – Somewhat later on you were lying still, several tubes led from your arms and legs to several bottles, you lay there bound like Gulliver and in secret gigantically strong in spite of your gaunt features that were so quiet; you had to have a blood transfusion, as became evident, and different treatment from what our hospital had to offer.

When you were taken away, I did not wake you up with the expression of a wish such as: all the best.

Silvio Blatter

The Stranger

He had already been there a long time, sitting silently at his table, before he was noticed by the others. Then suddenly they nodded across to him in greeting.

There was laughter, they stood up, stepped over to his table, held out their hands in friendly greeting, sat down beside him, straightened their ties and asserted that it was an honour and a pleasure to see the famous man here in person for once.

The embarrassment which could be seen in his red face was interpreted as modesty.

However, one of them surmised that there might be, in fact there must be some mistake, it was true the resemblance was extraordinary and deceptive.

The expression of embarrassment was now transferred to their faces. Hesitatingly they got up, nodded, but with hardly a trace of a smile, did not proffer their hands, which in any case were too moist, went back to their own table and sat down again. They possibly looked across again, stirred their cups with their spoons and forgot the man at the other table.

He had not said a word, had not demanded any attention.

He had remained the same person, but had been mistaken for someone else, had been elevated. It was an honour, they had said. As it transpired, it was a mistake. He had been repelled and dropped.

He remained seated at his table for a long time before he went, sat quietly, then suddenly got up and left quickly and without giving a greeting, and was never seen in that place again.

A Family Story

On Wednesdays a visitor comes. It is Aunt. She comes every third Wednesday. Aunt lives in the neighbouring locality. In summer she cycles. In winter she takes the bus. Aunt brings some gingerbread with her. She always bakes it herself.

Mother says, 'You needn't have done that.' Aunt replies, 'But I wouldn't have come with empty hands.' Mother and Aunt always say that. Three weeks are too long a time for it not to be mentioned any more. Mother puts the gingerbread in the kitchen. It will be eaten at tea-time at four o'clock. The children like their aunt. She never comes empty-handed, although she need not have done that, as Mother says.

What Aunt brings is always eaten at four o'clock.

Mother makes tea to go with it. Aunt prefers tea without milk. She takes one and a half teaspoons full of sugar and a dash of lemon.

It is handy to buy lemon juice in plastic lemons. Half lemons always go dry in the refrigerator.

Aunt comes in order to do knitting with Mother.

She has no children.

Martin still has to go to Grandmother's. She lives nearby. He does her shopping. She is not well. She suffers from inflammation of the hip joints.

'The inflammation will keep coming back', the doctor says. 'Unless she has the joints braced.'

But that is a risky operation at her age.

Mother will go and see her tomorrow.

Grandmother never telephones.

Aunt is the wife of Mother's brother.

108

They were already friends while still at school.

Her husband has a small business.

Mother cuts the gingerbread into pieces. Everyone praises it. Aunt laughs. She likes to bring some confectionery with her.

Her gingerbread is particularly good.

Mother puts a large piece on one side.

That is for Father.

Father works away from home.

He comes home in the evening.

He likes sweet things.

'It is five already', Aunt says, 'I'll have to – '

She will go in an hour's time.

She always goes before Father comes home.

In winter her bus goes at ten past six.

E.Y. Meyer

Island Story

He did not like the Rugby game at all, he found it boring, and it was no better as far as his friend and the latter's girl-friend were concerned. The rest of the people, however, seemed to be enthusiastic, for they were encouraging their team with loud shouts and hitting one another on the back or the knees whenever one of the players offered a performance that was even only moderately good or moderately comic. Even women let themselves be carried away to giving shouts, even if only a few produced very loud ones.

Actually he had not had any intention of participating in the outing organized by the firm where he was employed, not only because the outing this time had been supposed to be taking place in conjunction with another firm. But when his friend who was employed by the same firm as himself had said that this time the festivities would be taking place on an island, although he had not the slightest wish to know this, he had agreed to accompany his friend and the latter's girl-friend who similarly was employed by the same firm as his friend, to the outing. As soon as they arrived in the crowded ship on the morning of the normally free Saturday which he usually spent in reading, he had, however, noticed that he had formed false impressions about the way in which a works' outing on an island should be organized, for the entire beach was already overfilled with people who had been calling and beckoning to the new arrivals, and even when he had left the beach with his friend and the latter's girl-friend, so that they might make their way to the interior of the island, the crowds had not grown less. His friend, the latter's girl-friend and he had gone past people who were picnicking, a roundabout and similar fairground phenomena, as also a first-aid tent, and had then arrived at a playing field where a Rugby game between the teams of the two firms which had attracted a large crowd had been in full swing.

When two of the players from the team of the firm together with which the firm's outing was being organized this time, after the egg-shaped leather ball had been put down by their best player behind the opposing side's line, placed themselves back to back, to the delight of the crowd, and while they were thus leaning against one another, alternately dropping to their knees and then rising up again, his friend, the latter's girl-friend and he left the terraces of the Rugby ground, where an ever swelling peal of laughter now began to spread, and tried to press on further into the interior of the island, where it could still have corresponded to what he, and as it now transpired, also his friend and the latter's girl-friend, had expected. But after they had walked for a stretch through the wood with which the island was covered, and which likewise was overcrowded with people who were eating and drinking and playing hide-and-seek and other games, so that they often had difficulty in moving forwards at all and had been abused or ridiculed by angry people, they came to a monastery which like the Rugby ground was surrounded and besieged by a gigantic mass of people. The way past the newly available buildings round about to the old, original monastery building, where they now found themselves, was still quite passable, although it was being used by a great many people, but when they tried to enter the inner courtyard of the monastery through the Romanesque-arched gateway, they could only move forwards very slowly and had to stand in a queue, and when they had finally got so far that they could survey the courtyard where food and drink were dispensed in exchange for vouchers which had been obtainable from the firm, they saw that it would have been senseless to try to find a further place anywhere.

However, they did not succeed in turning round any more and they had to let themselves be carried along by the current of pressure into which they had been absorbed on through the narrow passage-ways between the innumerable tables and chairs that were huddled closely together in the courtyard. He did his best to try to stay by his friend and the latter's girl-friend, and when he became separated from them in spite of their mutual efforts, to keep them both in sight. For a moment he was afraid that he would have to go up a staircase (and since his friend and the latter's girl-friend had already safely gone past, he would thus no longer be able to follow the two of them) which led to the *Rousseau Room*, as was announced on a notice on the wall of the inner courtyard, above the starting-point of the staircase, but after turning in various directions he succeeded in climbing down again the few steps that he had been compelled to climb up. As he made his way from the staircase yet again, he became aware none the less that he had thereby lost sight of his friend and the latter's girl-friend; he continued vainly to scan the faces of the people in the monastery's inner courtyard, and it therefore also no longer mattered now in which direction he was being propelled.

If the courtyard had not been so overcrowded, he could have now looked at it more closely, while he let himself be pushed along by the people who surrounded him, but all that he saw was the end of the staircase with the notice that the staircase led to the *Rousseau Room*, the flashing window-panes of the rooms on the upper floor behind which opaque curtains were drawn and one of which had to be the *Rousseau Room*, the tiles of the monastery roofs which were built into one another, and the patch of sky to which the roofs formed a frame. After a while he once more arrived at the side where the entrance-gate was and where, as he also could now see for the first time, there were several cabinets and drawers of dark wood which had been provided with glass-cases and in which souvenirs were hung or placed. Cards, that were already turning slightly yellow at the edges, with pictures of the island and of *Jean-Jacques Rousseau 1712-1778* had been affixed with rusting drawing-pins on to boards past which he was pressed onward, then he found himself in front of the entrance-gate whose two wings were still wide open, and he would almost have let himself be carried away into the courtyard again, if his friend who was standing together with his girl-friend by a supporting beam at the side of the gate had not taken hold of him and drawn him back.

They waited together by the supporting beam until several people had been driven out past them from the gateway, attached themselves to these people, and in this way left the island monastery again without having made use of their luncheon vouchers. They decided that they wanted to leave the island again right away although they had also booked for a snack as well and, as in the case of lunch, had already paid for this too. Without wishing to delay again, they followed a footpath which led away along the length of the island and which, they believed, would sooner or later bring them to the landing-stage where they had left the ship. To their right, where the Rugby playing-field presumably was, they heard the shouts of the spectators who united periodically in a raging, or also only a loud shouting, so that they frequently almost had the impression of being pursued by a pack of savages and involuntarily began to walk more quickly; then, however, the howling in the distance fell silent behind them, and things became somewhat quieter again, although they still met a lot of people in and near the road.

Although they had not once encountered a road junction or a signpost, the path started more and more to pass over into meadowland, and the people they met became ever fewer until they were finally alone in not particularly long, but trackless grass, and after a time he suggested that he should separate from his friend and the latter's girl-friend and proceed on his own somewhat further to the right, in order to look for another path there, while his friend and the latter's girl-friend should continue to make their way slowly in the same direction as before. As the two were in agreement with his plan, he departed from them with long strides, but after the meadow had risen somewhat soon afterwards and then had gone down somewhat again, and he could no longer see his friend and the latter's girl-friend and had still not found any other path, he began to shorten his steps and to make his way more quickly, even though looking more to the left than ahead, hoping in this way to catch sight of his friend and the latter's girl-friend and at the same time to find another path. Now he often came past bushes and indeed trees, and just when he had made up his mind to go about a hundred metres further to the right and then to turn back in order to catch up with his friend and the latter's girl-friend, he ran headlong into a thorn hedge and in doing so scratched his hands and face so that for a time he dared not move at all, and then only started to work his way out of the hedge slowly, in so doing acquiring more scratches and also tearing his clothes rather badly.

After he had cautiously wiped away the blood that was running down his face in thin trickles and beginning to go into his eyes, he noted with surprise that he was surrounded by bushes and trees and that the thorn hedge, rather taller than he himself in both directions and the top of which had been cut not long previously, stretched out in front of him, and he was already deciding to go to the left along the narrow footpath that ran by the side of the thorn hedge, in order to meet his friend and the latter's girl-friend again, although his appearance would have perhaps frightened them and they would have perhaps wanted to go back with him to the first-aid tent which they had passed by, which he did not intend to do at all and which he would have resisted to the utmost, when he suddenly became aware of an almost inaudible groaning that was coming towards him from the hedge.

He tried in vain to endeavour to see something through the thorn hedge or to bend apart the branches and twigs; he only scratched his hands even more in doing so, but the closer he came to the hedge, the more clearly he could hear the groaning which continued to sound at fairly long intervals. Finally he began to go back from the spot where he could hear the groaning most clearly in the direction from whence he had come, so that this spot continued to be in front of him, and meanwhile his field of view of the hedge kept on expanding until he thought he could see on his left between the trees and bushes a place where there was a break in the hedge. He then went quickly forward to the spot where he had heard the groaning most clearly, and then, after waiting until the groaning had sounded again, he turned to the left, and shortly afterwards he really did come across a way through the hedge.

On the other side of the hedge there was likewise a narrow footpath which had been trodden into the grass and on which he now saw some distance away to his right a darkly clad figure lying over whom a second, likewise darkly clad

112

figure was bending, and in the two of them he recognized, when he had come close enough to them, an old man lying on the ground and bending over him, seated on the ground, an old woman. Both were dressed completely in black, also the straw-hat with the narrow rim worn by the old woman, who was bending over the man lying at the base of the hedge in such a way that he could see neither her face nor the face of the man, was black. Not until he had come to a halt before the two of them did the woman raise herself up somewhat, without however turning towards him, and he could see the blood-covered face of the old man who was bareheaded and whose clothes were even more torn than his own and which were likewise, even if to a lesser extent than the face, full of blood which in some places had even formed somewhat large, wet patches on the black material. The old man's head was lying in the lap of the woman who held a tin of ointment in her right hand which was lying on the torn and, as he could now see, formerly white shirt of the old man, while with her left hand she kept on stroking the old man's bloodstained, yellowish white hair. Without ceasing to make these movements, she none the less suddenly turned away from the old man and looked at him, but her eyes were curiously rigid in her face which was heavily made up and interlaced with traces of tears, as if she had difficulty in adjusting her vision to the distance where he was standing, and only after some time did she really seem to see him, whereupon she slowly stretched out her right hand, in which she was holding the ointment, towards him, waited until he had taken this latter, and then also handed to him the lid of the tin which had been lying in her lap near the old man's hand.

The old man's groaning which was sounding at fairly long intervals could be heard even here, directly beside him, only very faintly, but when he had applied the disinfectant ointment for wounds, as it was described on the lid of the tin, to the worst scratches on his hands and face, and had returned the tin and the lid to her, and wished to offer her his help, she indicated to him with her right hand that he should keep the ointment, and did not take up his offer. During the whole time that she had been turned towards him she had not taken her eyes off him, and when he had tried to return the tin and the lid, he had even thought he could discern the traces of a smile in her eyes, but before he could make sure whether the smile was real or only imaginary, she had turned away from him again, and now her head and her shoulders again covered the upper part of the body of the man lying on the ground. It was only now that he noticed that apart from the man's groaning there could also be heard some birdsong, but when neither of the two old people moved again, in the first place he cautiously stepped back some paces from them and then slowly went back further again before he turned round and went on at a normal pace, in the course of which, however, he kept on turning round intermittently, as long as he could still see the two old people.

For this reason too, while remaining on this side of the hedge, he had gone past the passage through which he had come, on the assumption that the hedge must come to an end again soon and that he would then again be near to the place where he had left his friend and the latter's girl-friend, but when the trees and bushes came to be ever further away from one another and scantier, and when finally the hedge, through which there had been no further passage-way, came to an end, he found himself on the edge of a plain where coarse grass and reeds were growing and which he at once started to cross, in order to reach an embankment which rose on the other side of the plain and from the top of which he hoped to obtain a better idea of his position.

Managing as best he could and taking care that as little dirt as possible got into the scratched parts of his hands, he climbed up the steep slope of the embankment which only had a small amount of grass still growing on it, as great stretches of grass must have been burnt off not long previously, for there were charred patches distributed over the whole slope, and those patches which he had crossed while climbing up the embankment were still almost hot, and then he saw beyond the sedge that the embankment kept on continuing on the right straight ahead through this open field, whereas on the left, in the direction where the island monastery must be, it came to a stop after a not too lengthy stretch and the track that was on it led further on the island; however, nobody apart from himself was to be seen on the embankment either in this or the other direction, so he determined to go back to the island, but when he was on it again, to go more slowly and perhaps even to stand still, in order that he should not chance going past his friend and the latter's girl-friend without noticing them.

When he reached the end of the embankment, where the path continued through a meadow with many hillocks, he finally came to a signpost which, however, only pointed in the direction from which he had just come and indicated that the path over the embankment was called *Heath Way*, but since up to that time he had seen neither his friend nor the latter's girl-friend nor anybody else, he sat down on the seat which was by the signpost and in the first place recuperated somewhat from his walking, but also from the strange change in the surroundings, by letting his gaze pass over the green meadow across which fairly frequently now the dark shadows of the clouds glided with which the hitherto blue sky was increasingly becoming covered, but suddenly he believed he could discern a movement in one of the shadows between two hillocks, and when the cloud which had caused the shadow had moved on and the sun was again illuminating that place, he saw that someone was there, advancing towards him, a man and a woman who at intervals disappeared in the green again, but when they had approached close enough, he saw that it was his friend and the latter's girl-friend, and he got up from the seat in order to draw their attention to him by waving, until he was sure that they had recognized him too.

His friend and the latter's girl-friend began to walk more quickly, and when they had come so close that they could not help seeing his scratched face and his torn clothes, they ran up to him to ask him what had happened, but he succeeded in calming them down while he told them everything; he also showed them the tin with the ointment for wounds and then asked them to be so good as to tell him how they had arrived at this point from the place where he had left them. As they told him that they had at first gone on slowly, as agreed, in the same direction as hitherto, but that when he had not come back, and they had become separated in going round a thicket which they had come across and in which, to their surprise, there were llamas, at which the girl-friend had continued to walk in the same direction as hitherto, so that he would have met at least her when he came back, but his friend had gone rather more to the left, in order perhaps to find a path there, and had then also seen the path which they were now on, and had come here with the girl-friend in order to be able to go and look for him afterwards alone; consequently the hedge, by the side of which he had gone after the encounter with the two old people, had led so far forwards in the original direction and away from the island monastery, that the scenery of the island had changed fairly abruptly.

His friend and the latter's girl-friend had met no one until they had come across him again, and at the thicket with the llamas there had not been anyone either, so that they made up their minds to leave the island by the *Heath Way*, as indicated on the signpost, but at the spot where he had come upon the embankment, to climb down again, in order to keep an eye on the two old people and to offer them once again their now combined help, but when they reached the spot which was characterized by the fact that his footprints were still present in the soil which was only slightly held together by the scanty and burnt grass, the old woman with her black attire and black straw hat was already standing at the foot of the embankment and asked his friend, the latter's girl-friend and him to help her to climb upon the embankment, and when they had climbed down and were offering the old woman their help also on behalf of the man, she said that that was no longer needful and that it was also not necessary to inform anybody else about it.

When they were once more standing on the path at the top of the embankment, the old woman asked if she might attach herself to them, since she no longer wished to visit the *Rousseau Room* in the island monastery on her own and wished to take again the path on the embankment which had formed part of her way there until they had suggested a short cut, and when neither his friend nor the latter's girl-friend nor he had anything against this, the four of them continued on their way on the embankment which after the sedge field led further and further away from the island across the lake. He had noticed that there was nothing more to be seen of the tear marks which at their first meeting had interlaced the heavily made-up face of the old woman and that this face appeared to have become fairly deeply reddened, but although he would have been glad to have learnt more from her, he no longer dared to speak to her again, as she did not turn either to his friend, the latter's girl-friend or himself, nor did she present any opportunity for this otherwise, and she walked with them in silence until they suddenly heard behind and above them the sound of flapping wings, and while they and also the old woman turned round, at which he could once more cast a glance at her reddened face, they saw that the most varied kinds of birds, among them also swans and other waterfowl, were rising in an uninterrupted sequence from the woods growing on the island and flying away above their heads, in the course of which the sound of flapping wings increased even further and the embankment lay in the restless shadow cast by the birds, but when they had looked after the flock of birds which after a time did come to an end, though it already extended as far as they could see, and they were again standing in the bright sunshine and facing in their original direction, the old woman started moving again without paying attention to the fact that it was now starting all at once to rain extremely heavily, although the sky was, so to speak, no longer covered with clouds, and a wind was beginning to drive the rain into their faces, which compelled them to continue further much more quickly than hitherto and to take it in turns to look after the old woman, two of them at a time.

When in this way, drenched through from hurrying through the rain, he was the first to reach the mainland at last, where there was an inn immediately by the lakeside where he, his friend following after and the latter's girl-friend who were together looking after the old woman could take shelter and look back into the rain, in spite of the sky having become somewhat brighter all that could be clearly recognized were the immediate surroundings of the inn and the beginning of the embankment across which they had hurried, for everything else had disappeared in the rain which, splashing up again from the ground, also penetrated beneath the overhanging roof of the inn, so that they withdrew along the side of the wall of the house which lay in the darkness caused by the overhanging roof, and when the wind veered and now drove the rain so fiercely in their direction that it even reached the lower half of the door, they pushed this door open without looking for further doors which perhaps were better designated as entrances, to find themselves in an extraordinarily long corridor which surpassed everything else that he had seen on that day and apparently on any other occasion in brightness, and which in its whole length, as far as he could estimate this on account of the brightness generally, was filled with people who, in spite of all possibilities of make-up, were of a beauty that was not to be expected and separated them only imperceptibly from the corridor, and who had all gradually turned round in the direction of the door, where the rain now began to penetrate into the corridor.

116

Heinrich Wiesner

Switzerland, For Example

There are small countries, large countries and fairly large countries. Germany, France and Britain are fairly large; America, Russia and China are large countries. Switzerland is a small country.

Switzerland is a country of opposites, different languages, different interests, parties, cantons. Large cantons, small cantons, even half-cantons. More small cantons than large ones, nothing but minorities. But large cantons do not attack small cantons. They bow to supra-cantonal law.

Switzerland is only an example. There are countries for which the example of Switzerland is apposite, especially small countries. There are more small ones than big ones. Perhaps there are also planets of other suns where Swiss conditions apply. Or not for a long time now.

Naturally everything is not as it is supposed to be. Things never are as they are supposed to be. Strikes, polemic, silent marches. Tomatoes are thrown. A Federal Councillor is prevented from speaking. But that is already the extreme limit. Even the newspaper thinks so. There are also cantons which want to come together again, half-cantons. Then there are separatists, parts of cantons with the will to autonomy. In earlier times a war would perhaps have made this possible. Not nowadays any more. Today everyone must observe the constitution. Force may no longer be used today. Switzerland is a constitutional state. Switzerland can look back on many wars, including wars between brothers. And groups are still at war with other groups, communes with communes, towns with towns, parties with parties, voices with voices. Many voices prevent one voice only from winning through. In Switzerland war is still going on. But it is a dialectical war. Switzerland has given up wars in which there are dead people, in face of the threatening danger. Switzerland is a constitutional state.

Naturally even in Switzerland there are individuals who kill other individuals, in drink, in the heat of the moment, perverts. Then the police step in. And later the law-court.

The earth possesses many nations, many languages, parties, interests, many minorities. But the big nations still keep attacking the little ones. They still do not bow to any supranational law, because there is no supranational law. The earth has still not given up warfare, in spite of threatening danger. The earth is not a constitutional state. The earth is much too large a country, people say, for it to be a constitutional state.

There are small countries, large countries and fairly large countries. The United States is a large country. Switzerland is a larger country in its relationship to the earth than the earth is in relationship to the universe. The earth is a small, a tiny country.

A New Platitude

Two states. Two big states. The largest in comparison with all the rest. Both powerful. They take precautions to ensure that neither of them becomes more powerful. They arm, they manufacture rifles and guns. Both about equal amounts. But all a little more, none the less.

Rifles and guns have long since ceased to suffice. One of them makes bombs. The other is compelled to make bombs too. Because of the balance of power, he says, only for that reason. The bombs serve the preservation of peace, they both aver.

Soon ordinary bombs and ordinary weapons are no longer sufficient. Nuclear weapons are constructed. As a deterrent. Only for that reason. Later, thermonuclear weapons. Both about equal amounts. Only the balance of power can prevent a war. In order to achieve the balance, each sets up a ring of bases around the other, launching pads for rockets. Bases alone are not adequate, they both recognize. The number of bases, their strength and their dispersal, are what count. Both are in agreement about this.

The two states are becoming ever more powerful, say the small states on whose land the bases are being set up.

In order that the large states may be allowed to set up bases, they make an alliance with the small ones. We undertake to protect you. In this way the small states feel somewhat more secure. Sometimes they think that the big state which is protecting them should take a more threatening attitude towards the one that is threatening them. At other times the attitude seems to them to be too threatening, too provocative. The large states do not have an easy time with the small ones. The latter are often discontented because they wish to have the same weapons as the big ones. Leave that for us to worry about, the large states then declare, and keep to rifles. Both states agree about that.

The number of bases is of no use, nor is their strength, as long as they are vulnerable. We must create an invulnerable apparatus of retaliation. Both states are agreed about that. They spend billions on underground installations. The one who makes the first strike must reckon with punishment; a risk that nobody is willing to take.

This the states call active defence. With all the active defence they forget passive defence, that of the population. It is not worth while, they both say, to build so many air-raid shelters for the population. They would not have any time at all to save themselves. What is more, they say, a few dozen million people do not matter, since this war that we want to prevent would be so terrible. We put our trust in the balance of terror. Only the balance can protect us from annihilation.

In the end both states are in possession of those instruments which can destroy the other one of them at any time and at any place. They are so powerful now that they stand facing one another powerless, two goats on the narrow path. The story is familiar. It is in the reading-book. One knows how the story ends. In the reading-book.

Ernst Eggimann

Before the Last Year

Naturally there are sects here in the Emmental, there always were, we know that, and in the back of beyond it is said to happen still that a couple of farmers shut themselves up every Sunday in the sitting-room and wish upon each other everything that one possibly can: colic among the cattle, thunderbolt and hydrocephalus. The one who wishes the more powerfully and no doubt also the more precisely is the winner. But what does a sensible person do in a case like this?

An intelligent and influential farmer who has been a churchwarden for years leaves his plough in the middle of the field and rushes into the house where his wife – woe betide her if she is not at home – must already have switched the radio on, and he listens to the first news report, perhaps only half of it, and returns at once to his work. But he is there again at tea, and at eleven, after all there is a news report every hour, even when he is working in winter a long way off in the woods: he wishes to know if the world war has broken out, he has read that it can happen quickly nowadays. If you happen to miss one news report, it may already be too late until the next one. I have been talking to his younger son who is a teacher in the neighbourhood.

Soon there was a farmer who vied with him, and I had to make reference to the atom bomb in my sermon. God protected our country in two world wars, we should not be lacking in faith. His two sons, in particular the teacher, wanted to dissuade him from the subject, and they told him that if nuclear war were to break out today, and furthermore a nuclear war involving hydrogen bombs, as can be confidently assumed, nothing would be of any use, not even the news would report events quickly enough. At that his fears increased further. He did not want to be taken by surprise, and carried on listening to the opening of all news bulletins, for the outbreak of a nuclear war involving hydrogen bombs would be reported right at the beginning. 'If it is reported at all', said the sons and presented him with a portable radio. However, in the fields there was no listening to music, that would have suited the farmhands all right, only to the news.

119

What did he want to do then? they all asked him. There was nothing at all that could be done. At least he would like to *know*, he replied. He would get a lot out of that. No, he was not religious, otherwise he would be in a sect: the sects are all talking now about the end of the world and are in the midst of an upsurge.

But all the same, something can be done, said someone who had just come from military service; what is more, it was really not all that bad, the captain who had been trained in CBR warfare had told them. In our country in particular there was scarcely any danger, though it was true, you need to dig out a nuclear burrow. So now they dug out nuclear burrows: Hans Schüpach, his elder son and his two farmhands who were slowly becoming convinced as well, a nuclear burrow in each corner of a ploughed field. That was reassuring; one could jump into it straight away, as soon as one saw a blinding flash, and one could drape over oneself the old military tent which everyone carried rolled up on their shoulders. That was against radio-active dust. The news reports would still be heard, he did not want to be taken by surprise. But his wife went to the Jehovah's Witnesses.

The fellow who had told Schüpach about nuclear burrows was not able to laugh for long about his trick; a few days ago he too dug his burrows. In the *Bear* somebody calculated: 'If an H-bomb fell on Bern (that's what they say, the first ones were A-bombs, now they've already got to H!)', he understood something about it!, 'one would be bound to fall on Bern, the capital city, here in the country we should be protected in a nuclear burrow from radiation, heat and blast'. And many people started to dig out nuclear burrows and to listen to the news. 'You don't say, an H-bomb! Don't give me that! They've already reached Z, I swear to you!' a little old man said, 'that has been foreseen for a long time'. 'People exaggerate', said the man who had taken an atomic course in military service, 'it is really not all that bad, that's what the CBR-colonel said, the enemy only want to intimidate us. Throughout history it was always like that: against every weapon a counter-weapon is discovered. By the way, we shall soon have atomic bombs, I've already noticed, during the last manoeuvres our troops also made use of atomic bombs'. – 'In our country', somebody said, shaking his head. 'Oh, it's not all that bad, believe me, after all they must know: when you see the flash, you throw yourself on to the ground or into the burrow, and then you count to fifteen. You drape the tent round you and put on your gas-mask. By the way, these bombs are only tactical.' – 'I see, only tactical', everyone said in astonishment. 'Just look! If I had only just so much atomic power and ignited it – one uses electricity to ignite it, of course – there would be nothing more to be seen of the *Bear* and of all of you!'

'We don't have gas-masks either', Hans Schüpach said, and somebody commented: 'There's not a grain of truth in it'.

A week ago – by then there were nearly a hundred nuclear burrows in my

120

parish – I saw a small, yellowish mound of earth in front of Schüpach's house. The mound has been growing bigger and bigger, and in the homestead another one is already arising. They have not cut a single blade of corn over there, they have more important things to do now. He has become a mole, and I am told that he no longer shows himself above ground. It is entirely possible that the others will imitate him. It is almost four o'clock, shall we quickly switch on the news or at least the beginning. . .

Paul Nizon

From *Diskurs in der Enge*

The lack of noteworthy art-centres in Switzerland must on the one hand be seen in the context of the nature of our state and of our political attitudes – we are a structure consisting of 25 small 'state' units, a plurality (even as far as the languages are concerned) without a genuine capital and without a dominating centre. But more definitely: we are a people of primarily peasant-farming character, in spite of industry, connections with world trade, banking power and flight from the country. . . The country regions played a more important role in our history than the towns, and they still do so today – particularly in our thinking and feeling.

Strictly speaking, we are only acquainted with pure, urban civilization in the case of Basle and Geneva – during the age of humanism Basle was indeed an advance post of the modern spirit of the times, and on this account it attained European importance in cultural affairs too. But that is the exception. In our country many small market-towns and bailiwicks came into existence in the course of history, but not the *town* as a radical differentiation from country, countryside and 'natural life'. Apart from Zürich (which just about reaches the proportions of a big city), the phenomenon of the large town has remained unknown to us; what is more, flight from the country results in these parts by no means in grand urban conception, but rather in a proliferation of village ideas.

The development of a dominating urban concentration and thereby of an urban wedge-shape with the function of a (civilizing-cultural) 'locomotive' appears to be opposed in Switzerland by factors of deeply rooted resistance. Without doubt the 'country', the rural province, offers here much more that is homely and sympathetic and binding than the town.

A state of this type possesses different cultural assumptions and traditions from those countries which have been moulded by princely or ecclesiastical courts and which have inevitably become centralised; such countries have made world history at one time or have indeed been the navel of the world, and therefore of world culture. It was not merely that our history for understandable reasons prevented the development of courtly brilliance – our system in itself made a cultural programme of corresponding scale unthinkable, it did not allow a comparable demand to come into being at all. Typical of this state of affairs is the fact that we do not have any academies of art; there were no requirements that would have justified such luxuries. Cultural needs were satisfied rather in an incidental manner, either in a provincial framework and criterion or by importation. The matrix of our public art collections illustrates this situation obviously: their original constituents were not provided by princely galleries of paintings and sculpture, but by church relics and armouries, whose outstanding works often consisted of booty. With exception of the exclusive Basle, we find among the old masters predominantly regional masters, frequently 'anonymous'. The original constituents of our collections are characterized by a modest middle-class or patrician artistic sense.

This multiform small state which grew from self-help measures into a federation and applied all its energies to surviving and wriggling through between the great powers that surrounded it; which in its way of thinking still feels more firmly embedded in the 'country' than in the 'town' and has managed in cultural matters somewhat frugally: this our modern Swiss Confederation, once it was established, has strictly denied itself, for reasons of self-preservation, all ambition in the direction of world-historical adventures or of involvement; it has guaranteed itself its abstinence in this context by means of the neutrality maxim. Good. But in the eyes of someone who is hungry for experience of the world, it slightly resembles a married couple that have withdrawn from active farming; they are concerned carefully to preserve and protect the granaries, whatever has been brought under cover, what they esteem as the work of their hands and revere as a stronghold of freedom; and the gables of the barns fuse a little with the old snow from the Alps, and out of the picture of peace there also shines forth the personification of one's own virtue; and a radiant wreath confirms the myth of their advancement. . . But the rest of the world, changeable, progressing, frivolous and demanding as it is, pursues the couple with suspicious glances.

A country that keeps away from world conflicts, but more than that, which consciously keeps at arm's length world events and consequently history itself – such a country is able naturally only with difficulty to crystallize that world-significant, fateful atmosphere which we have recognized as the presupposition for important art-centres. There is the danger that the irrigating stream of history may pass it by, so that, who knows, its waters may become brackish.

In Switzerland artistic life has no capital city and stronghold, no actual focal point which might attract artistic energies: it takes place, with varying significance, in many provincial centres, indeed it is distributed among the smallest units, the largely autonomous communes.

Culture in Switzerland is basically a matter for the local commune, and for

122

that reason the Swiss are by nature local artists who, in the absence of a centre that could offer wider competition and greater repute, are compelled to strive for local honours.

This is the reason why the bolder artists have always emigrated. They are seeking a link with the main currents of their time and the competitiveness that goes with them *outside* Switzerland.

It is characteristic that in the case of those artists who have an international name, it is almost always a question of such emigrants. Apparently Switzerland cannot make an artist great. It is the same with art as it used to be with mercenary soldiers: Switzerland lets her sons disperse to the world-significant centres abroad, and she receives the returning wanderers again and·with them the emigrants who for their part establish in Switzerland diaspora-communities of foreign art-movements. In other words, they bring home with them intellectual booty or 'world'.

Culturally Switzerland lives 'in contact'.

Kurt Guggenheim

Switzerland, Province?

I

An adjective that hardly occurs in Swiss-German dialect, but which is used in our press and our literature, is the word 'provincial'. In larger countries which have a capital city, a metropolis that sets the fashion, province has a geographical meaning. In a country like Switzerland where there is no actual metropolis the word 'provincial' is intended to express what is behind the times, petty and small-town. Hence something ridiculous, comic and pitiable, something to be ashamed of.

Since in Switzerland with its three languages there are only principal cantonal towns, there is no such thing as 'province' in Switzerland. Each canton, each valley, each locality not only has its own autonomy but also its cultural individuality. None the less, the word 'provincial' is used again and again, by non-Swiss who make unsuitable comparisons with their own countries, but unfortunately also by Swiss who, because they believe they have felt the wind of the great world blowing about them, often look down with mockery and irony on to their little native country in its narrowness, as they say. Their models are man-of-the-world and cosmopolitan. There is no continent, almost no part of the world, to which they are not transported by 'plane in a few hours. Unfortunately, membership of the German and French linguistic area misleads many people in German-speaking and also in French-speaking Switzerland to the assumption that we, that is, German or Romance Switzerland, are a cultural province in the German cultural centres of Berlin or Bonn, Frankfurt,

Hamburg, etc., or that the literature of Western Switzerland belongs to an intellectual region that is dominated by Paris.

In speech and in writing, in the language of press and literature, radio and television we often have to note a tendency to competition with, indeed to imitation of the great and successful representatives of the larger language area, not only in written texts, but also in action and conduct, in manner, and in criticism of Switzerland. Here French or German cosmopolitanism is demonstrated.

But see, precisely this *is* pure provincialism, for the provincial is recognizable by his constant fear of being considered provincial. Switzerland has no provinces, but at the same time she is not a province.

II

It must certainly have occurred to everyone at some time or other that there are two kinds of the country Switzerland. There is the normal Switzerland of our working day, with its traffic, shops, factories, schools, offices and so on, with the thousands, hundreds of thousands, and millions of people who are occupied there, day after day and at night as well, and things work out, not always, but most of the time, after a fashion, and all who are involved there try to fulfil their tasks with more or less good will, according to the ways of human beings.

Then there is a second kind of Switzerland, the one that people talk and write about. This second kind is not the real Switzerland, it is an imaginary Switzerland, it is a so-called projection of Switzerland, and this picture of Switzerland which is talked and written about, extends not only into the past, but also into the future. It is the conception of Switzerland, the conception which the individual has of the country. This conception is made up, according to circumstances, of regrets about the good old days or gratitude for the prosperity of the present or anxiety concerning the country's future.

The conception of Switzerland is also accompanied by criticism of contemporary Switzerland. This criticism too is based on a picture which the critic in question makes of Switzerland in his imagination, with wishful thinking. He compares the real, present-day Switzerland with the country as it ought to be, according to his conception.

In such a confrontation between present-day, prosaic, everyday, egoistic Switzerland and the idealistic, good, tolerant Switzerland of the future, the real, present-day one naturally comes off very badly. It contains within itself the unpleasant and deplorable qualities of average humanity: it is petty, greedy, unjust, obstinate, sick, does not deserve at all to be defended any more, should we not simply let it slide? We could become very fearful on hearing all these shortcomings of Switzerland and the verdicts of these stern judges. Indeed, one feels positively embarrassed to be a Swiss, and it is with a feeling of guilt that one declares one's fondness for Switzerland.

124

These judgements make an impression on us, naturally, because they contain a germ of truth. How could it be otherwise. This state is man's work, and nothing made by human beings is perfect. Switzerland is precisely the sum-total of all the merits and faults of the people who live there.

But fundamentally and after due consideration we should be pleased at the severe judgements of the critics. They derive from the vision of the future, the conception which they form of Switzerland in times to come. This Switzerland is to be just, generous, tolerant and humane. There is to be no more poverty, no more distress. In a word, this Switzerland of the future is to be noble and healthy.

This makes one's heart swell with pride. The harsh critics do therefore expect Switzerland to become better. What is more, they believe in it. Now, I think, if they believe, they also love, for there is no faith without love.

III

There have always been people who have suffered from the pettiness and narrowness of Switzerland, their home country. The mercenaries of earlier days, the emigrants, the Swiss living abroad cannot be explained only because of the lack or inadequacy of opportunities to earn money. For many of them their homeland, divided up into cantons and confined by mountains, was simply too narrow. They felt the lack of distance, of great, flat stretches of land, of mighty cities, of the sea. They felt their breathing constricted, they were afraid of suffocating, they found that the people were petty too, incapable of worldwide ideas, also less happened in the valleys than in the wide world outside, and when anything did happen, it was taken too seriously, inflated in the 'piccolo mondo' of their home country. A restrictive cantonal spirit reigned in their homeland, and their fellow-citizens were philistines. There was no space, no understanding for the longings of youth, for the sense of adventure, for boldness of conception.

This need for greatness is understandable and justifiable, and of course people become particularly urgently conscious of it in a small country, in narrow confines. Other peoples are the object of envy because of the size of their country, the superior scope of opportunities there, and the so-called unlimited potentialities.

In literature and art there was striving for ever more international spirit. Artists aimed at world reputation. Basically they were striving for the same world-wide influences as the export industries, trade, the banks, insurance businesses and the multi-national firms. In matters of technology that was always more easily possible. The mass-media, cars and aeroplanes link up everybody with everybody else, space becomes smaller, times grow less – there is nothing to prevent even the littlest ones any more from having access to the big, wide world.

In the material world, in the industrial, mercantile world this striving for worldwide success is rewarded with power and wealth, in the ideal world of science and art it is rewarded with fame and admiration.

It might be thought that if this is the case, it becomes in fact increasingly less important where someone is born. Everyone could indeed leave his place of birth and seek out for himself the place where he would like to live. But at that point we have to admit that only a few of us could put up with such uprooting and replanting. Trade, industry, finance, science and art are international, but an individual human being is like a tree: occasionally it is possible to transplant it successfully, but its fruits ripen more certainly in the valley where it originated, however narrow the valley may be, and among its own sort.

Urs Widmer

From *Die Forschungsreise*

It is dark now. I take the pocket torch. I go on to a moraine. When I come to the ice, I carry on without hesitating. I believe I can distinguish a track. A stormy wind sweeps down from the mountain-top. 'No one has ever as yet looked down on the other side', I say, 'or at least I never have.' My voice fades away in the wind. I go in a ditch of ice which leads upwards. I keep on slipping. I am obstinate. My pocket torch goes out. I throw it away. I light one of my signal rockets. It hisses, I see the glowing wick, then it is dark again. 'It has got wet, no wonder, in this weather'. The storm tears the protective helmet off my head. A flash of lightning strikes in the peak above me, for a moment it is as bright as day, and I can see above me a black shadow in the snowstorm. It takes my breath away. 'I am terribly frightened', I stammer, and I stare into the impenetrable darkness. Sparks spray over the metal parts of my ice-pick. I hear the rolling of the thunder, violent claps, loud crashing. I now climb very quickly, on the polished ice. The beam of light from my dynamo lamp which I keep on driving with my hand, glides past towers of ice. The ice-pick falls from my hand when a flash of lightning hisses down with a violent thunderclap. After the thunder has died away, I hear the pick fall into the depths of a crevasse. The storm shakes my rucksack this way and that. I take a turning on to the ridge at the mountain-top. I am walking upright now, in the raging storm. Below me the ridge path, narrow as a knife's edge, gleams white. I make my way in hard-frozen tracks. I brace myself against the icy wind. The handle of my dynamo lamp is freezing. I can feel the resistance continually increasing. I throw the lamp away. When I feel out into the night, near to the icy-hard tracks, my hand clutches at thin air. I become rigid for a moment. Groaning I make my way on further, upright, upwards. I open my mouth, I try to sing a loud, plaintive tone, but the wind presses my singing breath back into my throat. It tears away my ammunition pouch. I hear how it slithers down the icy precipice, more and more quickly, and how the

charges of dynamite explode, scarcely audibly. 'Ohh!' I say. I go more quickly.
The air howls. The strap of my rucksack snaps over my left shoulder with a
crack. The rucksack is hurled about at my back, I totter, I scream, I am just about
able to unwind myself out of the loop. I stagger. I put my icy hand to my brow.
'Really now, this too is no longer of any importance', I cry out in a voice choked
with tears. I feel my way forwards in the snow with my one remaining glove. I
am aware of the hard edges of the tracks, as if from mountain caravans or
gigantic feet. The snowstorm clogs up my eyes, my mouth. I go on all fours. I
groan. The wind catches in the hood of my anorak, tearing it away. I have ice
before my eyes. Suddenly my hand knocks against something hard, large, firm.
'The cairn', I stammer, 'of course!' A hot wind blows into my face. I call. I
shout. I howl. I listen. 'Ahhh!' I say. With both hands I feel over the stones at the
summit cross. I grasp at every cleft in the stones, my lips tremble, and for a
moment the terrible wind at the summit stops. There is a smell. I can feel the stiff
cloth of the flag on the summit, the flagpost, the wooden cross beneath it, the tin
cans that are lying about everywhere. I stare in front of me. Flashes of lightning
flicker before my eyes. I beat my fists against my brow. I howl, I bite off one of
my fingernails with one bite. Suddenly I stand up. My heart is beating. 'Ye gods
and little knapsacks!' I say. I seize my theodolite with a sob and throw it down
over the south wall. I listen. Then, while the wind is again thundering against
my ears, I take the rope, the specimen box, the oxygen apparatus, the compass. I
hurl them all into the black void before me. With my searching hands I feel the
drawing-block, the record book, the book for taste impressions, the relief-map,
the pocket first-aid kit, the altimeter, then the camera, the decibel meter, the
cassette recorder with the scientific impressions from on the way, the spirit
level, the slide rule. I throw them all into the wall of ice. I hear the wind, like a
howling, like a thundering in the ears. I stamp my foot. Once more I caress the
cairn, then I turn round and start my descent. In the far distance on the horizon I
see a narrow strip of light. I stumble downwards, going head over heels, while
slipping I recognize once more, in a violent flash of lightning, the flag at the
summit, with its flapping cloth. I wave my hand, then I crash against a piece of
rock.

Gertrud Leutenegger

From *Ninive*

The most unassuming happenings in the streets have an air of leave-taking about
them. The thin glass panels of the weather telegraph are replaced by more
weather-resistant ones. The waiters of the Edelweiss Hotel stand around in front
of the hotel entrance already by noon, as if each day here could be their last. It
seems that a chambermaid has moved into one of the hotel rooms on the dark

side that has been empty for some time now; one morning, from my window I can see her waving goodbye from behind half-closed curtains. She stands there, a slightly blurred figure, immobile, in a pale-coloured nightdress; down below her lover, a waiter from the Mediterranean, is ready to depart. He too is standing immobile, a monument in the square, and is looking up to the window where the chambermaid is leaning against the curtains with an almost completely negligent tiredness, like one of the guests whom she has observed and served long enough. She raises her hand from time to time. And waves. Then the beloved down below also raises his hand and waves. Very slowly, just a few times to and fro, as if he had to wipe away from his face the distance that was already becoming greater, or is it the blurring in front of the chambermaid's form. Then they both let their hands fall again and stand motionless. In the end the waiter has to make for the bus that is due to depart. At this moment the chambermaid lifts with bare arms the curtain away from her face and lets it fall in a definitive manner, now yawning fleetingly as the curtain drops. A few days later this chambermaid also seems to have departed. The shutters of the bedroom where she had stood waving goodbye remain closed. The high-winged doors of the ground-floor rooms are boarded up with bulwarks of piled-up wooden slats, as if people were afraid of avalanches that might come down into the locality; even the balcony doors of the high bedrooms are blocked with boards to prevent snow drifting in. The breakfast rooms and dance-halls seem to have been deserted in precipitate haste. Through the windows of the doors that are boarded up to three-quarters of their height one can still see coffee-pots and further back, in the direction of the dance-floor, the seats disturbed from their arrangement, as if the guests had just gone to take part in one of the dances whose repertoire still consisted of flowers in bloom and Alpine glow.

While there is increasing liveliness inside the workers' house as the season draws to its close, in the public rooms of the hotels I take my evening meals in growing isolation. According to an old agreement, as curator of the museum I receive free meals in all the hotels of the mountain locality, and I do so following a particular rota which had been made known to me in a most detailed schedule on the first day of my arrival. While the snowflakes begin to fall again outside, I sit at my small table in the dining-room of one of the last hotels that have not yet closed. I am the only guest. The last one. Behind the glasses which are set out at their varying heights, the reserved seat ticket, 'Curator of N.', is still kept there for me. I have been placed against the wall of the centre of the room, a large number of white-covered table places extends around my table. Gleaming rows of glasses. The plates sparkle, it is only the reservation tickets that are missing and the stiff, high-standing serviettes. In spite of that the waiter, silent and polite, hands me the complete menu card for the day. With impassive facial expression he brings in one course after another, the Poulet de France doré is there, the Poires Emmy Destin are there at midday, and in the evening the

Knickerbocker Glory. The glass doors of the dining room are not used one single time. The hotel seems to have adapted itself to my solitude. Next evening, when I try to reach my place amid the white sea of tablecloths, the chandeliers which usually lavish beaming light hang extinguished in the dark at ceiling height. It is only above my table that a chandelier has been lowered and is still dispensing a brightness which gives emphasis to the half-light of the rest of the room. I am kept waiting. Sometimes a course is missing. I spend less and less time with my eyes on my plate. The supporting pillars now stand white one behind the other, more clearly than when the room is fully lit, and the estrades extend high up against the room walls, fenced off by dainty lattice-work. From these estrade-like mural walks there now and again appears the glazed eye of a stuffed chamois buck which is thrusting forward its horns as if ready to leap, as if the popping of champagne corks had terrified him to death and as if at the next moment he would come hurtling down from the height of the ceiling over the dainty estrade-balustrade and into the mountains of blancmange and lakes of vanilla. Plate after plate is brought in to me, it all tastes the same, I now think, overcooked, the warmed-up remains of the high season; up there the chandeliers are hanging in the dark. I should like to talk a little to the waiter, would be glad to hear, thrusting aside the quietness of the room, his mocking laughter at my formal solitude at table, but he withdraws. He stands with folded arms in front of the winged door, in statuesque quiet. Everything about him expresses superiority. He surveys the rows of glasses, the flashing formations of cutlery. It seems as if in a ghostly way the crowds of people who used to talk here in elegant whispers and for whom the places are laid beneath the unlit chandeliers as if for a final course are assembling once more beneath his gaze and are silently conforming to his long held-back triumph. My sweet is not available. The waiter bows. I can still hear the echoing from the opening and shutting of the winged doors while I am hurrying down to the lake through the meadows that are intersected by low stone walls.

The half-light over the meadowland with its rough grass seems to be the same as that in the dining-room, the same definitive grey, light in weight, motionless like some sort of material. A grey curtain has fallen over the world. The theatre wings are still there, the estrades in the unlit room, the mountain shadows by the lake.

Hermann Burger

The Happiest Day of Your Life

In the darkened sitting-room the projector is humming. The figures are moving on the screen, in the small, flickering rectangle. By mistake I have caused the film to be shown in reverse. Doris finds this almost perverse. I promise her that I will not look at our happiness the wrong way round. The figures stride backwards with incredible confidence, and when they go forwards, one notices that they do so with effort, as if they were moving in some sticky, transparent substance. It is a festive party of replete adults. Long dresses are conspicuous, ladies in fluttering trouser-suits. The gentlemen in dark suits, with a rose in their buttonhole, the older ones still wearing grey-black striped trousers. If it were a sound film, one would be obliged to hear the jokes of Uncle Max. Exaggerated cordiality on the faces, perhaps it is only the dazzling sunlight. It may well be a brilliant October day, the cherry-trees are aflame. The church-clock points to ten minutes past four. Some guests stand stiffly at the edge of the lawn where a group of six lines up. The photographer who has just taken the snapshot comes into the picture, and while kneeling directs his victims: come forward a little, move apart a little further, really stylized, please! The people become continually more restless. There are glances in all directions, only not at the camera. Has the photographer overlooked the gravestones in the background? Or do they belong to the requisites of the happiness that is dazzling the six Kodak-brown faces? They will be noticed later when the picture is passed round among the grandchildren. But fortunately the film has been put into reverse. The father-in-law's hat, which has stood fast for a while in front of his stomach, all at once no longer knows where it is to go. Firstly it wanders behind his back, then it makes an appearance again, and for a moment it looks as if it were going to splinter off to the side. The group now breaks up, parents and parents-in-law step away backwards. They avoid the bridal couple who are standing on their own in the sunlight, the long white silk dress glistening. Soon Uncle Max will take the cigar out of his mouth and put it back in the case where the speech about happiness is written down in catchwords, after the match has jumped from the grass into his hand. After all, Uncle Max is always the same.

Doris finds herself quite impossible, but also the rest of the ladies. Surely a fur doesn't go with balm-red chiffon and a frilled collar, she says. And Aunt Lisbeth's dress is terrible. It clings to her body like a glittering snake skin full of coffee stains. 'Doris', I say, 'you are the most beautiful bride I have ever seen, I would have been proud of you. Give me a kiss!' But Doris anticipates herself on the film. Just as she is about to bend over to me across the hot projector, she impresses a tender film kiss on the bridegroom's cheek. 'Do you remember?' Doris says with a sigh. 'But Doris, in the second year of marriage one doesn't yet remember.' 'You have no cause to grumble at all, when you forget our wedding anniversary every year!' The guests are just stepping backwards into the picture in a disorderly procession, in order to congratulate us in front of the church on the happiest day of our life. And it is this day of all days that I keep on forgetting. As a punishment for this I have to watch our wedding film. Men just do forget wedding anniversaries. Do they not get married to oblige the women? On the other hand the women forget the names of mountains.

The seventh of October. A golden date, as if created to be the happiest day. There is nothing entered in my diary under the seventh of October. All the other pages are full of appointments, the seventh is blank. Where was I on the seventh of October? Doris maintains that I married her, and she has never as yet lost a bet. The film acknowledges that she is right. I appear in it, disguised as bridegroom, rather clumsy in my movements, rather awkward, as one should be in face of happiness, with my hair rather too short. I see myself standing about anxiously and walking backwards as if stepping upon eggs. My trousers are too long. I scratch my hair, to get rid of the stinging dandruff. You should be able at all events to control the movements of your hands on your wedding-day! What must the relatives be thinking who are now congratulating us? That is to say, they withdraw their good wishes and cautiously disappear in the semi-darkness of the church doorway. But at any time I can change over the red lever on the camera, and then they will congratulate us again; I can even fix it at slow motion, if we want to observe happiness quite precisely. However, can one bear so much happiness all at once?

I don't know how this gap came in my memory. The seventh of October does not exist in my recollection. If we did not possess the wedding film and the photograph album, I could not believe that we are married, Doris and I. I am said to have uttered an enthusiastic 'Yes', my cousin who is moving away to the rear in a mink coat has assured me. Funny that one can say such an important 'Yes' without being there. Where was I on the seventh of October? Of course, one looks forward so much to this day, the big day, the day that belongs wholly to the bridal couple. One has nightmares that end in profuse sweating. The women dream that they say 'No' at the last minute or stumble up the steps to the altar or lose their veil. I did not even dream that I had been there. I would have come too late, for the ceremony in my dream just as gladly, if I could have been there on the seventh of October, when I am supposed to have uttered a dry, but none the less enthusiastic 'Yes' in our bleak parish church to a completely bright fortune in the shape of a minister in Protestant dress.

'Typical, your imagination', Doris always says, when I ask her to describe our wedding to me. 'Just as you imagine that you have been in places where you certainly never have been, so you imagine that you weren't there on the seventh of October. What is more, you were so considerate, the way you set free my veil when I was pressing it with my back against the back of the chair. You were a model bridegroom.' In the film I am in fact standing by the doorway, like happiness personified, and shaking hands, with the sun in my neck. Doris blames my imagination – how could it be otherwise with feminine logic! – for a day that is missing in my memory. I might equally well ascribe this wedding to the imagination of our relatives. If I adjust the lens so that it is out of focus, we are only two more smudges, swimming in a brightly coloured sea of smudges. That's how a wedding should be celebrated, without programming happiness, I think, gleaming colours that merge silently into one another. 'You always imagine everything much too vividly', Doris says, 'so that afterwards you no longer have the strength to experience it in reality. Presumably, on our wedding-day you were already on our honeymoon, somewhere in the sunny south.' I don't disagree with her. Yet I have precise memories of the honeymoon: when we arrived in Venice under cover of darkness and the band was still playing in St Mark's Square, when we heard a bell tinkling all night and the gurgling of the canal water. Venice too I visualized intensively, and yet I experienced its presence at the time. We were happy without realizing it.

What did Lucky Johnnie in the story in fact do with his good fortune? He could not rest until he had got rid of it, until he had sunk the stone in the well. Happiness is not something you can ride or milk, or slaughter or drag along, you can merely forget it in order not to disturb it, if possible. Doris thinks otherwise. Uncle Max said in his speech, she says, that one must simply learn to take hold of happiness, it is always there. 'There you are then', I say. 'I wasn't there on the seventh of October in order that you could not take hold of me'.

Doris wants me to show the congratulatory reception again in slow motion, forwards, for instead of the marriage ceremony the photographer has sought out a symbolic October motif: shivering poplar branches. I would not have been surprised if the entire film had taken place in the trees. Surprising, how many aunts we have together! And they are all radiant on our account and are expensively dressed. Mirror, mirror on the wall, who is the fairest of them all? The bride, of course, it is her due. Or is it Aunt Vera? How ever can one display so much bosom? It is shameless of Aunt Vera to keep on bending down in the film, as if she had dropped something on to the ground.

It was not our day, it was your day, dear Aunts. Our marriage was of minor importance. The main thing was that you could participate in the experience of how two young people accept each other in marriage and become happy. Perhaps I was not there because I was afraid of having to be happy to order. Even at an earlier stage I could never unpack presents in the presence of grown-ups. I did not wish to let myself be compelled to deception, to a radiant smile for a book which I had already read, or for a set of railway-lines with the wrong gauge. Should one not be allowed at least on the happiest day of one's life to be happy, or indeed unhappy, for once according to one's own judgment? The congratulatory telegrams prescribe happiness too. One happiness seldom comes on its own. To be loved is the greatest happiness on earth. Everyone is the architect of his own fortune. It's the lucky man who brings home the bride, etc.

The film has torn. A dazzling white on the screen. Happiness goes on strike, it is off and away. Doris insists that I glue it together at once, the happiest day of our life. I suggest silhouettes, such as the wolf eating up Red Riding Hood, or the elephant losing its trunk. But don't let us quarrel on our wedding anniversary! I get out the implements, fit both strips of celluloid into the little piece of equipment, make the torn parts rough, cut the ends straight, dab on the glue with the little brush, and make it close with a snap. What movement, what pressure of hands has been lost?

'Do you remember', Doris says, 'how the minister came too late because in the heat of the moment we had forgotten to call for him? Do you remember how Klara couldn't play the organ because of her gastric 'flu? Do you remember how my shoe got stuck in the lawn as we were walking up to the church? Do you remember how the children snatched at the flints?' No, Doris, I don't yet remember. We shall have to make good the day in my much strained imagination, without alerting our relatives, without having to draw up a table plan with an Uncle Max who must be not be given a place by Aunt Vera or else he will take sidelong glances at her décolletage, without flints, congratulatory telegrams and producers, without photographers who capture on pictures what can't be captured. Happiness that does not go by the calendar will be there without putting up the banns, and it will not need to smile into the camera. It will be a day that belongs completely to us, a day like any other, as white and bright as the flickering rectangle on the screen.

The film has been set in motion again, we can carry on getting married in the dark. The marriage ceremony has long since been put into reverse, the minister has slurred over his first words, the notes have found their way back into the organ pipes and the bellows. The church door opens, and the picture becomes dark because of the many backs. Finally the two bridal attendants, the mother with the bridegroom and the father with the bride. Then there follows the packaging into beribboned and highly polished limousines. They all drive backwards much too quickly, it's a miracle that there are no accidents.

Jürg Laederach

I and Crime

I was called to the main station in my capacity as police inspector. Again I came too late. At the scene of the crime I waited for morning to come.

I was the police inspector. I was called to Basle main station. Had it happened, as I maintained, in the waiting-room? The dead man had disappeared. I waited in my cape for that dull morning to come.

I had scarcely arrived at Basle main station when I felt that I had become a police inspector. At all events a promotion had taken place emanating from my office. Unfortunately I came too early. No dead man was lying in the van of a goods' train carrying corn that had just arrived from Alsace. I asserted to a permanent – way inspector the view that the murder had not yet happened and, with my presence as a warning that was visible from afar, that it would not happen. There was something fishy about the business. In all the bother that was to follow in this puzzling case I started from the assumption that I had definitely come too early; this was proved solely by the fact that all the survivors were alive. Back in my office, I fell down one increment and broke my ankle.

Since I was almost out of action on account of rheumatism in my shoulder I had spent the whole day admiring Fahrner, the confiscated Basle painter and a man possessed of a Schopenhauerian fury. When I was attempting the splaying out of my hands which I did every evening, a telephone call summoned me to the main station. The threadlike-thick rain that was falling on the customs buildings could be proved to be of prime importance for the depth of the night. Had it happened, as I surmised, in the waiting-room where they were all eating sausage with bread-rolls, waiting, knocking back plum-brandies, waiting, carving obsessions into the corner-seats with their switch knives, waiting? A dead man lay in the van of a goods train carrying chemicals that had just come from Alsace, which surprisingly meant that the train with chemicals only consisted of one van. Sulphuric acid had worked havoc with the corpse, and with presence of mind I ordered inquiries to be made in all chemist's shops on the Continent, as there was no question of Britain and Jersey being scenes of the crime, I repeat, no question. As the train carrying chemicals had come from Alsace, the customary nasty business reverted in essentials back to the French. Being without knowledge of French, I had this observation translated. A trail of blood led me to my dilapidated house nearby. I followed it, without querying much to myself, as far as my basement where I sat down on the executioner's block, spread out my fingers with a wedge driven in between and took out a sterilized knitting-needle from the Indian wrap. The next morning I was informed that I was dismissed without notice, that my salary was graded back to zero and that I had forfeited my pension, because of incredible hired car expenses; but in spite of the strictest official veto I continued to occupy myself with that case as a free-lance amateur, and before my rheumatism reached my coronary vessels, I was provided with the wholly negative findings from the checks made of the chemist's shops; these findings I quickly redirected to the nearest plenary session.

At the main station night, deep. The dead man in the van, half decomposed. Resembled my father like two pins. When I there, he away. Blood on the wall of my house, lamb's blood. The case in its parts without relation to other parts or to itself or to me. I alone. The dead man scarcely held in check. No solution to look for the solution. Place of the crime the size of a pinhead, minute clot. Can't, I said. At the customs tomorrow, daylight. Can't, I said. First van. Fallen back on to the desk. Under the cold tap to prevent nose-bleeding. Snatched egg-sandwich. Next file into the fire.

Hugo Loetscher

'Who Discovered Switzerland?'
translated by Peter Spycher

It was in Latin America that I heard the best question ever asked about my country: 'Who discovered Switzerland?' I wanted to give an answer, and in my novel *The Man with Immunity* I wrote about a possible discovery of my country. I would like to share the beginning of this chapter with you:

We fought our way up the river. Never before had we seen this kind of water, the only kinds we knew till then were fresh or sea water, but what we found there, in such a strange region, was indeed a new variety of water. It smelled rather nauseating and had a brownish colour; the current was sluggish, the white crests that formed were not caused by the flow of the river. One morning we discovered fish drifting in the water with their pale bellies turned up.

We asked the prisoner who served as our interpreter what this means but he seemed to be puzzled by our question. We offered him a ladle filled with this water, he drank it without any hesitation and then looked up beaming. He said that in all his life – he is still a young man – he had never seen any other kind of water in river beds. We ordered him to drink a second and a third time, but it did him no harm.

Since we failed to get a clear explanation about the nature of the water in this river, we called it the River of the Dead Fish. But after all, we did not want to stay on these banks, we wanted to push ahead up the river; for we had heard stories about a secret country, rich in gold, an El Dorado, where immense wealth was supposed to be hoarded. During a stopover on an island that is situated close to the mainland, we had learned that this hoard was guarded by gnomes.

But what impelled us to forge ahead towards the province called Helvetia was not just this treasure guarded by dwarfs, but also the existence of fountains of youth promising eternal life. Their magic charms and formulas are said to be kept strictly secret. Yet we hoped to find ways and means to provide our own great ruler and our people with such blessings, too.

Suddenly, our prisoner called out: 'Here we are!' We were surprised because what we saw was, at least for the moment, no different from what we had hitherto observed along these banks. But our interpreter was quite excited; he told us that we had arrived at the meeting point of three countries. To be sure, we had not yet reached the province proper of the gold-guarding gnomes, he averred; but we were at the border of their territory. What we saw in front of us, he said, was the legendary location of the fountains of youth.

We marvelled greatly at the sight, fell down on our knees, and gave thanks to our mighty god for this unexpected, but most generously granted, privilege;

thereupon we sharpened our swords and readied our bows and arrows.

At first, we thought we had been detected and word had been spread concerning our arrival, because there were smoke signals going up wherever we looked. Soon enough, however, we learned that those smoke signals were not intended to broadcast any messages; this was not possible, for one thing, since they were not replaced by visible fire signals at night.

Rather, people were performing sacrificial rites. All along the river bank, smoke was rising towards the sky. Earlier, we had wondered why people would erect tall buildings without any rows of steps, yet we were told that they construct stairs inside and also that these stairs keep moving of their own accord, which, naturally, caused hearty laughter among us. They also build houses for the smoke, round and slim ones, looking like tubes. This was not a holiday, though, but rather an ordinary workday; these people do not sacrifice human beings, slitting open their chests, as we do, taking out their steaming hearts, and offering them up to Heaven; nor do they sacrifice specially chosen victims who prepare themselves for the deadly rite by singing hymns; they sacrifice indiscriminately; they subject their victims to a lifelong sacrifice by forcing them to work; it is not a large number of people who sacrifice a few, it is a few people who sacrifice a large number of others.

Nonetheless, we remained sceptical. On our way, we had already lost one ship, a loss still weighing heavily on the minds of our crew. The natives have larger and faster crafts, but so far our own flat-bottomed ships have proved to be superior. To be sure, we had heard that the tribe of the gold-hoarding gnomes was peaceable; that for a long time they themselves had no longer waged any wars, but had kept a careful eye on wars waged between others, refraining from taking sides, doing business with both participants. On the other hand, we had found out that the able-bodied men annually turn into warriors and play war games that last up to three weeks.

In order to test the willingness of this tribe to keep the peace, Kamilk, the brave son of the Kaziks, swam to the river bank in the dark of the night, where he laid out peace offerings; precious wood, some jewelry, and many perfumed cloths. The one who found the gifts examined them at length, then he ran away, and we waited for him to return along with his chieftain. Yet he turned up with two identically dressed men. They were two policemen, as they soon told us themselves, at least that is what they called themselves, pointing with their fingers at their chests; we were to find out soon enough what that meant.

First, they searched the bank, until they discovered us floating on the river. Then they waved to us and boarded one of their fast boats. It would have been wrong for us to try to escape them; thus we made preparations for a fight and took shelter in our ships, being firmly resolved to sell our lives as dearly as possible. But after they had approached us by way of a loop, one of them made unmistakable peace signals in our direction. We returned the same signals to express our gratitude and let the first of them come aboard. The man wanted to see our papers, but we did not know just what he was looking for. Even when the interpreter explained to us the matter at hand, we did not fully understand what he meant. Soon enough, however, we noticed that he was not satisfied to simply look at us and our ship with his own sound eyes.

All natives carry papers with them, on which the place and date of their birth are entered. This is all the more understandable since their hairdo and attire no longer indicate their different origins. The life of these people starts, not with their emergence from the womb of a woman, but with a bureaucratic entry. We would have loved to know if the same applies to death, too.

The native in uniform scribbled something on a piece of paper and held it out towards us. We thought it was a return gift and broke out into a shout of joy. But our mood became more subdued when we learned that it was a penalty. It was really baffling news to us that we should be penalized for having laid out perfumed cloths, jewelry, and precious wood. But the man informed us that there was a regulation against anchoring ships here and swimming ashore. We laughed at him, and this made him angry. We realized quickly that this was just a stratagem on his part to engage us in an argument. The man denied it; he repeated several times what he had told us and insisted again and again it was indeed a regulation, which made us curious to find out what this word signified.

He produced these regulations from one of their sacred books, which he was carrying on his person; it contains innumerable regulations arranged according to symbols, which resembled a double gallows and noose about to be drawn tight.

These regulations may be likened to those slowly working poisons that some of our Indian tribal members extract from lianas, maniocs, and cactuses. Except that the regulations are extracted not from plants but from the juice of brains that have been trained for years. These regulations do have an effect, although afterwards you could not determine exactly how long ago it was that you 'swallowed' them. Many of them have such a neutral taste that you do not notice anything special when swallowing them. Thus their effect sets in without a noticeable transition after years have elapsed. The regulations lead to some kind of paralysis, without slackening your zest for work; on the contrary, the result may be an outright obsession for work. The most conspicuous effect is a gradual loss of memory; thus, under the influence, most people forget the dreams of their youth and the things for which they once struggled.

The regulations also cause a certain degree of intoxication. Yet this intoxication is experienced not by those who swallow them but rather by those who enforce them. We could distinctly perceive that the policeman's pupils, while he was reading the regulations to us, were dilated with ecstasy and that the cornea was changed to a lustful red colour.

137

Hansjörg Schneider

From *Lieber Leo*

Every evening during the following weeks there was a students' occasion in Basle, and each one was taken seriously by the newspapers. I did interviews with women student leaders, I asked bearded young men about forthcoming large-scale demonstrations, I reviewed the books about the student unrest, the Vietnam war and street theatre which were being published by the dozen. Everybody expected a major operation by the Basle police, for what had been happening abroad had to happen in Basle too, it was important, and I had a flair for this type of reporting. I liked doing this, dear Leo, although I had not forgotten the all-consuming avalanche of cars in Paris. A big student meeting had been planned, when student leaders from abroad were to speak, at this meeting the future of the Basle university should be decided, the professors who were still hesitating and using devious tactics were to be brought to their knees once and for all.

I had already been at the Petersplatz for over an hour before the start, dear Leo, I watched as the last benches were put in place and the loudspeaker cables were assembled, there was already an audience of several hundred. They laughed rather too loudly at some joke or other, they looked up very quickly when there was equally loud laughter somewhere else, evidently they were all afraid. When the first speaker took up the microphone, the square was full of people. It was very quiet when the voice from the loudspeaker said that they had waited long enough, now they wanted to see action. The University would eventually have to become autonomous, that was to say free from outside influence, private capital which had nothing in mind apart from its own aggrandisement, and what was more, at the cost of human lives and human happiness, should not be allowed to have any further influence on research and knowledge, and professors were the servants of precisely this private capital, only the students were free from outside influence, and for this reason they would have to take over power in the University. They themselves would have to determine what and how they wanted to learn, only in this way could there be a guarantee of genuinely free research and knowledge, and this free and independent research and knowledge would radiate into all spheres of human co-existence and would make this co-existence free and independent.

This short speech was followed by concentrated applause. Then the man of the evening made his way to the rostrum. He came from Paris, he had fairly long, well-groomed hair and was wearing glasses with round lenses. He waited for some seconds, he seemed to be concentrating. Camarades, he then said, c'est assez!

After these words there was shrill shouting, the French student-star had to wait a fairly long time until it was quiet again, he stood there without moving, then he went on speaking.

I knew the statements that he was making, I knew that they were admittedly right, but useless, and after a time I noticed that I was no longer listening, but observing the people around me.

They were sitting crowded together on the benches, they were very young people, and they had insignificant faces. There was nothing to be learnt from these faces apart from the zeal of good intentions, they were well protected faces, without despair and without passion.

I looked at the backs of the heads of those sitting in front of me, I only saw hair, always the same shampooed long hair, sometimes blonde, sometimes dark, for the most part it was lightly waved, and suddenly I saw Bea's relatively short, curly, reddish hair.

I immediately looked away, dear Leo. I did not want to see Bea now, I did not want to see her at all. I considered for a moment whether I should get up and go away, but I could not do that, I had my notebook on my knees and the pencil in my hand, I was here in order to use my flair in reporting what the man from Paris with glasses had to say to the Basle student body, after all it was my work, and I remained seated.

I tried not to look over there. I succeeded for the length of several sentences. I concentrated on these difficult French sentences, they were concerned with the relationship of eroticism and the performance of duty. It was no accident, the well-groomed student leader was saying, that the revolt had started in Nanterre with the fellows no longer being willing to sleep separately from the girls. That had not been a trivial matter, he explained further, for the European performance of duty, which had brought so much misfortune upon the world, had only been possible thanks to the domesticization of eroticism.

I found myself in agreement with this sentence, I noted down the expression 'domesticization of eroticism', I concentrated on the sentences that followed, but it was of no help at all. In vain did I direct my attention to the blue-tinted paper on my knees, my eyes turned away in a quick glance to the front. In fact she was sitting on the front bench just below the speaker's lectern, she was holding her head slightly to one side, she was gazing motionless at the bespectacled face, what is she doing here, I thought, does she know French at all?

Ernst Bloch, the student leader was saying, was no doubt right when he reproached Freud for only studying the problems of well-to-do Europeans. The problems of the rest of humanity were not in fact erotic, but nutritional in character. But as far as we who had come together in the old humanist city of Basle were concerned, Freud had in fact been right. For we were not under-developed from the nutritional point of view, but we were erotically, and that was why we were also so eminently subject to manipulation. We must now be bold and take the final step towards permanent revolution, we must shake off the repression of the old father-professors, in any case this would be very easy, for in the face of sufficient spontaneity the authoritarian bogey-men would collapse like paper tigers.

I wrote the words 'paper tiger' in my notebook, dear Leo, this phrase hooked itself firmly on to my mind. I saw in my mind's eye a tiger made of light paper, I could not shoo it away, it stayed there, it was painted bright-red and yellow, and had white patches on its flanks, its head was cheerful, it was holding it slightly to one side and was blinking at me.

I stood up, pressed my way past the bench full of people, I knocked against strange knees and heads that were bent forward. There was some space before the front row, I could get through here comfortably. I saw Bea, the way she was sitting there, the upper part of her body bent slightly forward, her head supported in her right hand. She seemed to notice me only when I forced myself in beside her, the individual at her side made room protestingly, the man with glasses on the speakers' platform came to a halt for a moment, then he went on holding forth, by now he had got to Mao and the permanent revolution. Bea nodded briefly to me, she seemed to take it for granted that I was there, it almost seemed as if she had expected me, she moved away a little so that I could sit more comfortably, she immediately immersed herself in the further development of the hypothesis of the dialectic interplay between theory and practice.

I waited until my pulse was beating more quietly, it took a fairly long time, dear Leo. Then I opened my notebook and went on writing. I noted one idea after another, I did not show my feelings, it suited me that Bea could see how exactly I worked. Without looking up, I also took notes on the other speeches which were given as well, they too were concerned with permanent revolution. Bea remained seated beside me until shortly after eleven, she looked inquisitively into every speaker's face, she did not seem to grow tired, she was evidently fascinated by these characters, I didn't know why, at all events she could not understand anything.

When the last speaker had finished, Bea joined in the applause, which was not very enthusiastic, she clapped lightly with her small hands, evidently the evening had been to her liking. Then she gave me her hand to shake, she took her leave in a friendly way and went. I did not hold her back, dear Leo, I stayed seated and followed with my eyes, as she disappeared in the throng.

French

Maurice Chappaz

The Obscure Saints. Villages Sold for an Apple, Bought back by a Heart

'My grace is sufficient for thee!' Is it true? I call the idiots to mind. They were huge, they dragged themselves along with faces eaten away like tree-bark. They tried to speak, but only cluckings and bellowings passed their lips. More than other disabled people they appeared to me as debris of nature, and I looked on them as if they were human streams or human trees. They were very strong as to their arms, very weak as to their legs. They worked hard with their four limbs. A stray cat jumping up on them could cause them to fall down. There was the cretin Locâ, the cretin Hat and the big cretin with the cigar. More mysterious than these, the one who was only taken out at night to walk him in the direction of the river, and whose head was enclosed in a sack. He had the face of a horse.

The youngsters from the schools occasionally teased the idiots. They held two pieces of wood in the shape of a cross under their noses and bawled out songs to them. It was believed that an enormous and passive sexuality could be discerned in them. They were sometimes tied up in stables and maltreated, but we well knew that the only folly is malice. In the village they were known as the innocents. In general the families looked after them as well as possible, and I never felt the slightest contempt towards them.

'They alone', someone said to me, 'since they have no reason, have not sinned against Christ'.

They affected me as if I were bearing within myself something monstrous and perhaps sentimental. I said to myself, there are the flesh and the entrails of man: touch them. They were terribly stunted and wounded. What is more, I reckoned that I must be related to the idiots because of my excessive timidity.

I would not wish to blaspheme nor to deceive myself. Saints are born of the infirm, saints emerge from monsters. They have their share of evil, and their humility makes them so curiously ordinary that either we do not see them or else we see only a fault, only a wound. Today the idiots of the Valais are concealed. It is above all from them, these placard heads of the procession of miseries that this truth was deduced that everyone needed a healer as in the Gospel.

The villages were certainly too poor in science, but they invented their own remedy. It was the heart, it was the church within. How was misfortune to be borne? There was a response that was not a form of flight.

We knew shame, we also knew a wonderful balance.

Faces of those who become purified. My mother used to say: 'There are saints in existence who have not been to Rome. They do not have a distinguished presence. They are banal and straightforward.' Well! Our little Saint Theresas remained unknown with their bouquets of roses that we denied them. Unknown also these powerful and simple saints from the highland pastures, the cheese-maker who came down every night to help his sick wife and who went up again, saying a Pater that lasted two hours, through the fir-trees.

Villages, convents full of ill-feeling or considerateness, certain ones of them succeeded in understanding and in controlling themselves. Witness this small Alpine town where no one swore, no one clamoured; these people, like Rousseau, would have ennobled a piece of cheese. Witness still more this hamlet of three or four houses where a man or a woman in each family got up in the night to recite the Office of the Dead. I heard some movement in the rooms. I went to the window, I looked down into the gentle little black gardens. I looked at the earth. These nocturnal prayers made us all, dead and living, in love with the Creator.

An idea of chastity was on the watch: in these villages the bread passed from the kitchen to the other room. I was chatting over supper round a big table, and one of the guests, while telling a story, came out with a strong obscenity. A sign with his finger from the master of the house, and one of the waiters took up the bread and disappeared. 'Why is this?' I said to my neighbour. 'So that it does not hear', he told me, and he added: 'With us the bread must not hear either anything that is impure or a lie'. 'Then it is the kingdom of God here, for short periods at least.'

My friend Paul is stretched out in his bed. He has very red cheeks. As for me, my shoes are white with dust. I have crossed three valleys to come and see him. And it is three years since he left school for a strange sort of long holidays. Because we all knew that it was to die, and the form-master (a priest) had asked him to offer his life on our behalf. Of course he had said yes. And now he was asking for news of us. So-and-so, So-and-so: is he still studying? And is that boy from Trogne still friendly with the lad from Veysonne? and does Jacob continue to go down into the grottoes on Thursdays? and what about your rock-climbing? And what do the masters say to you? And Peter? And Gilbert?

Paul had been abandoned.

The attention and tenderness which everyone had at first promised him had been exhausted, lost. At the end of six months, a year, six months more, he had held out in his chalet in the forests, looked after by his mother, a little dark-haired countrywoman who was almost childish. There was only the group of those who were called writers because of their enthusiasm for weekly editions (A mowing-machine goes into the meadow – winter interior – interminable snow – springtime in leaves of glass) of which it was said they read a volume a week; they alone occasionally made the climb in order to find Paul in his mountain.

'Maurice, write me a poem, even if it's a short one, even a rough draft: so that I can reply to you!'

What he liked were three lines about nature. We thought we could not live without creating each day a little image to say how beautiful the earth was and to express this starting from the place where we were, from the people we met during the twenty-four hours. What importance we attached to the weather, the sun, the snow, the rain!

What Paul liked was jokes and puns about angels. He also used to throw down this formula like a gambler: 'Villages sold for an apple, bought back by a heart!' We believed in too fragile and too strong a fashion to be able to discipline our imaginations except in this way. We looked upon our lives as a game of cards with Adam and Eve. And then behind the spirits there opened up the idea of death, and death was Christ Himself, feared and revered. We never spoke about Him. We well knew that Paul was obliged to imitate Him, in the same way that he could not forget us.

The fourth spring was filled with the approaches of death. Let no one weep, let no one wear mourning! He suffered for a long time from thirst. He begged his mother to remove a small advertisement for chocolate which depicted a cow drinking large draughts from a bucket and which mocked him from a chest of drawers.

When the crises had passed, we smiled. He never lost his hold on happiness. I have known a compatriot who held sadness in detestation. In the face of suffering he would say, shrugging his shoulders: 'When you think what we deserve'.

S. Corinna Bille

Café des Voyageurs

A fierce Easter wind was blowing down upon the Rhône valley: the föhn! It took hold of you completely in its paw and shook you like a dice-box, mingling the smoke from brushwood fires with whirlwinds of dust and their wood-embers with the petals of the grey peach-trees.

A young man was walking along the road which was occasionally flanked by a poplar-tree, the survivor of a magnificent avenue that had been laid low (not by the wind, but by men) and which had provided travellers with its shade and its organ music for a hundred years. Germain had got out of the train at the last station but one, preferring to arrive on foot at the town of his childhood. 'I shall be home soon enough. Meanwhile I shall have taken in a great basin-full of air, of that air of my own country which is unique and which I have missed in my years as a student . . . ' When he saw a cab coming towards him. It was surprising to see a vehicle of this type on a road where the only traffic now consisted of motor-cars, buses and lorries.

The cab advanced slowly, with some hesitation, and Germain saw that the coachman was sleeping. He hailed him in a loud voice. The man who had been sprawled out started up, and his head and shoulders appeared above the outside-seat. Seeing his ruddy face and his coarse appearance, Germain expected a salvo of abuse. There was nothing of the sort.

'Excuse me, sir, do get in, sir . . . '

While he was standing in the road, surprised at this invitation, he heard the other man muttering in a humble manner:

'Do get in sir, please, the seat is yours.'

He was being mistaken for someone else.

'I think you are making a mistake . . . '

143

'No, sir, I never make mistakes. You or someone else, it's all the same to us.'

'Where are you going?' Germain asked, more and more perplexed.

'Where we have to go', the man said in a sudden bad mood that threatened to become intensified.

'Ah, but . . . I was going to Sion and you are going in the opposite direction.'

The driver did not understand, or at least did not want to hear.

'Take a seat, I tell you, we shall be late!'

Germain clambered up over the step, and the contraption creaked under his weight. The strange driver threw him a rug without looking at him. The vehicle emitted a sour smell of wine and of old, cracked leather.

'He's completely drunk', Germain again said to himself, as he saw him struggling on his seat and whipping up the horse. But this frenzy did not appear to agitate the poor hack which continued with its quiet progress. The coachman turned back to the student:

'You won't be sorry you came. Mme. Victoire is anxious that you are looked after. She has never done so much for her own customers!'

Outlined against the grey sky, he was talking in a dignified manner now. The wind missed him, not daring to touch him; it was swallowed up in the hood of the cab and caused it to distend. They took a side-road leading towards the Rhône. Surrounded by meadows where willows were growing, a hamlet rose gradually between two hills.

They stopped in front of a house which bore the notice, in large brown faded letters on the façade:

café des voyageurs

'Good', thought Germain, 'here the adventure is to stop. I shall give up being the person I am taken for. And I shall be able to set out again on the main road to arrive at Sion just in time.' He leapt down. But he was pushed by the man into a decrepit passage-way, and he found himself confronted by an old woman who exclaimed:

'At last! There you are!'

She regarded him avidly, gave a little cough and said in a knowing manner:

'I was expecting you.'

The young man, although intrigued, remained cool on the whole.

'Robert, show him up to the little drawing-room.'

The little drawing-room was a dreadful, small room whose floor was blood-red in colour, where polish had been put on over dirt; it contained a round table, an old piano from which the pompons of a crocheted covering were hanging, a threadbare armchair and some other chairs.

Caught in a trap, Germain remained standing, looking out of the window as if looking for a way out. Through the curtain he could see some roofs of barns and the golden slope of the hills. The musty smell of the room was so unpleasant that he sorely missed the lukewarm breath of the föhn wind.

144

He rushed to the door. But the coachman-turned-butler came in, obstructing his passage with a large tray bearing a bottle and two glasses. Then shutting carefully the door behind him, he came up to the table where he put down his burden.

'You will be comfortable here, won't you, sir?'

He pushed the armchair close to the table opposite Germain and withdrew.

The young man, believing that he was going to have to clink glasses with this individual or the old woman, was annoyed at having given way. 'But in heaven's name, who do they think I am?' The driver came back, he had forgotten to lay a table-cloth; with a ridiculous alacrity he removed the tray, placed it on a chair and unfolded a white table-cloth, put the tray back on it. He then added two plates, some knives and forks.

'She will be here soon', he said in an artful manner and without looking at the young man, as if he had understood that it was necessary to be more discreet in his words.

'This time', Germain said to himself, both surprised and intrigued, 'one could have sworn that it was an amorous rendezvous! . . . ' But he was only just starting to take pleasure in this thought when the old lady came in. 'It is on her own account, after all!' he thought, feeling disappointed. However, she did not sit in the armchair and installed herself modestly in one of the other chairs.

'You had a good journey? You are not too tired?'

'Er . . . no', he replied.

'It must be a change for you to come back here?'

'Well, yes, I suppose so.'

Gradually Germain came to see in her another person, a much younger person beneath the features of an old woman. The wrinkles seemed false, the grey hair as well. What was beautiful and true was the eyes. They became large as he watched them, they became sparkling and gentle. The mouth too: it was no longer drooping and bitter, as it had been during the first moments, but the lips became rosier and were smiling.

'I am pining, I am pining away from being on my own', she went on. 'But you so wanted to go away and study . . . '

'If I am being taken for a student, there isn't all that much difference!' And he felt more at ease.

The man returned with a plate of dried-up meat and some bread. In a respectful manner he filled the two glasses and withdrew without saying a word.

'How different from here the life must be there!' the woman again said.

'Perhaps less so than one thinks', he replied at a venture.

He ate with an appetite. The ride and the bizarre nature of his situation had made him hungry. But he was eating alone.

'Aren't you hungry?' he asked.

There was no reply. At first he had not noticed, but he soon perceived that she had come a little closer, and that her hand, much older than her eyes and mouth, covered with reddish brown marks, with its gnarled fingers and slack skin, was slowly creeping towards his own. Stopping on its way, pretending to be wishing for something else, but it was coming closer. It possessed a life of its own, an animal's life. He was afraid of it, he tried to hide his own hand beneath the table. Too late! The animal had seized his wrist and was squeezing it, so vigorously that Germain cried out. He no longer recognized the woman's face. The over-large eyes had become wild-looking, the mouth trembled and was murmuring phrases that he could not understand.

But the man came in. He simply took hold of the old woman's two hands and drew her out of the room. She offered no resistance, suddenly docile, humble.

When he returned, Germain who was very pale had got up. He had understood.

'Is she insane?'

'Ah, if you only knew! But it's the first time she has done this. The first time! Why?'

He regarded Germain with an angry look.

'Perhaps', he added, 'because you are too much like him'.

'Like who? Who do I look like?' Germain's voice rose.

'Like her son. I can tell you about it now. He died twenty years ago, on Easter Day! Getting out of the train . . . The train went over him. He was a student. He was coming back for the vacation. It was like today.'

'Terrible . . . '

'I always went to the station to fetch him . . . There was the föhn wind, and you are like him, how very much you are like him!'

'But why, why make me come here?'

'She never would believe in his death. She sent me to look for him with the cab . . . Every year I picked someone up on the road. A young person if possible, a gentleman, or anyone at all! She was satisfied, and he was too: he had a meal. Mme. Victoire stayed quiet and looked at him. Afterwards he left. As though he had never been.'

He showed the young man to the door:

'But you've brought him to life, you have! Only too much. For me too, it seemed all the time that it was him. Goodbye.'

'Goodbye', Germain said.

And the Easter wind took hold of him in its powerful hand, removing from him the traces of the other one.

Jean-Pierre Monnier

From *La clarté de la nuit*

When he had drawn up his bed-clothes so that they could cover him to his shoulders, he put out his lamp and, all at once, the window appeared behind the curtains. It was like a light mist, a scarcely definable void out of which the snow kept on rising.

In the room there was the light of the fire dancing against the wainscotting, the slightly squat shape of the seats; by the side of the cupboard the medallion of the barometer. The minister felt himself being borne onward by the day which was coming. 'A new day', he said to himself, 'one more day'. He was aware of all the duties it would bring. Hour by hour, he knew what labours, what tasks there would be. He also told himself: 'I shall see it beginning. In a moment night will be over. I shall get up.'

Each morning, up to midday, seemed to him to be a gift. It went quickly. It had hardly been gone through before he had finished living it. Beyond midday it was longer, it was even distressing. The sun was setting, the light was going down, evening was slowly merging into the night of the next day. The time of daylight was over. At first there was that particular time which was full of living things. Then there was the time of dead things. 'To die in the night', the minister said to himself, 'nobody is asking you to decide about that. It's completely stupid.'

He thought of the day that he had before him, all that Sunday. In the week that was beginning, some moments stood out, some hours, like landmarks. Further off lay the future, the snow melting, the snow returning, the north winds of March. Finally there were the Easter celebrations, spring. He could no longer say, as he once said: next month, the following week. He took a notebook out of his pocket, he registered his engagements for that particular day, for the next day. He said: 'I shall expect you on Monday, not later'. He added: 'It's safer'. He had made a habit of this, and people understood because he concerned himself with them without delay. But his wife reproached him for moving too quickly.

The little Lacour woman, obviously, was a special case. What was more, she had never taken the trouble to ask for an appointment. She would ring the door-bell, she would come in as if she were at home. One day she had made arrangements to see the minister in the village streets. Later, when she had begun to avoid him, things had changed again. But for some weeks past it was no longer possible to be unaware of her intrigues. 'She is going to launch another attack', he said to himself. 'However, I shan't do anything, I shan't budge'. He also said to himself: 'I shall wait. I shall give myself time'. The prospect of an adventure that concerned him personally affected the minister like the lash of a whip. This was new. This was unhoped-for. He had the feeling as if a horizon were opening up before him. Death was moving away at last. Walls were falling. Barriers . . . But the adventure, however probable, was not a risk to be run. You had to believe in it, you also had to desire it, and the minister was a long way off here.

He tried to go to sleep again, he remained for some time with his eyes closed and hands clasped, then when the household was awake, he turned towards the light.

The window was quite large. On the exterior panes of glass there were patterns, palm-branches and sheaves. It was the frost. The daylight which came from on high seemed to grow longer like a strip of smoke. Lower down, the mountain was becoming visible in parts. It was exposing its ridge which made an irregular line with hollows, humps and the cross at the summit would could not be seen but could be assigned its place. Beneath the bare branches of the trees the nearest houses had emerged from the snow. The more distant houses were still hidden behind the veil of mist which was slowly dispersing. It was as if the fine weather were coming back, as if the sun were about to appear. Some lighter trails of mist which were moving about in the sky released some patches of blue behind. They had scarcely closed up again when they opened once more a little further off, came together, stretched, and finally triumphed over the last vestiges of the night. Behind the window-panes the garden lamp was still burning. But its light was so weak that it was difficult to distinguish it. 'It is the finest moment', he thought. 'It is now.'

When he heard François coming down to the kitchen, he dressed in order to go and join him. It was his custom to have breakfast on his own, before everyone else. He heated some coffee and had it in his bedroom, then he prepared his timetable for the day. Visiting took up time, often too much of it. Meetings took place in the evenings, committees in the afternoons. For a parish of three thousand inhabitants, it was a lot of work. Since becoming ill he knew very well that it was wrong of him to persist. But it was his work.

'You are making a fire?'

'I'm trying to.'

François, who was filling the kitchen-range had his face covered with soap. His pocket-mirror was placed against the window frame, his sponge-bag on the stone of the sink.

'You are going out?'

'I promised to be there at ten o'clock, and from here to the lake you know what a tramp it is.'

He had said the previous day that he would be going ski-ing in the Bernese Oberland. The girl he was meeting at Bienne knew some people there who had a large chalet near Kandersteg.

'I see', the minister said. 'A girl friend?'

'If you like.'

'Is it serious?'

'No', said François. 'Not yet.'

He added: 'It's to have someone'.

The two men, who never went very far in their intimacy, understood one another fairly well. In any case, they were sure of making sound conjectures about each other. The minister had grown into the habit of waiting. He was reserved. In his attitude to his sons he had a certain bashfulness. It was not so much that he guarded his own thoughts but that he did not wish to know theirs'. None the less he often had the impression that they were freer than he was, that they had got away to a better start, that they were making more of their lives. This impression was perhaps inevitable. When one is old, all the things that one has not been able to do appear very important.

'I am asking the question', the minister said, 'because you travel a lot, you know a lot of girls'.

'Good friends', François said. 'But nothing else just for the moment'.

He added: 'If it were a great love affair, you can count on it that I wouldn't want to conceal it from you. You would know.'

He talked in an unhurried manner, with a voice that was happy and balanced. The words seemed not to be a part of him, as if the things that he said did not concern him directly.

'In the main', he went on, 'I am afraid of thinking it's a great love affair, to be sure. I am afraid of being caught'.

'You know best', the minister said.

There was a silence, then the two men separated. François turned back to the window and went on with his shaving, while the minister started preparing breakfast. He felt better for the presence of his son. More cheerful, more confident. He wanted to talk at random about a host of things that came into his mind. He thought of his own father, his mother, the small house they lived in, the room where they had died. These old images were joined by new ones, other faces. Furthermore, there was this fine winter's day which was rising on the Jura mountains rather than elsewhere, this great silence and all this snow.

'It is a part of the country that I still love', the minister said.

'If I were you, I couldn't stay here any longer.'

'Why?'

'Everybody knows you. You know everybody. It's too small.'

'Precisely', the minister said. 'You don't get away from it.'

François, who was still shaving, stopped. He put up with his father's odd remarks better than anybody, and above all better than Simon. But this particular one was going too far. Moreover, it touched him in a spot that was too sensitive.

'I don't understand you', he said. 'You have had the most unfair treatment, they have done all sorts of unpleasant things to you, and if you don't leave this village, it is because you don't want to get away from it?'

'No', the minister said. 'But this parish is no worse than plenty of others.'

He added: 'Men are all the same, like villages. They are pretty well the same everywhere. But it's me, it is my fault if I hold fast like this, and sometimes it is wrong of me to take everything seriously.'

With one movement he unrolled the oil cloth, he carefully covered the end of the table with it, then he fetched the cups and the coffee-pot. His face was pale, his eyes tired. It could be clearly seen that his breathing was laboured. He found it hard to regain his breath.

'You got up too early', François said. 'Up till ten o'clock you would have had time to say your office.'

'I could not sleep any longer.'

'Don't you ever take sleeping pills?'

'Yes, occasionally. But sleeping pills don't help much.'

He would have liked to say quite simply what he was feeling. To say that he was happy still to be standing upright in this kitchen where he had someone with whom he could share his breakfast. The only thing is that very simple words very quickly become embarrassing.

'You ought to ask for Father Jeanrenaud's advice.'

'It's all right at night', the minister said. 'It's in the morning.'

He poured out the coffee which spread its aroma throughout the kitchen, then he waited for his son. Through the window, above the heap of snow that they had had to clear away, the sky had become completely cleared. It had clearly spread beyond the horizon, and its colour had changed.

'If it had been up to me', François said, 'I would have sent the whole lot packing when the right moment came.'

'You know very well that you wouldn't.'

'Why not?'

'Why, because there are people.'

'People', François said, 'for all the good they do to you, you could forget them.'

'You think that one can choose to forget!'

'Can't you?'

'No, I can't.'

He opened his large hands and all at once, to demonstrate to him that there was nothing more obvious, though in a muffled voice, he added: 'It is inside me. It is stronger than everything else.'

150

Georges Borgeaud

From *Le voyage à l'étranger*

I have already alluded to the immediate liking which I had taken for my mentor's wife and which was reciprocal. The smile which she had at once directed to me passed through the usual stages without pausing. I had surmised the subtlety of a mind to which gestures, bearing and bodily elegance bore witness, so true is it that the body is the visible expression of the soul. At the same time I realized that I would have to restrain the impulsive quality of my feeling, that I would have to employ in my approach all the delicacy of which I was capable, while avoiding behaving like a lover, which moreover did not occur to me. My response was very much marked by timidity, discretion and the wish to show more the profundity of my spirit than the inexperience of my youth or the freshness of my complexion. More simply, I decided to love while taking into account only qualities of heart and intelligence, while playing only upon our sensibilities, intuitions, enthusiasms and opinions. I longed to be visited in the most secret part of my interior life. At least my religious education had led me to turn aside my instincts which would have so much changed my life if I had abandoned myself to them.

These are thoughts which I have today. I admired Madeleine like a flower whose scent I was refusing to breathe. One day when I was walking in a park, and this memory is not alien to what has gone before, leaning towards a rose in full bloom and biting it with my teeth in order to fill my mouth with its petals, I heard behind me a girl's laughter. I blushed because she was perhaps intelligent enough to understand that my gesture was revealing my privations to her, an immodesty. Nature, oh my lover!

I did not have a time of my youth that was carnal and triumphant, others would say that I did not live out my virility. This is probably why Madeleine respected me. I was intact. This was different for her from the abrupt vitality of her husband, and I had difficulty in conceiving that she could accommodate herself to him. I am not afraid of saying that I opened up noble vistas to her, that I proposed subtle exchanges with her where her intelligence was at ease and animated. One recognizes in women that age at which the attainment of forty years leaves them with a panic in their souls which becomes assuaged by protecting somebody's youth. Probably I had not been capable of making such an analysis, of even supposing it to be the right one, but Madeleine was obeying an almost maternal instinct which discouraged within myself the physical attraction which I felt for her.

In private conversation she pressed me in my stronghold. Basically she had a mind to confidences, while I longed to be listened to, looked at, loved, recognized, disconcerted, set free . . . She herself spoke in a language that was transparent, inventive, fresh, unforeseen. Nature moved her. She became excited about life, about certain authors, about painting and music. I do not believe that I have as yet said that I was not entirely innocent as far as literature was concerned, especially with regard to anything that could arouse my emotions, coursing from the artificial to the natural, from the museum and library to rural musing, from ideas to Nirvana.

I cannot prevent myself from recognizing that I was a young man by whom women, generally older than myself, were captivated, less by the possible lover than by the cloud that surrounded him, the web of visions that clothed him.

However, I was not ugly, but it was in the bowl of my spirit that they picked and quenched their thirst. No woman has ever ravished me, and I regret this.

Probably the very fact of my origins, whose position I revealed to them, drove them to offer me a little compassion, all the more willingly as I was unpitying in the judgments I made about my mother. How many of these great hearts of old ladies, of very old ladies, have I come to know, gradually as I lost my youth while retaining my childish freshness. Good ladies, attentive to my diet, to slipping in the hot-water bottle between my sheets, to tucking me up. This too is the lot of the unlucky members of society which loves them as one loves the negro children in the parish-churches.

Today I have reached the age when my case is no longer of interest to anyone in this way. One feels sorry for a cat that has been abandoned, not for an alley-cat. A young woman occasionally looks at me, and I have the illusion of believing that she is saying to herself: 'He's not so bad', while relegating me to the ranks of the fifty-year-olds, unpitying among themselves, on the watch for the inevitable signs of ageing upon the faces of their neighbours. After all, is it not a splendid time when one reaches life's summit from whence the panorama is vast and magnificent, before beginning the descent, but it has already begun, amidst the fallen rocks and loose stones, the foot less sure, in haste to find one's hole, the little shelter more or less bathed in sunshine, like old cats that spend more time curled up than in hunting?

*

Between the Count and Léon Cédrat, the partner, there was a certain familiarity. Neither of them gave expression to this in the same way. It was distinction on the one side and good nature on the other. Whereas there did not exist the habitual complicity between their wives. The Countess had no liking for sharing with anybody either opinions, which she did not have, nor holidays that she would have preferred to spend on her own, although I do not see how she could have established any difference between the time spent at Soye and that at the seaside, since she only lived through periods of leisure which she cluttered up with futile obligations, childish caprices, ruminations, minutely scrutinized justifications, distracted by anxieties, by prettily useless activities like the preparation of glass-cases and historical figures. It is understandable then

152

that the invasion of her habits by strangers was a burden for her, when into the bargain she had to saddle herself with all the duties of the legal wife of the Count who only tolerated her because he did not live much with her, because there was a child, because his reputation obliged him in appearance not to offend against a tradition of a rural aristocrat whose bad example could have had disastrous consequences for his house.

Madeleine Cédrat tried, without much success, to make tractable what it was agreed to call the Countess' unsociableness. Thus she could be seen to suggest to her a walk by the seaside which she accepted without pleasure. They were more miserable when they came back than when they left. It was almost the only exception that she made in her habits, for she systematically refused, without anyone succeeding in making her change her mind, to accompany her husband and his guests by car when it was a question of gastronomic expeditions, for she had discouraged Léon Cédrat from renewing such invitations to her. No Vatel would have succeeded in deflecting her from her dietary rules. It is true that his own wife, without extolling a diet and lemon-juice, was not co-operative either, as he said, in plying her knife and fork. But at least her austerity was not perceived. Madeleine tasted the courses without finishing them. The Countess' refusals had some slight justification in the fact that she was responsible for Christian, since the governess, Mlle Anne, always went away on holiday at this time of year.

One day when I was in my room at an unaccustomed time, I heard without wishing to do so a short altercation between the Count and the Countess which alarmed me by its fury. I recognized there something that is part of a well brought-up background where people say terrible things to one another while using the polite form of address. The whole difficulty of living together is revealed, the shabbiest part of each person finds its outlet there, and I am certain that I should not have escaped myself if it had been my lot to share my existence with someone. Why, why is this so? I have often asked myself. I admired the actors in a small incident, though it was large in its significance, two young people who had vowed to take their own lives as soon as their love should become involved with mutual reproaches, suspicions, accusations, as soon as hurtful words and justifications should make their appearance . . . They were found drowned in the lake, still holding each other by the hand. Great sorrows have the advantage of annihilating a situation, while mediocrity saps it by degrees. Suddenly the strings become slack and the instrument can no longer make any sounds.

All the attachment to my childhood cannot be explained by the illusion of having been happier then than at present. On the contrary. I have memories of inconsolable bouts of distress for which I knew no expedients. The confidence which I had quite naturally, I would even say my freshness, very quickly came up against the dead reality of grown-ups, against the impact upon my fragility of

153

their opinions, their constraints, their choices, their lassitude, like bad blood in their veins, of a whole range of shared weaknesses. I did not understand how they made sense, and I turned my back on the sad mental landscape of adults. Not to go elsewhere. Far from that, I upheld myself, thanks to the simplest of realities, to what I had before my eyes, the sun, the plants, my crayons, the transparency of a glass of water, the pink pips in the raspberry jam, my face in the mirror, the entertainment I had in looking at that little tip of flesh at the base of my belly, without understanding why my mother insisted so much on my not touching it and even on my not taking too much interest in a mystery which, by this action, she stirred up. If something arouses a child's sense of wonder it sets at defiance all prohibitions, but there now, his parents put him on guard against obstacles that are inconceivable for him. Then everything becomes confused. Reality becomes formidable, it becomes confounded in taboos, it stops having frank relations with him, or so he thinks, whereas it is only education which is separating him from it.

Georges Haldas

From *L'état de poésie. Carnets 1979*

8 January

There was nothing in this life that one has not loved. More than anyone can imagine. So much so that sometimes I would like to begin everything again, in an eternal youthfulness. One kind of music alone in which this music of Heaven and Earth can be recognized: Mozart.

Take every thing away, this joy remains. Which contains everything. Where all things – beings and objects – appear again at their best.

May my last years – if there are to be such – be a hymn to this happiness in being. To repeat everything, to say everything, in this state. Which is the very state of Transfiguration. The State of Poetry, pre-eminently. At the heart of a world both catastrophic and full of promises.

Among so many things loved, I repeat: the blackbird's song, mornings, Venice, Mozart.

This happiness, be it said in passing, perfectly compatible with the suffering of exile and the great patience in the painful genesis of all things.

Insomnia. Awareness of a body that is everywhere becoming out of joint, fissured and cracked beneath the silent assaults of old age and death. Which in no way prevents the great music of what we have lived from rising up within us, carrying and transporting us forward from the past and also the present, into that psychic area where they cease to be past, present and even future. Certain insomnias, in this respect, resemble at the same time submersions in time and new ascents towards what transcends time. One is crippled with lumbago and

154

arthrosis, rheumatism, cramp, ills of all sorts, overwhelming and comic. And none the less, from the depths of these ruins something sings like a bird that is perpetually young.

The continual gifts that life gives us. Life at its most immediate. Gifts like seeds put down in the obscure humus of being within ourselves: the silence this morning; this faint cry of a bird in the snow; an echo of music, while M., in the bathroom, is doing her hair. Brightness of the lamp on the table when the day has scarcely broken. All things, yes, which are granted to us in a discontinuous manner, but which a particular disposition within ourselves – at the most intimate level – puts together with infallible precision in harmony. With the result that the silence, the faint cry of the bird in the snow, the music perceived intermittently on the radio, the invisible presence of M. doing her hair in the bathroom, the brightness of the lamp on the pages of my little notebook are suddenly found to be *connected* with one another. And as if forming parts of a whole which is musical too. But not of an audible music. A music of *being*. Preceding all music.

In this sense, when the so-called external world penetrates us – this is its seminal quality – it immediately discovers that it is involved in this great music, of which we are less the creators than the interpreters and instrumentalists.

This inward defeat – the sting of nothingness, or what is called nothingness – to which I do not wish to yield. The hour is coming when there will be no room in the world for words of despair. When one despairing word would be equivalent to a murder. For murder is there: around us, within us, everywhere. Henceforth in no way must we stretch out a hand to it, nor pronounce its name, nor even give it a wink. And precisely because all is murder, every word that we have to offer, if we are to remain human, should be an anti-murder. I hate optimism. It is the lie of lies, the imposture above all others. But things have reached the point that what made us cry out in despair yesterday makes us today speak – not cry out – in the name of hope. Or rather, of this hope in Man which is constructed out of our transformed states of despair. A thorny stretch of road awaits us. By our manner of living or dying, let us enter it.

9 January

All is war. And you can only live by agreement. So to establish agreement, it is always needful to embark on war. And they say that it is I who am a tissue of contradictions.

The stronger the resistance around you, the firmer you must be. The more the sand piles up, the more demanding is the need to open up the Way. Keep this constantly in mind. Live it in your work.

You are now writing with death at your heels. It is the best stimulus of all. To be sure, death itself is not the stimulus, but the fact of accepting it and at the same time of countering it. Not to let oneself be affected by its advent. The opposite of

155

death, therefore. The seed of true life. Joined to what one loves.

Once more, and for the thousandth time: to transform your lyrical energy into exactness of touch. The rest is only magic. Falsehood.

Each one of our remarks, each one of our actions – even as far as simply lifting a glass of wine to one's lips – subtends a metaphysical creed. Let us say, a relationship to the whole world which is most frequently unconscious. Hence any description of a state which, in one way or another, does not take into account this metaphysical dimension is null and void. Whatever, in other respects, may be its relevance in the short term.

If one wished, for example, to give a characterization of Shakespeare's genius, it is there that one would have to begin. By showing – but what is the use of showing? It *is* so, – that the least remark, indeed the least gesture of his characters imply this dimension. This relationship. Containing Heaven and Earth.

Would have liked to do this with *The Book of the Passions and the Hours*. But am a long way out. Someone else will do it for me.

The reasons for my failure? I let myself be imprisoned by the power and allurement of the present moment. Of undecanted experience. I am aware of all the faults and weaknesses which result from it. No point in reproaching me with them.

All this again because I have been too subjected to sensations, to passions, to the *desiderata* of the ego. And because the sword of transcendence has not split them sufficiently asunder. But who can add a cubit to his stature? One is lucky even to be aware of this.

To pass from the idea of summing up to that of starting.

Young Rock singers – French – on T.V. No real inspiration. Agitation and caricature.

True affections are never lost.

I do not prove or demonstrate anything. I say: I have lived, I have thought, I have felt that. Confronted by a certain thing, I have reacted in a certain manner. (What is important is to render a faithful account of this manner: here is the first step towards truth.) Who am I? It is for you to tell me. To be is to propose oneself to others simply. Not to impose oneself. And in that way to become a subject for discussion, and at the same time the basis for a relationship. In each one of my writings I am proposing myself. Nothing else. And in life too. At least I hope so.

I keep in my heart what needs to be kept. And am calm: it will not die.

They only shout so loudly because they have not found their foundations. And then, he who truly seeks, does not shout. He seeks. Hoping, in the silence, to find.

Only he who is deprived of all hope has the right to cry out. There are millions of these. The strangest thing being that they are not the ones who make the most noise. But those who often live well and comfortably, and claim to be shouting in their name. I have done that myself. I know what it is about.

Television does not reveal to us the state of the world. It reveals to us the manner – the lamentable manner most frequently – in which the state of the world is interpreted and presented.

The foolishness of basing a relationship between two people on sexuality. Another foolishness, to base it on non-sexuality.

A 'sharpened' thought. Always the point: the weapon and the sex organ. Masculine.

11 January

It is not for me either to discover or to invent. Even less to preach. My part is to be astonished and to ask questions. As children do.

This mixture, at night, of terror and unshaken confidence. Everything is intermingled in insomnia. And it is here that one best takes by surprise, with its wonderful components parts, the very substance of our life and what it is that determines our fate. To evoke one day some of these insomnias. As communicative as dreams.

Alice Rivaz

The Pushchair

People talked about her poor appearance, had you noticed this recently? The other day in the lift she did not even make a response to the good fellow on the fifth floor who had greeted her politely. She appeared not to have seen him, her eyes were like two empty holes, images from outside were no longer reflected there, and those from within remained hidden in their terrible prison.

People said that things had not been going at all well with her for a very long time. And yet, remember, such a pretty wedding! These fresh veils, her regal hair-style and her large eyes cut like diamonds, black as night. But everything had rapidly gone downhill after the birth of Marinette, when her younger sister, she too as pretty as a picture, had formed the habit of coming every day to take the baby for a walk in a pushchair with big wheels along the pavement outside the property. For soon, everyone had noticed, it was not merely her little niece that she took for a walk in this way, but also her brother-in-law who had appeared as if by magic near to the pushchair, moving forward at its side like a dog on a lead. And gradually this pushchair seemed to have become a sort of drawbridge between their two bodies which called to one another with a muffled violence to the point of keeping them both silent while they walked slowly like sleepwalkers, pushing the little vehicle in front of them. And as soon as Marinette had begun to walk, the father disappeared, making off with his little sister-in-law.

Yes, people kept on and on saying, everything had started to go badly from that moment on. However, things could have turned out differently. Such an attractive woman, even if it is only her younger sister. But what man would wish to bring up another man's child? And yet, what a delightful little girl this Marinette was, every year a little prettier, she resembled at the same time her delightful aunt and her charming mother. Fifteen, and a real beauty! And the few lovers of the mother became enamoured of the little one, just as at other times the father had become crazy about the young aunt.

People said why did she not try to get work, this helps in such cases, and who knows if she wouldn't have met a good man, that is to say a serious-minded, marrying man with whom she could have built up her life afresh. She did once take up a job as saleswoman in a shoe shop. But this way of kneeling from morning to night in front of anybody, like a servant before her lord, you can understand that she did not like that. It was then that there started this aimless, insubstantial life, which had nothing within itself to look at and stir up, like an empty bucket, the bottom of which she was constantly examining, while she had the appearance of keeping a watch on the road, leaning on her sixth-floor balcony, as if she were waiting for somebody. It might well be asked what she could be thinking of all day long, leaning over the void like that. And some good fellow would get as far as her door-step, never much further into her life, sometimes for a few weeks or months, never for longer. And little Marinette becoming prettier and prettier to look at, enough to send every man and boy wild! And some film man staying for a short while in our town had to meet her in the street and to get her to come to Paris with her mother, for a test. Once in Paris, she stayed there, not to work in films – it seems that she did not have sufficient talent for this – but to get married to an architect there.

And meanwhile her mother came back home, henceforth still more lonely, her mother with her large jet-black eyes, always unbelievably pretty, but such a sad look, you hardly dared to look her in the face when you chanced to meet her; her mother most of the time leaning on the balcony to observe nobody knew what, and after a few years no longer taking the trouble to make her bed or prepare her meals, making do with a cup of coffee and a croissant which she had once daily in a local tea-room, growing visibly thinner, her gaze vacant, her lovely eyes curiously moist at times, her expression sagging, which had led to rumours that she drank and took drugs, but making so little noise, taking so little room in the lift and increasingly less in the lives of others, hardly going out any longer except to drink her café-crème, a veritable shade, and how transparent she seemed, a phantom without a voice, and nobody in the block had even known that she had thrown herself in the Rhône six months before. She had been fished out just in time, but since then she had been under surveillance. A social worker knocked on her door every other day. That is how she was found. They had to dismantle the lock because she did not answer, and this had worried the social worker. Then they sealed up the flat and sent a telegram to Marinette who arrived the next morning from Paris by the night train.

They said two tenants were gossiping about the event while waiting for the lift at the moment when the young woman arrived, carrying her little suitcase, always so pretty, like a picture, a real charmer who would turn anybody's head, but her eyelids were swollen and red, she looked very down, perhaps she had been crying during this sad journey.

When she saw her entering, one of the two women who knew her from childhood – but you won't tell me that that particular woman had any delicacy of feeling – hastened towards her with a distressed mien, calling out as she came, even before she had greeted her:

'So, Marinette, your mamma has hanged herself?'

It was disgusting, the other neighbour said, to receive her with such words, but what could you expect of a woman who had no delicacy of feeling?

They said that Marinette immediately took the train back to Paris once the funeral was over, without even taking leave of the tenants who had, after all, watched her growing up and had clubbed together to provide a lovely wreath.

It was the aunt who came to clear the apartment. What a surprise! Nobody knew exactly what had become of her since she had gone off with her sister's husband. Meanwhile she had got married, but, it seems, to somebody else. You could scarcely recognize her again, she had put on so much weight, she was no longer at all pretty as in earlier days, you remember, at the time when she took Marinette for walks in her pushchair in her brother-in-law's company, neither of them opening their mouths, as if they had been muzzled, since every word like every glance had become useless to them.

Jacques Mercanton

Except His Face

Coming from Faro on the main road, instead of going over the bridge across the Arave, you take a small road on the right which runs along the estuary: Ferragudo, a quiet little market-town which faces Praia da Rocha on the other side of the river, laying out its white houses in tiers as far as the church and dominating the sea. No hotel, not even an inn. In the street which climbs between the closed façades there is nobody to be seen. Two or three open doors. I cast a timid glance. The woman with the black fichu over her shoulders, slender in her long black dress, who has been leaning over the fire-place, sits up, smiles, beckons me to come in. On one side the table surrounded by straight-backed chairs, on the other two or three beds separated by tulle curtains. Above the fire-place, some saucepans hanging from a line, two or three copper buckets with lids. A sparkling cleanliness as in a Dutch interior scene, the curtains immaculately white. She follows my glance as it travels from one corner to another of the room, doubtlessly the only one in the house. Beneath the veil her face is all burnished and lined, but with a delightful freshness. I try a few words in French, in English; with her delicate hand she indicates that she does not understand. Two or three words in Spanish: she replies to me in the purest Castilian and seems to be amused at my accent:

'Francés?'

She comes from Estramadura, a village near the frontier, close to Badajoz. My light cyclist's clothing does not seem to surprise or embarrass her. One must suppose that some tourists venture as far as this lost, silent little place opposite the noisy clamour of Praia da Rocha. 'No', I say, 'I come from a little further away, from a big hotel by the Alvor beach.' Her face lights up.

'The Alvor Praia Hotel. Two of my boys, the youngest ones, work in this hotel. Both of them as porters. The elder is already married, and he lives at Portimão, with his wife and a little girl who is already a toddler. You must have noticed him: fair brown hair, which is rarely found on the boys of this locality. He comes to the hotel every day by moped.'

I had noticed him, indeed, because, having got out of his livery, he stopped me in a Portimão street in order to introduce me to his wife and child; this he did easily and naturally, and in this young man so obliging and agreeable in his duties, no trace of servility, which is a habitual feature in the south, not only in Portugal.

She has set up two folding-chairs by the doorway and invites me to sit down.

'Do you often come to the Algarve on holiday?'

'Yes, but up to now always in the autumn, when the land has been burnt by the sun. It is the first time that I have come in the spring and found it so leafy and flowering, and in such varied green that you scarcely know it.'

'But the sky over the sea is often storm-laden. Without much wind. Where it faces Africa it is a gentle ocean. It changes on the west coast where it can be violent.'

She is silent. Then:

'Pedro is satisfied with his work at the hotel. It appears that he is appreciated and that he has been promised promotion. He will have to earn more if he is to have a large family, as he wishes to. For my part, I am glad that he has chosen this job, because of the quite recent development of tourism. I lost my husband and two of my elder sons at sea. The sea is no friend of man.'

Facing her close at hand, I am struck by the refinement of her features, which are very regular, the nose slightly arched, sinuous lips. And an expression that is still youthful, even when she is talking about her bereavements. Probably older than she looks, for she mentions yet another son living in Lisbon and a married daughter in Seville. But she has not said anything about the younger son, he too,

160

like Pedro, an employee at the Alvor Praia Hotel. When I mention it, her limpid look darkens.

'Aïssa', she says. 'He is much younger. Fifteen, and with only a junior post. He is not like his brothers, much more fragile. He was born after I had been a widow for three years, his father was a young man who had come from Algeria, a Kabyle. He was tormented, restless, unstable. However, he was faithful to me, but he never settled with us. Haunted by memories of the civil war. He took flight not from the French, but from his own people. At least, our little one was a great joy to him. I believe he saw himself a bit in the child. He taught him verses from the Koran which the child repeated without understanding them, in that guttural language so different from our own. He has forgotten them now. His father died of a malignant fever which carried him off in a few days.'

A silence, then in a low voice:

'But a year ago Aïssa suffered a great blow, too cruel for his strength, which he can't overcome. He is still so sensitive! In the hotel he stands at the door, and with others he looks after the luggage. You will easily recognize him: a very Berber type, a long, narrow face, eyes stretched out beneath the temples. Smiling, but since his grief so melancholy, out of touch with boys of his own age, indifferent to girls who are attracted by his mysterious beauty. He relates strange dreams to me.'

'He comes to see you often?'

'Whenever he has a day off, but even here, with me, I have the feeling that he does not get away from his haunting thoughts.'

She reflects, her eye-lids half closed. She is not questioning me, a chance visitor, but herself, and without doubt she does so frequently.

'What worries me about him is that he appears to live only in the moment, as if there had not been a yesterday and as if there will not be a tomorrow, with so little attachment to life, ready to give it up, as I see him escape on his bicycle, disappearing at the end of the road. Not only since his misfortune, but already earlier. I used to tell myself that it was his childhood. No! I've met nothing comparable with my other boys. They are impatient as boys are, whereas there is no trace of impatience in him. He expects nothing. But his father was like that, serene even amid sadness and grief. He died so lightly, as if the time had come for him to die. And he was still young.'

Her look clouds over again, but I do not see tears in her eyes. She is contemplating an enigma: this Arab or Moslem sense of the ephemeral, which eludes her, enigmatic, indeed, to her passionate Spanish temperament. Suddenly I catch sight of the reflection of a conflagration on her beautiful face.

The young boy's misfortune? Banal, but grievous. She recounts it in summary form, without detail, in a low voice. Together with his much loved friend Aïssa discovered an abandoned boat on an isolated beach beyond Lagos.

161

After doing some repairs the two boys judged that it was seaworthy. They made some tests without going far from the shore, and these appeared to be conclusive to them. Then they came one morning at dawn, at the time when the stars were disappearing, and embarked, firstly using oars and then hoisting a small sail. All at once the boat began to fill with water. They tried to bail it out with the help of scoops which they found in the hold. In vain: the boat sank in the sea that was very calm. Then the other boy, Manoèl, told his companion to swim to the shore, which was not difficult, but impossible for him because of a heart condition about which he had never said anything. And he stretched out in the sea with his arms in a cross, like a young, naked Christ, knowing that his death would be close at hand. It was not slow in coming, while Aïssa was trying to hold him up. He did not die of drowning but because of his heart, and the tide carried off his body. He was only found a few days later, thrown up on the shore by the waves.

'How could my little boy have endured this loss, in these circumstances?'
Now it is she who is dreaming.
'For women there is a secret in this love between boys, which women do not know: so chaste, so pure, with such depth of tenderness, a love to which they surrender themselves completely. A love perhaps which has issue only in death.'

In the hotel vestibule Pedro pointed out his brother to me among the other boys. I should not have needed his help in order to recognize him, as his mother had described him. The elongated face, very brown beneath the curly black hair. But did she tell me that his eyes that were stretched out and had long lashes were bright, with a silvery sparkle? He comes and goes, carrying luggage to the triple glass-door where someone else takes it so that it can be placed in the boot of a large de luxe car. Why do I not venture to speak to him, nor do I do so a moment later when I pass him on the staircase and he greets me with a gracious smile, showing his pearl-like teeth? He is extremely thin, shaped into his fine royal-blue uniform, adorned with gold lace at the collar and the sleeves. It seems to me that a single word on my part, the most banal of words, would be an indiscretion.

At the foot of the steps that twist between the bushes and the shrubs which lead down to the beach, instead of continuing it indefinitely towards the west where you can see the port of Lagos with its white houses and above them wooded uplands, at low tide you can proceed towards the point 'dos Três Irmãos', where you can go from one cave to another, little beaches which go deeply into grottoes of copper-coloured rock, bristling with headlands and reefs, making a way here and there through small tunnels, a place where entwined young couples seek refuge. It is on one of these little solitary beaches that I find him stretched out in the sand, his bronzed body girded with bathing trunks as white as swansdown. He gets up at my approach, stretching out his thin body and long legs where there is no anticipation of the type of robust and often broad-backed figure which young Portuguese develop some years later. He has recognized me as a hotel guest, and when I sit down beside him, he offers me his slight hand to shake.

'Why do you come here all on your own instead of playing handball with your colleagues on the long beach, or on the football ground near the main road?'

'I like solitude. From now on it will be my only companion.'

'You are not afraid of falling asleep when the tide is coming in?'

'I would hear it in my sleep. In any case, I know the times of the tide although they change every day.'

'You could escape by clambering on the reefs?'

'No, the tide is too fast and strong here. The high waves would crush you in the heart of the grottoes. If this place is known as the Point of the Three Brothers, it is probably in memory of the three boys who died here.'

Who has taught him this French which he speaks with facility, rolling his 'r's, with a hoarseness which still indicates the husky quality of the breaking voice? His father, no doubt, who will have come from Kabylie.

'My mother has told me about your visit to Ferragudo.'

'How do you know that it was me?'

'You are the only hotel guest who uses a bicycle. It isn't easy to cycle along our narrow roads. It's obvious that you are in training.'

There is little risk of his going to sleep, for he keeps on turning and turning back again on the sand, sometimes lying flat on his face, leaning on his elbows, lifting up his chest that is smooth like the rest of his body, sometimes lying on his back, his knees bent very high up because of the length of his legs, and he talks as if he were only half-wake, from the depths of a dream, in a state of restlessness that is both childish and languid.

'I didn't know that Manoèl could not swim, because of his heart. Otherwise I would not have taken him that far out in the boat. And I didn't understand why he lay stretched out on the water instead of swimming with me towards the bank. It was then that he told me to leave him and that he was happy to die because we should not be separated for long. I tried to lift him, telling him to hang on to my shoulders. The sea was calm; I could have swum without difficulty while carrying him on my back. He smiled, then he closed his eyes. All at once he became very heavy, and bending my face towards his, I saw that his eyes were wide open and that his fixed look no longer saw me. I realized that he was dead. We had been torn from one another, for ever. No! I can hear him calling me. I shall not impose for long upon the brevity of the days which separate us.'

His voice gives way. He lets the tears fall. I take him by the nape of the neck, his face is concealed from me between my arms and takes refuge against my breast. I only see his curly hair and his body that is still stretched out, shaken by

163

grief. I think of his mother's words: this boys' love, mysterious, without resemblance to what we call love, with its chaste vitality, its inflexible sweetness. Above the sea, towards the sunset, the sky becomes greenish, with grey clouds that turn white as they disperse.

'But you are not thinking of shortening these days which keep you separated from your friend?'

He raises his head, and his silvery eyes which stare at me in surprise are still moist.

'It is true', he says, 'that Christians commit suicide, as if they believed it possible to escape from God. But God guards us in His hand until He lets us fly away again. He alone chooses the moment in our ephemeral existence because He alone is not, like us, destined to die. Mamma thinks that I have forgotten the words which my father repeated to me in Arabic and which I did not understand. But he whispered them into my ear afterwards in French: "All things perish, except His countenance". I repeated them to Manoèl, softening them for him so that he might perceive them in more delicate form: "All things pass, except His face". He liked them because, like myself, he knew that he was not destined to a long life.'

'Did he go to mass?'

'I sometimes went with him in order to please Mamma. He made the proper gestures, but I don't know whether he prayed. For someone who knows love, this love for God which the Christians talk about must be filled with bitterness, since it is a God who often abandons them. For myself, I expect nothing except from His mercy which does not let us slip out of His hand.'

'Even since you have lost your friend?'

'I haven't lost him. He has left me so that we may love each other more, in a way that one never completely succeeds in loving on this fragile earth. But he lives in my heart and sings me prophetic songs in secret.'

There is so much desolation in his wonderful face that I find it difficult to believe that his dreams console him. But it is a face that will not pass because God is looking at it. The boy smiles: a sparkling star in the night.

Jacques Chessex

Dylan Thomas's Mirror

The spring was full of traps like a beautiful green wood which the poacher's boys have criss-crossed in all directions. Jean Serre would go into a café and come out again . . . A bad way for a lonely man to spend his time. However, the afternoon and the weeks that followed were to turn out differently for him, thanks to a brief encounter.

So he went inside a café in the rue de Bourg and sat at the bar by the door, he ordered a beer and looked around him without pleasure. Very few people at this time, one or two couples were in the seats, at the other end of the bar a young fellow with grey hair who stood out sharply in this dump and who was drinking his white wine in quick snatches. In a few moments he had finished the small jug-full. He at once ordered another. He ordered it with a jerk of the thumb towards his glass, and Jean Serre was fascinated by the scene, this way of drinking suited him. The afternoon was already moving on. His neighbour dispatched his fresh wine with magnificent speed. Hell, this fellow could put it back. Jean Serre began to forget the bad company. He watched: another jerk of his thumb, another jug-full. The man's face was red rather than bronzed, on the thin side, not very tall, his hair greying at the tips, a little of a badger's grey. It was not that Jean Serre was inclined to use images that afternoon, but it looked just as if the personage had a wig of badger hair, short, thick-set and silvery at the tips, which gave him an appearance that was wild and not at all drunk. On the other hand, his nose was strangely marked at the end as if some forceps had squeezed it very hard in infancy and had left its double mark there for life. Which gave its owner, in spite of his application to drinking, a surprised look, making him appear young.

After a moment he looked at Jean Serre, the expression on his face became even more surprised, he got up without putting his glass down, seized hold of his jug and came up to him.

'Good afternoon', he said with a strong Anglo-Saxon accent. 'I'm fed up. There's nobody in this town.'

He sat down.

Jean Serre said nothing, impressed by the attack. Because this man's accent suddenly made him see a forest of oak-trees beneath the gloomy rain and red-faced peasants in gaberdines going unhurriedly into a pub with a thatched roof.

'I'm Welsh', he said. 'You know, Wales, in the south-west of England.'

Jean Serre understood at once that for this man 'Welsh' was of decisive importance.

At that moment something came into his mind, but he did not know what. A seat by the seaside? Lead coloured, perhaps, or silver and green in the veins and in his bad memory. A willow-tree? A bard suspected of concocting philtres by the gull-headed women, his neighbours? A mill kept by the younger sister of a bull-dog of a man with a hat of dressed leather, a spinster who eats cutlets at twilight in her kitchen, the only room, between a battery of copper saucepans and a hired television which produces more waves than pictures? Rain falls in front of the trees and the grass. In front of the unattainable water of the sea.

Yes, an air of surprise.

'Are you staying with beer?' he said. 'I get fed up in this country. All right, it's very beautiful, the countryside, the trees, everything. But I can't talk to anybody. The people are shut up behind their prison-bars. You wouldn't care to

165

have a glass of wine with me?'

Jean Serre was willing. Another jug of white wine slid across the bar in their direction.

'I come from Wales, you know. My wife is Swiss, that's why I'm here for a few days. But I can't talk to anybody. Here everybody is in their dungeon. German Swiss, my wife. The people are sort of . . . chipped. Like a poor person's crockery hidden in a beautiful cupboard. I want to talk to somebody, I go to the café . . . Never a soul. Has someone thrown a spell over them? At home, I've written a play. I'll send it to you. People have discussions in my country, they laugh, they swear at each other. They are alive, that's what. They are alive. I'm from Wales. The country of Dylan Thomas.'

Jean Serre looked at him blankly.

The man did not see his reaction. He talked while staring at the bar, now he was drinking his glasses of wine in single gulps. Dylan Thomas. Swansea, the house which smelt of rot, the animals, the damp night, then Laugharne, the faces with big nostrils, the wildly waving shadows, a herd of black pigs biting each other and running amongst the tufts of grass turned salty by the spray, a drunken minister making up hymns, an oat-haired Sunday-school boy, the pub door banging above the sea, the night thronged with people, the wandering about on the cliffs. And in front of these visions, the Laugharne cemetery with the little white-painted cross, In memory of Dylan Thomas, R.I.P. The spongy countryside and the clusters of trees filling up with poems, there, at the start and at the finish of every voice, in the uninterrupted undertone of the ocean.

'I knew Dylan Thomas', the man said, without changing the tone of his voice.

He was talking flatly. As if reciting a prayer repeated a hundred times to drive away an evil influence.

'I was quite small. I used to go and fetch him beer. He lived near us. When he died, it was I who received his mirror.'

And he repeated several times, as if spell-bound: 'his mirror. His mirror. Yes. Dylan Thomas's mirror.'

Straight away Jean Serre felt that he had been caught, that the incantation would never let him go again. That the words that he had just heard from this restless and distracted mouth were like wells.

'You knew Dylan Thomas', he said stupidly. He could not escape from the urge to repeat this name in his turn. At the same time he was overtaken by a stupendously sudden sadness. The eyes of Dylan Thomas in his mirror, in his eyes lost in the mirror. The unfathomable look of the look. 'The Lord shall preserve thy going out and thy coming in.' What, Reverend? Dylan Thomas shaving. The lather on Dylan Thomas' chin. The scraping of the blade, the mad howls after vomiting, the eyes again, drowned in alcohol, the round, lathered cheeks, the head full of horror and poems, the gentle, guttural speech, and in the mirror the dreadful apparition of the mortal brother stops and never stops. Why did he think at that moment of a phrase from Isaiah: 'the youths shall faint and be weary'. As if the whole distress of a man had come to be fixed in the backing of this haunted mirror.

Jean Serre cannot remember what they said afterwards.

Wine, dreaming, silence also; then they left each other, wrote, from Wales Jean Serre received short messages, the promised play, and a souvenir book showing the sea, some trees, some stones, the boathouse at Laugharne, 'My sea-shaken house on a breakneck of rocks', and a photograph of Dylan Thomas, with a sad and sulky look, buried to his waist in the wild vegetation of a cemetery – just as if he had been struck motionless, caught in a trap while walking, stuck in a stagnant pool that was heavy around his thighs. Behind him, black railings open on to a jumble of tombs, pell-mell. His head is inclined to the right, his right hand is plunged into his jacket pocket, his eyes gloomy and sad, the sullen and sad mouth of a child that has been punished. And beneath the roundness of the face an absurd, black, ridiculous bow-tie, as for a funeral, like those worn by the waiters of his time, like the one which the Reverend Eli Jenkins at Bethesda Chapel must be wearing world without end. As for him, he has passed by Currant Avenue, Donkey Street, he has drunk fifteen glasses of stout at the Marine Arms, now he advances motionless in the paralysing ivy, he walks, he walks, you see, he makes no advance, remaining a dark patch in the cool green trap, for the dead are calling him and taking hold of him. That's it. Stuck with his back against the dead. His legs and thighs caught in the funereal green stagnation; at his back, the gibberish of the dead jabbering and complaining and crying out his name in the silence of the end of an afternoon of alcohol and summer.

Jean Serre never goes back to that bar. But every time he passes, he hears the stuttering of the dead from the depths of the ossuary and the grass. And in a certain mirror he makes out a long, sad look, laden with tears, which the spring of living waters and of light, he knows, will never wash away.

Anne Cuneo

From *Le temps des loups blancs*

Gradually I had learnt French. At the start the language was a problem that did not preoccupy me very much. I was hungry, I was cold, the shock of this new life was almost unbearable. I saw my mother from time to time on Sunday afternoons. She was done for, had no energy to spare for me, and I did not succeed in talking to her. I contented myself with wolfing down all the food which she brought from the kitchen. I soon stopped asking her to take me away: I realized that there was no solution. I would live there or in Italy, where I had no wish to return. I wanted to be 'free' in Lausanne, not to be in Milan.

167

The first thing I liked in Switzerland, after the scenery, were the duvets, unknown in Italy. The second was the shopping arcade.

At that time there was a shopkeeper behind every door and every shop-window. The different storeys were linked by a strange lift whose open compartments kept on moving the whole day through. You jumped in when they came up to your level, you got off when they reached the desired floor. I adored this. I made use of this paternoster until about 1966 or 1967 when the postal authorities stopped up the openings for fear of an accident.

I could pass hours (during which I was thought to be going to confession, or to be having extra French lessons with Sister Saint-Denis) seated at the corner of the staircase reading a book borrowed from a second-hand bookseller on the first floor. All the shopkeepers knew me, and in the end a number of them made use of me to run errands.

I was frequently offered clothes, footwear and other things. For most of the time I was unable to accept them, at least at first, because I did not know how to explain them to the Sisters. When I learnt to tell lies it became easier.

My fixed, overmastering thought soon became this: to get out.

I feverishly made up stories, the confession of fictitious sins, imaginary visits to my mother, special lessons at school. The shopping arcade and school were my ports of call. I asked the mistress to let me stay behind while she did her marking. I explained to her that the Italian Sisters could not help me, and sometimes she agreed. I also had the Chailly bakery and in fine weather Saint-François or Ouchy.

One day my mother sent me to look for a book for her in the City Library, and the Library soon threw everything else into the shade. I must have been about thirteen and looked it, so the librarian kept on repeating to me:

'Does your mother really read all that?'

'Oh, yes . . . '

'She reads the whole night through then?'

'Oh, I don't know, she told me to come, that's all.' We had this little dialogue for some years.

'If the Children's Service had seen what you were reading', she told me later, 'I would have had to pretend to believe that it was for your mother'.

Sometimes it was she who recommended books to me, and I am indebted to her for some marvellous pleasures.

For instance, I remember Charles Morgan's *The Voyage*, the most unforgettable book of my first period in Lausanne. It was the story of a girl from the provinces in the nineteenth century who had become a singer in Paris and who was passionately loved by a gentleman wine-grower.

'Your mother will like this', the librarian had told me. I read it and re-read it, five times, ten times. Some passages from this book are as fresh in my memory as if I had read them yesterday.

She got me to read the Brontë sisters, my first crime stories, my first American classics. She introduced me to contemporary drama: Giraudoux, Claudel.

How did I live?

I try to see myself: weariness, anxiety, a longing to get out of this situation, the certainty that I never would – that the convent was going to shut down upon me like a trap. The first six months, a permanent nightmare. The Library and the other things only came later. Cold, frustration, difficulties with French. The first winter seems to me to have been interminable.

I have no exact memories apart from those that I have recounted.

At about Easter time (this came at the end of the school year) the problem of my education presented itself.

I spoke French fluently, it was no longer possible to trace my Italian origins in my speech. But I did not succeed in writing French. Sister Saint-Denis called in the Italian Sister:

'She is young, she can repeat a year. I will keep her, and in a year's time she won't have any further problems.'

She likewise asked to see my mother.

'You ought to send her to the secondary school, she is rather wasting her time with me. Not immediately, but in the autumn, I am sure she will be ready.'

My mother explained to her that she could not afford it. At that time secondary-school education was fee-paying, and books, and exercise-books had to be bought.

By the Spring I had outgrown my clothes. My mother obtained for me two or three skirts and some sandals to replace the clogs. A young lady who lived at the guest-house where she worked gave me some lessons in French and grammar. One day everything suddenly fitted together, and I wrote my first real French composition.

I was already becoming bored with Sister Saint-Denis' lessons, in which I came top of the class without any effort. She kept on repeating that I needed to be put somewhere else.

The summer holidays came. It rained without stopping. We were confined in our sham chalet, knitting, praying, threading never-ending chains of haricot beans which were to be dried for winter. Reading had been made difficult, if not impossible. It was impossible to go out without permission. 'I am fed up with this bloody country where there's damn all in the way of sunshine, I want to go to the seaside', I said one afternoon when we were knitting in silence on the verandah (the French that I had learnt was that of the working-class districts).

Sister Carmen threw a fit of temper and sent me off to spend the afternoon on my knees in the chapel. I settled down comfortably there (sitting down, of course), and I set about telling myself a story. I remember the incident because it was one of my first open transgressions. I decided that it was stupid of me not to tell myself stories every time we went to church, and I believe that from that day on I gave up praying altogether. I did not even go through the motions any more. Everbody was entitled to know that as far as I was concerned religion was a load of rubbish.

It was during these holidays, I believe, that, driven to despair by our daily pious performances and by the flat tedium of our days (we got up as usual at half-past six, and then spent the days in silent immobility, without reading, with no possibility of doing anything else but housework and needlework), I began to take an interest in the small children.

There was a new two-year-old, I even remember that she was called Graziella, she had big black eyes and curly hair, I had a mind to look after her. At the same time the other little ones needed looking after, but I quickly grew fond of them all. For hours on end I would recount, in two languages, all the stories that I knew to this little group gathered around me on the cellar steps. The little ones kept quiet, that suited Sister Jeanne who was left with a group that was more homogeneous and easier to keep occupied. I believe that it was the discovery of this pedagogic gift that enabled me not to leave Switzerland.

If the Sisters had expelled me, and they were not far from doing so, I could not have stayed; as my mother was a seasonal worker, I was not allowed to live with her, even if she had been able to take me. I should have had to go into another boarding-school, and there would not have been any money for his. However, I stayed, because in spite of my increasingly aggressive ways I became useful.

From now on my aggressiveness had one aim: to defend 'my' children. When the Sisters and in particular the deputy Head punished me, I was for the most part incapable of reacting. I scarcely said a word when I was deprived of a meal, and reacted to 'penitences' with a silent hatred. But if anyone took it upon herself to touch one of the hairs of 'my' little ones' heads, I would make a scene.

No longer knowing what other stories to tell them, I suggested to them that we might give a dramatic performance of the stories which we knew. They were between two and seven years old – they agreed, of course, all the more so as I must have been for them a substitute mother.

We formed the troupe of the 'Seven Dwarfs', our first show having been Snow-White, much appreciated by the other children. On one occasion we even performed in a parish-hall.

After the holidays Sister Saint-Denis asked to see my mother again.

'She must do something else now', she declared. 'She must take an intensive course in French, and then go to a secondary school. I have found what you need: the Commercial School.'

As soon as I heard the proposal, I was overwhelmed with emotion: would my mother consent? And the Italian Sisters? Would I be able to keep up? I should no longer have to traverse the town in a crocodile two abreast. Could I afford to dress in such a way that nobody would notice that I came from the world of the poverty-stricken?

It was arranged.

Everybody consented, even – after she had made Sister Saint-Denis plead with her for a long time – the Head of the orphanage.

And one September morning, dressed in a skirt, a pullover and mocassins which my mother had routed out second-hand and which made me appear almost elegant, I arrived at the Commercial School.

Nicolas Bouvier

A Depression from the Kuriles

North Japan, August 1965 – March 1976

My train is transporting its cargo of bill-hooks, of axes with greased, blue blades that have been carefully wrapped in canvas, and of sleeping passengers with faces blackened by tiredness, fast and straight through the green night, for there has been a lot of rain on the banks of tender grass and on the fields adjoining the primitive forest. And now that the train is stopping, let us lean out of the window: it is a little station after nightfall full of coils of rope, sacks of sawdust, and bowed shadows that move about as they unroll this rope and call to one another as they yawn. There are days like this one when, do what you may, all the people one turns to appear not to see you and to be counting in their heads up to a thousand while waiting for this thing to go away, days more fuliginous and lighter than soot . . . I know, I know, I haven't been able to get used to it yet.

For twenty-four hours I have been living off the benefits of a large crab eaten in the evening of the day before yesterday with a little vinegar, as fresh as if I had been the shark. I still have the two or three thousand yen which I need to cross over the strait of Tsugaru and to rejoin the large island. With the lack of money, perhaps this journey will become a little lively! Always – except in a brothel – one pays in order that nothing shall happen, in order not to sleep out of doors, in order not to share in the stories, the fits of delirium and the fleas of a dockers' doss-house, in order to put one's backside – I did so through weariness the day before yesterday – on the useless plush of a compartment opposite to fellow-passengers whom education has made too timid for them to dare or to deign to address a word to you.

No more plush here. This train – a locomotive with a bronze bell which disperses into the night its flourish of pearly smoke, one coach only – is as if the woodcutters from these parts had built it themselves by recollecting the notions from school manuals (inertia, friction, pi=3.14, compression of boilers) which save the castaways in 'The Mysterious Island'. The badly planed cross-pieces of the seats are still exuding resin, and it can be feared that by means of a shunting operation this wild little train will return neighing to the forest from which it has emerged . . .

A new stop: another station frozen in the great ice-pack of sleep well before Wakanaï which I shan't reach tonight now. As the waiting-room is icily cold and as there is nowhere to sit at table in this place which consists only of churned-up black peat, giant umbels, heaps of squared tree-trunks, lairs, crows and isolated lighthouses by the side of an ever-grey sea, I have settled myself behind the ticket-office window on the desk of the station-master who, it appears, has gone to his mother's for a meal. The ticket-collector who is his subordinate counts and recounts on a kind of abacus the day's takings while nibbling hazel-nuts of which he has offered me half. From time to time he stops in order to kick to pieces an old 'Suntory' whisky-case and feed a small iron stove. In between his addition sums he informs me that on the Wakanaï line since the beginning of the year the bears have killed three calves, a horse and a schoolgirl, and have attacked two agricultural workers who drove them away with pitchforks. The radio is transmitting a baseball match at the other end of the archipelago which he has stopped listening to as he is dealing with an old woman with a fichu who has come several hours in advance of her train and who appears never to have taken a return-ticket before. She is worried and insistent, and does not listen to any of the replies he gives her. To be so uncertain not only of leaving but also of coming back: she will only believe this when she has seen it (the majority of those who have come to settle in this 'island without memory' have not done so altogether of their own free will). A fairly recent luxury, this certainty. In other days poor people did not go elsewhere to look for their meagre living except under constraint and with a heavy heart. Often they had to get into debt or become beggars in order to leave, and what is more to reckon with the redskins, wolves, icebergs, bolting coach-horses, the plague, highwaymen. Whence this harrowing folklore of ports and stations which used to surround – and too frequently still does surround – the slightest departure. The silent families, the women who kiss the ground of the platform between their cases that are tied up with string and filled with bread and onions, the faces discomposed by tears, and the handkerchiefs which chapped hands wave in the cinders or in the direction of a mast which is being consumed by the open sea . . .

. . . Return of the station-master who comes in polishing his lamp. He is taken aback to find this stranger installed at his table where his scrawled notes are spread out. He hesitates for a moment between forced cordiality and circumspection, regrets almost at once this hesitation which I have noticed, and looks for some way to oblige me. He telephones to get the weather report for me, and he recites it with raised finger. 'Ashta ga furi so desu', it was raining yesterday, it is raining today, It will rain tomorrow. A depression from the Kuriles. All the better! The rain in this country, with so little to be said for it, is always a little something extra. By the way, I very much like those

172

temperaments that don't make symphonic music, but only know a few notes and repeat them without tiring. In this little something which resembles myself I feel at home and find myself, in a word I have the feeling of understanding what one is trying to say to me. What is more, this station has just reminded me of another one in Canton Vaud where, at the age of six or seven, I often dozed with my legs dangling and my nose in my mittens while waiting for the milk-train. After all! you will say to me, this low, polar sky, this dead water, this want, these crows, why Canton Vaud? It is the light of this opaline lamp with counter-balance which is suspended too high above the table, the way in which the brown parcels tied up tightly with string are piled up behind the ticket-office window, the noise of this big round clock whose seconds are as broad as fingers, in short these nothings which come together and conspire to form a climate. For it is not by the identity of the things themselves, but by the associations which are secretly established between these things, that places which would have nothing in common suddenly become resonant together with a logic that is hallucinatory and entirely new . . .

. . . Four men wearing fur hats whose profiles have been effaced by the wind have just entered the waiting-room and are reading in this light like moist sugar – it is a wind generator that is providing the current – manuals for windlass repairers or sawyers. It is precisely thus that I used to imagine the 'North' (sledges, natives, pemmican) when I read the description of Hokkaido in the 'Journal of Travels' for 1894, a thick, bottle-green volume with dog-eared pages lent (it is called 'come back') by the pointsman at Allaman station where I was waiting for the milk-train. Boilles, halo of streetlights, scarlatina, tiny dancers in tutu in the musical slot-machine. And I was six or seven.

The Wakanaï train will pass through tomorrow morning. Leaning against the ticket-office window, my chin clasped in the palms of my hands, I was borne off to sleep like a straw in an unfurling of memories where everything, even the shadows, became mercifully miniature.

Roger-Louis Junod

From *Les enfants du roi Marc*

At the time when my father went bankrupt, not more than a few months after the death of Pierre, he was inventing letter-scales and recording machines to measure the length of telephone conversations. His letter-scales only interested a limited number of clients, while the machines with their clockwork mechanism could be replaced with advantage by any sand-glass. He got up at four in the morning to fiddle about with the prototype of a typewriter which was to work by means of electro-magnets, without keys and levers, and which would have cost, according to his estimation, a third of the price of the traditional machines. He intended to construct it on his own, on a large scale, and to become wealthy, to buy for us splendid furniture, new curtains, clothes, a superheterodine radio like the one belonging to the manager of the metal-spring factory, for Mamma a gold necklace, for myself some skis with a Kandahar fixing device. How he caused us to dream about these luxuries! He would pay off his debts in less than a year, would have the outside of the house repainted (this house which, if it had not belonged to Mamma and her brothers and sisters, would have been sold at the time of the bankruptcy, and from which we should have been evicted). But the iron bars, the corrugated iron sheets, the spools of electric wire, the aluminium spindles, the cogs of tempered steel that he accumulated in his retreat in anticipation of the day when the industrial production of typewriters would start, all this put him even further in debt. Bills poured in: he would await the postman in the road, concealed by the group of elder-trees from Mamma's curiosity, and hide in his pockets the letters which he did not want her to see. When she was not present he would ring up his creditors, begging them to be patient. I heard him protest in an anxious voice that a knife was being put at his throat, that he was neither a thief nor a dishonest man, that his word could be relied on.

And Uncle Emile! Uncle announced his visits by telephoning, two or three days in advance. From that moment on he was the sole subject of conversation: 'Emile will arrive by the train at 15.12. Let's hope that Emile has good weather! Emile shouldn't see your new shoes. Emile adores country ham: let us buy 250 grammes.' Should we offer him wine, or not? A glass of wine will give him pleasure, but perhaps he will imagine that we drink it every day. Uncle Emile bought me little presents: a yoyo, a tin trumpet, a bag of sweets. He placed his grey hat with its navy-blue hatband and his gloves on the sideboard. He drew himself up like an officer, with his chin held up high. With his moustache and goatee, his big ears and his intelligent-looking forehead, he resembled Mallarmé in profile. He spoke to Mamma with the politeness of a minister, and to Papa in the tones of command and reproof employed by a master when addressing his worst pupil. In his presence Papa lost all pride. He gave me the impression of having become once more a child who is afraid of being punished. Uncle Emile inspected the apartment. 'Why, Charles', he would say, 'you didn't have this pretty candlestick last time'. He went to take hold of the object that had been placed on the piano, held it up in the light, tapped the metal to make it resound. 'It's my birthday present', Mamma said in a courageous voice. 'But Violet, you don't need to make excuses. I am glad that Charles can find the means to indulge you in spite of everything. Now Charles, this is no trifle; it must weigh about 800 grammes. And pewter costing what it does . . . ' 'I bought at a bargain price', Papa pleaded, 'on the day when I went to Bern to take out my patent'. 'Come now, yet another patent? You don't say so. These gentlemen in Bern give you your patents for nothing, do they?' 'Listen, Emile, we haven't had time to talk about this yet. I'm on to a really first-rate idea, a typewriter . . . ' He cleared his throat; he suddenly lost his voice. 'They told me at the Patent Office in Bern that this typewriter was absolutely revolutionary!' Uncle Emile had cut him short with a look. He placed his hand on Mamma's arm: 'Violet, you ought to stop him. It's all very well to dream when it doesn't cost anything. When it gets to be expensive and you have the sort of debts that Charles has, you have to say no.' Turning to my father: 'None of your inventions has brought you any money at all. And look at you, stubbornly chasing a new illusion. But good heavens, Charles, how old are you? Patents! A typewriter! Perhaps you think you can compete with Remington? If you had sworn to put your family in the gutter, you wouldn't behave any differently.' 'I will show you my plans. You will understand at once that it can't go wrong. They told me so in Bern. Everything is on my side.' 'In the meantime', Uncle Emile said, 'I should like to have a look at your accounts'. My mother and I went out, leaving my father and my uncle in the sitting-room. From time to time, Uncle Emile's voice was raised, scolding, angry, and Mamma would sadly shake her head or bite her lip.

When we came back after accompanying my uncle to the station, Papa resembled someone who had just escaped from danger. He took my hand in his and clasped it joyfully. He told me stories going back to his childhood which I knew by heart. Four years older than Emile, my father had taught him to read and to count, had helped him with his homework, but above all, it was he who had initiated him into the secrets of woods and streams. Later on, when Emile had started at the Commercial School, it was he, the elder brother, again who had found money from his pay as a workman to provide Emile with the pocket-money he needed. And it was to him, the elder brother, that he used to entrust his affairs of the heart (I held it against my father that he had been so indiscreet). 'He was never very sure of his French nor of his spelling, so that the letters he had to write, yes, even his love-letters, he often asked me to rough out for him. We were friends through thick and thin, Emile and I were. He never undertook anything without consulting me. And in short, there has been no change in this respect, although he has become an accountant and earns as good a living as a doctor. Always the same trust between us: through thick and thin.' Mamma awaited our return with impatience, curious to learn 'what Emile had said.' Emile had said that the sale of the letter-scales would have to be extended to German-speaking Switzerland. 'What else?' 'That the situation could be worse.' 'But what about your debts?' Emile was in favour of an arrangement with the creditors. 'So it's bankruptcy, Charles?' 'Not really. We can escape that. He explained everything to me in detail. We have made a plan. I will show you the papers this evening.' And he returned to his odds and ends, certain of the forthcoming success of his typewriter.

On Tuesdays and Thursdays Mamma went to the rehearsals of the parish choir, conducted by the minister Weber himself. She played the harmonium (which we youngsters called the 'hymn pump'). She esteemed the minister more highly than anyone else in the world. What devotion to his parish! He wore himself out visiting the sick and the old. It was useless to tell him to take care of himself, nothing held him back, neither snow or cold. And the simplicity of this man who knew how to be in tune with everybody, whether rich or poor, intelligent or limited! He never proclaimed his own superiority. You could see him digging his garden beds himself, pulling up weeds, pruning his rose-trees. Those who came home late from a journey or from an evening with friends saw the light in the window of his study. He did not read his sermons, which were too short for Mamma's taste, for she could have listened to them for hours without tiring; he spoke them as if he had learnt them off by heart, consulting only occasionally his notes on a piece of paper. And his voice which was so well in tune and time, and had such a good timbre, rose above the rest of the congregation when hymns were being sung.

It was much later that I realized that my mother thought she had married badly, and that she would have liked to be the wife of a minister. She never said so explicitly, but I began to suspect it when she developed the habit, during Mme Weber's illness, of spending time at the rectory in order to perform a number of services there. She who had complained for years of not having sufficient strength for her own housework was overflowing with energy as soon as it was a question of 'helping this poor M. Weber'. She was radiant when she came back from her expeditions to the pastoral hearth. She had been sewing, ironing, cleaning windows, putting the parish magazine in envelopes, copying addresses, going on errands and preparing the meals of the invalid, her husband and her son who was three years older than myself. Papa was uneasy: 'You are doing too much, you will tire yourself out'. She replied with a smile that was full of goodness and a sweetness that reminded me of the first years of my life, that she was only doing her duty. She had become cheerful; she sang once more as she fulfilled her daily tasks and even found time to play the piano in the evening.

Louis Gaulis

From *Zig-Zag Street*   *Only what happens in the street is true.*
                                                                    (Henry Miller)

It would be a mistake to believe that Zig-Zag Street was only inhabited by bizarre or colourful people. In fact most of its inhabitants lived confined behind their window-shutters, which were closed almost the whole year. In summer for protection against the sun (and to shelter from the light their dear curtains, their dear carpets, their dear bedspreads), in winter because of the cold. When they went out, once a day, they passed quickly by, avoiding God knows what dangers, as if reluctantly, already impatient to regain their lairs. For most of the women, completely enslaved to their housekeeping, their greatest entertainment was to sit on their balcony at sunset and look at the street, and even there, at this magic hour when beauty should transfigure us all, they appeared like sinister nurses seated by a patient's bedside.

I had asked the hairdresser if he knew what Zig-Zag meant. According to him it was a Turkish word that meant: not straight. I told this to the imam who retorted to me that on the contrary it was a Greek word meaning: bizarre and complicated. I finally discovered that it was a word invented by the Germans, adopted by the French, then by the whole world, which signifies: in the shape of a Z. The reason for this name was not only that it described very exactly the shape of the street which was like two Zs, the one on top of the other, but also and above all because it could not have been given a Greek or a Turkish name without bringing about a minor civil war. At one end of the street was the mosque, and at the other the Pension Hellas. In the middle the hairdresser's shop made the link between the two cultures, even adding Hebrew to them, represented by the signs of the cabbala.

The street had been pacified, but to bring agreement truly to everyone, it would perhaps have been needful to invent a flag? There wasn't one. At a later date the flag of the young republic hardly ever flew in the street. It was not to be seen anywhere. The Greek flags flew on the one side, the Turkish ones on the other. On holidays, it was a variegated and pretty sight. You can't be too mistrustful of flags.

Asia started just after the Old Romantic Bar and the hairdresser's shop which was its frontier-post. How could one guess that one was in the Orient? The same cafés, the same faces, the same calm immobility. However, certain signs appeared as one approached. The flies perhaps, more numerous, more persistent. Outside noises, sharper, breaking a different kind of silence. The music too, more modulated, with interminable ornamentations which ended by swallowing up the melody. Less talkative too, the Turks, somnolent mystics, they appeared, as they smoked their narghiles, as if totally open to time, allowing it to flow through them without offering the least resistance, which is in fact the reverse of the manner of the mute for instance who, while constantly active, was struggling against time, breasting it like a swimmer, against the current. On the Greek side, one killed time. They wore it away. But wore it away by loving it, as one loved one's wife.

The silence which they observed as the day ended was the silence which falls upon lovers, when the moment becomes more mysterious and charged with life than their bodies, suddenly paralysed with attention. They know for ever that this for ever is short, ineffably present and measured; and what makes them happy belongs to an order that is older and more generous than anything that they have been, and will be, able to understand.

177

'Pray as if you were to die this evening, and work as if you were eternal', the Prophet has said. What the prophets say is not always easy to live. The Christians know something about this. It cannot be said that much praying or work was done, in the Turkish end of Zig-Zag Street. People were less hard-working there than in the Greek end, and so poorer and more modest.

There were also some Moslem gipsies who had come from Turkey after who knows what avatars. They lived on the edge of the neighbourhood in derelict shanties, and the Turkish community showed extreme tolerance towards them. They wore immense magnificent drooping moustaches, and smoked with elegance their long de luxe cigarettes. They were very skilful at mending and converting, and could make you a lorry from two wrecked buses, a fishing-boat from a lorry, and a newspaper kiosk from an old boat. The fathers showed a solicitude and tenderness for their children which I have never met elsewhere. Never a voiced raised, never a rough gesture. For that we respected them. It would not have occurred to us, either to the sons of the mute or to myself, to pick a quarrel with the gipsy children. However, they too were among the victims, although they never waved the smallest flag.

At this end of the street, my father was the only person who spoke and understood Turkish perfectly. But the Turks had this advantage over us that almost all of them understood Greek. Our Esperanto was English. Hardly anyone made use of it.

At the Turkish end, the pitaride (itinerant musician) did not sing. The poetry of a language is something too intimate. One should not colonize hearts. And the Turkish heart is not a desert, not an Anatolian steppe: it is a furnace of despair. The pitaride moved around from table to table and from one pavement to the other, offering his lottery tickets.

He had worked out a very personal system of selling. Usually the salesman speculates on superstition based on numbers: everyone believes in some numbers which he supposes to be luckier than others. So you have to proclaim in a loud voice the numbers which you are offering, in the hope that some of them will correspond to the superstitious belief of a passer-by. There are two solutions: to stay always at the same spot, at a street corner, what could be called 'angling', or to move about, to cross the market and to traverse as many streets as possible, while trusting to the law of averages, 'trawling'.

Neither of these methods satisfied the pitaride. They were both equally tiring and disappointing. Staying in one place is not more restful than striding through the town. But in the market or in the very crowded streets the great quantity of ticket-sellers, all shouting varied numbers at the same time, made the crowd deaf and indifferent. It was necessary to find something else. It was Kyrios Kostas who solved the dilemma for the pitaride by suggesting that he replaced the superstition of numbers by that of days, related to the signs of the zodiac.

Very simple: every week in Sunday's horoscope, it was easy to read which was the lucky day given for each sign. There were approximately two different signs every day. Instead of merely shouting his wretched numbers into the void while waiting for his customers, he made them come to him by announcing simply: 'Tuesday, lucky day for Virgo and Pisces!' He had quickly noticed that the signs were distributed in a regular manner. For approximately every six passers-by there was either a Virgo or a Pisces who felt that little shock, as we all do, when something springs out of the general indifference and seems to be addressed to our particular selves. To a certain extent it was fishing with a lamp to attract the fish, at night.

He made quite a decent living.

Phoivos was a polyglot, or thought himself one. He was a gentle and nostalgic man, who came from Alexandria in the first place. He had travelled widely in his youth, before taking flight from Egypt with his savings and setting himself up here as landlord of the Old Romantic Bar, a big vaulted café that was always empty. In addition to the three languages of the island, he knew Arabic, French and Italian. Phoivos believed in tourism. He used to let three rooms on the upper floor. In order to attract the clientele from Nice or Monaco, for whom he had been waiting desperately for years, he had placed everywhere placards drawn up in several languages.

Today the Old Romantic has changed ownership, but the placards are still there. At the entrance: 'Here you will find a cordial and physical ambient atmosphere'. Over the bar, for 'cognac de Paphos' can be read in English: 'Paphos of Brandy'. At the foot of the staircase: 'There is leaking water in all rooms', and in the toilets: 'The tetragonal papers placed for this purpose will not go into the pipe, if you please, but in the waste-basket, thank you very much'.

Phoivos liked to recount his travels. He would describe in minute detail all the hotels he had stayed in. The finest one was the Hotel Brighton, rue de Rivoli. He related how moving it was to wake up each morning opposite the 'Palace of King Louvre'.

But all his efforts had finished by giving the inhabitants of the street the impression that this place was not made to welcome them. They did not feel at home there, and the Old Romantic Bar was always empty. Phoivos played backgammon with the two waiters – waiters who often changed, but were always young, with eyes that were too big and bistre-coloured, whispering, never knowing the price of things, even of a cup of coffee. Phoivos was not married.

The finest place in the street, perhaps in the entire town, was the roof of the Pension. The important person who had had this Venetian-Moorish palace built, each window of which had its balcony, gracefully curved and adorned with wrought iron, had indulged in the luxury of a roof terrace, a kind of hanging garden from whence one could see the sea, the masts of the caiques in the old harbour, the spurs of the Troodos Mountains, and the first escarpments of the road leading to Paphos. A parapet with stone balusters acted as a protection against the drop in space. One could sit down there, side by side. In summer the stonework remained warm the whole night through. Yanoulla kept potted bays there, and bushes of geraniums, jasmin and many other plants which were cultivated in assorted cans painted in bright, clashing colours. The date-palm in the courtyard added the shade of three or four of its fronds which ruffled the girls' hair when the evening breeze arose. Yanoulla used to hang out the finery of these ladies, my dear aunts and cousins. These rows of motley-coloured little panties fluttered and flapped joyfully, giving a festive air to this privileged place.

Koulla had shown me how to get up to the terrace without going through the Pension. One had to enter the courtyard, which was always open, and go along by the arches beneath which the Governor's open carriage stood, and beyond the old stables a small staircase led straight there. I used to go there to fly my kites, along with other youngsters of the neighbourhood. We fixed razor-blades to the tails of the kites. The object of the game was to cause the contraption to perform evolutions in such a way that its tail would whip the opposing kite. After two or three slashes the wind enlarged the wounds, and the kite came down and became entangled in the telephone wires where it hung dead, losing its colours, for months on end.

Etienne Barilier

From *Prague*

You know, my impression is that each thought and each word, when they are floating between the mind and the written state, are still, are really life itself, even more precise and therefore more intense than the unformulated feeling. But the instant afterwards there they are, immobilized and enshrouded in their silence. This makes me think of the most fascinating moment of a stage performance: when, after dancing before these meagre audiences of blankly admiring, incompetent, crudely thinking middle-class people who thought they were attending some gymnastic festival, I came forward with my partners to take a bow. In spite of the level of the performance and that of the audience, something happened, I think, which must happen for the greatest star of the Paris Opera: your body and your mind are intoxicated with the show that has been given, intoxicated at having given themselves, invested and glorified by all the beauty that has passed through them, inhabited by the still fullness of what is transient. Without counting the relief, joy and happiness which are provided by these rounds of applause arising from the shapeless darkness, like those scents which rise up from the earth after sunset. To know that they are looking at you, to know the proof that the magic of the performance, through our mediation, comes through to these dull creatures who are rebellious against beauty. In short, the supreme moment when you see doubly and proudly: you return to everyday life, you give up what makes you different, your nature as dancer, in order to become a woman again, but at the same time you retain that wonderful privilege of yours (costume, stage-setting, etc.). During the performance you were, as far as you could be, divine, but separated. Now you are divine amidst your human brothers and sisters, and is it not finer to be a lily amidst the thorns rather than amidst the lilies? Oh, these unique moments, I would give my life to find them again, and he who has not experienced them cannot know what they are. I shall not wound you, I imagine, in telling you that they surpass love itself, for they are love without the anguish, they are the apotheosis of the gift. If ever I have been princely, princely for myself and without pride, it was at such moments.

But why have I talked to you about this? Yes, because of writing. I wanted to say that between those moments of ineffable glory where you are sacred at the very heart of the profane, and the final return to the profane, the transition is imperceptible: the last rounds of applause resound thinly, you make your last bow and give your final radiant smile; all that is left on the floor of the stage is a few poor dismal lights, the curtain will not rise again, you free your hands from those of your neighbours and you become aware of their dampness. You are exhausted, deprived of your fairy magic, your costume is a cumbersome disguise. I wanted to talk about this imperceptible and yet abrupt transition from glory to nothingness, from triumph to desolation. That's how it is when I write to you. From words that have been dreamt to words that have become fixed. Nothing has changed, it seems, and yet it is death.

I would wish not to write any more because I do not wish to die. Dizziness, unimaginable sadness. Exhausted at the ceaseless picturing of our union, our communion, in a city that I don't know, which has taken hold of you and which eludes me. Worn out at making constant calls upon our memories, upon cities we have known in the past. The precise urge to seize hold of you and to see you here in front of me, in this bare room, without mystery and almost without memory. The urge to recognize you in even more humdrum surroundings, a corridor, a trolley-bus, a street without anything picturesque about it, without shop-windows, without monuments. On the other hand, neither railway platform nor hospital corridor. I want neutrality, banality, I want to cut the nerves of the past. Nothing to tear us from ourselves alone, nothing to lift us up nor inflate us nor provide us with borrowed images. I want to dance for you without scenery, do you understand? To be sure that it is I that you love, you that I love. I shall kill you if you compare me to anybody else, I shall ask you to put out my eyes with your fingers if I should see hovering behind your face the cupola of St Nicholas or those forests in which these last days I so much enjoyed losing myself in thought.

Shall we survive if we survive alone? Should we still know what love is, if our memories did not relay old desire? I am not sure, but I wish it to be so. You know, I sometimes think of those violet-coloured skies which one can contemplate when one is at the top of a mountain, at a height of three or four thousand metres. And the air burning with purity, and the strange happiness at seeing only ice and stones. Suddenly vegetation, intrusive trees, over-bland pastures, even flowers (apart from gentians), all seem superfluous, vulgar, offensive. Green is now only a half measure, compromise, frivolity. But those skies, I wish we could look at them together from the plain, from my urban balcony, between black façades, above factory chimneys. Do you understand? I would like to discover them without assistance, without any spiritual stool to stand on, without poets. I no longer wish to see through the hollow eyes of centuries of great lovers, nor do I wish you to see my phantom dancing on the wet pavements of the city of gold. Nor to recount our foolishness any more. Nor even to re-invent love, but perhaps to invent another kind of love. No more of those endearments which Daphnis and Chloë had already conceived thousands of years ago, nor of those sacrifices and acts of violence already catalogued by Sade. Vanity, puerility, even stupidity? Possibly, certainly. Very well then, let us invent nothing but forget everything, and let us be ready to kill the first lovers who would dare to imitate, without having known it, our way of holding our forks.

Why this rejection? I know very well why: Prague. I have the feeling of a sort of 'cruel story'. Illegally, taking advantage of some slackness of the frontier-guards, I have penetrated, following you, into this city. But without documents, money or anything. Sooner or later I am going to be challenged, my deception will be found out, I shall be shown to the gates. I can travel in all directions and at any pace across the city, I can see it on its finest day, be in several places at once, move without passers-by catching the echo of my footsteps. But I cannot grasp hold of anything, not even the stones. And the least distraction, the least loss of concentration can suffice to expel me from paradise for a long time: a door that slams, a bell from a tower, even a telephone. Yes, one evening I was walking like this, without making any noise, in the Street of the Alchemists, and I was looking at the house of Master Athanasius Pernath, wedging my temples gently but firmly between two bars of the railing. Suddenly my attention was attracted by a huge open bay and by the brightly lit room which it revealed. A stooping shadow fell on one of the walls. And I thought that I could see its arm move above an invisible moving object. Then a groaning sound came to my ears. I pressed my head more strongly against the bars, as if by so doing I could get past the railing. All the time I could see only this large shadow, calmly leaning. Beneath it, someone stretched out on a bed. I tore

182

myself from what I was contemplating, I ran, I bent down, then knelt down. I was weeping, alone in my flat in Lausanne. Just like this evening when I am writing these extravagances to you, caught between this fascination with your universe, this wish to get past the bars, and this revolt, this will to accept things in their concrete commonplaceness: I am here, you are there, let us tear ourselves away from the spells of the imaginary and of memory, let us love each other without magic, without dreaming, and even perhaps without beauty. Let us live.

Yes, here I am quite naked and quite desperate, in my turn. Each time, for some days, the same thing has happened: I fight against your moods of sadness, I demonstrate in a thousand ways that they are without cause, then I start again talking to you about myself, more dolefully than you ever do! I don't see how our dialogue of ailing convalescents can end before your return. What happiness that this will be in the near future and that we may finally give ourselves up to silence. When one is in love, to talk is always to lie.

Odile

Monique Laederach

From *La femme séparée*

Anne.

That is her name since that day, that first day, that axis of before and after, the day of the break, not really that day the break, but that day the one she moved out: she takes her furniture, she goes away. *I leave my husband.*

Jerome away somewhere in the mountains in order not to see it, and it is better that way, this upset in the house, linen furniture suitcases, and how would you take leave; besides, the two *cronies*, Terence's cronies of course, Fred, Jean-Louis, who are already bringing down a mattress, the bedside-table, some boxes and:

'What else?'

– the little red rug at the entrance to the lounge. Red. Anne at the edge of the red rug as in former times, ten years ago, when they (Jerome and she) had put it there, ten years previously, at the same time as the settee the arm-chairs the pictures.

'We shall need curtains', Jerome said.

And Anne, hesitatingly:

'Green ones?'

Jerome surprised, hardly that one glance, and with absolute certainty:

'Green ones? Definitely not.'

Obviously. And Anne taken aback: 'why not green?' This overwhelming knowledge of Jerome, his certainties, and her, Anne's, no less overwhelming ignorance, always like a blind person, you would have said, the colours the shapes the words escaping her unceasingly, viscous beneath her hand or her eyes, Anne floundering in doubts and may-bes, and desperately trying to guess what Jerome was expecting; Jerome never made a mistake, but as for her.

And still now, these curtains – red ones – which she is looking at, their obvious rightness for ten years, Jerome was right, and all of a sudden this anxiety for the other flat, *over there*, where she has absurdly decided to transport her furniture her books her bed her bits and pieces, this suite of three rooms, she sees them so distinctly, but now compared with the red curtains they appear like a dark star, one of those stars which, it seems, absorb the whole memory of centuries and give it back again each day in surprising images. But what do I give back? I shall not have retained any certainty, even after ten years, *Don't think of it*, inadequacy, there is nothing to be done, but fortunately Fred behind her, impatient:

'What now? What has to come down?'

The red rug, which at last Anne rolls up. Then in the kitchen some plates and dishes some pans some dishcloths, *strict minimum*, Jerome must not go without anything, later on *I shall buy what is missing*, another dizzy spell, short-lived: what with, what money?

She is leaving like a thief. She thinks: 'Like a thief'. And it is not a revolt, not even leaving Jerome intact. At all costs. Jerome must not notice. But when she goes round the flat again, the empty spaces seem to her to be sharply defined, as Jerome will see them this evening, she goes round the rooms as Jerome will this evening, she is Jerome, his sadness, the shocks, the hatred gradually for Anne-the-thief, the treacherous, how can she do such a thing? but she continues to *do* it, divided up like a space marked in squares for hopscotch, but she never seems to get out of hell, and yet she keeps obstinately kicking her stone further and higher, Heaven help you.

Tidy up a piece of paper, a handkerchief. *Don't leave any traces*. The absurdity of her reflex action. The hand-basin, clean out. Change the towels. The other things too heavy all at once, and her own haste all at once. Don't re-open the wardrobes yet again, the drawers, never mind, I shall come back. Fred and Jean-Louis are on the door-step, their silence within her silence: 'a woman who is leaving her husband', they would like to laugh, she feels, to act abruptly, to shake off this heaviness that has suddenly come down on to the house; but there they are, hands in pockets, assiduously trying not to see, attentive all the same, and their bodies enveloped in the dust of the light coming from behind them, fraternally:

'You haven't forgotten anything? You have everything?'

'One minute', Anne says. 'Just a minute.'

Her suppliant tone of voice, which she immediately detests.

Something has been forgotten, but what, but where? She goes round the rooms again; the bedroom, the still bare tree in the window, its branches where on clear nights she could follow the curve of the wood, her waking dreams, the dark riding of unreal horses. Her flight. How many arguments hanging there, how many bouts of insomnia? How many faces imagined in summer in the changing leaves? And Jerome slept, he slept alone, she lay watching alone. She was watching *him*, it seemed, as if she knew the traps in which he could have been caught in the depths of his sleep.

'I am accepting responsibility again', Anne thinks.

Nothing else but that: the rejection of all rejections. This vomiting. I cannot be angry with him because of it. But there is no vomit, only the slight weight between the ribs that she is familiar with. And this unbearable feeling of a mistake somewhere, but she looks for it in vain: it is precisely what she wanted. Don't go back. She closes her eyes; in any case, whatever else is true, if there is a chance left, it will be ahead.

She slightly opens the door of the bedroom, as usual. Nothing opening suddenly on a view of emptiness, this evening Jerome will pass through the corridor, and the door will be as always. But she is well aware, how could she not be, were it only because of her own tiredness, that there is no remedy against the emptiness that she is going to leave.

'I'll be with you in a minute', Anne says, and the two boys go down the staircase.

She locks the flat door; drops the key in the letter-box. It is too soon, she thinks, much too soon. She isn't ready for this. But who is ready? Furiously: 'Nobody would ever do anything'. And accepts the sense that something has been torn apart. However, she stays there looking at the box, its grey metal, almost derisive; *their* name on the letter-box. And the key right at the bottom, scarcely visible, *her* key, *my house*. I am no longer anybody.

At her back, beyond the door, she is conscious of Fred and Jean-Louis by the van; again they appear to be laughing; but when she looks more closely she sees a kind of gleam on their faces, the same for the two of them, electric, strained. They have lowered their eyes. 'They are waiting for me to shed tears', Anne thinks. 'I'm not going to.' And in the lightning flash of the breaking away, at the moment when she is crossing the threshold, another Anne is smiling, thinking:

'That's all they know: that a woman cries at such moments.'

'Off we go', she says.

Vivacious. Except for her voice which is as if laid bare, which is like the branch of a tree after an October wind: rough and dark. But the boys by good luck take the words as they come, they move forward very quickly, moving against the immobility, climb into the vehicle, with Anne behind. She repeats:

'Let's go.'

Her voice better already. But they do not look at her. Jean-Louis starts the engine, they talk to each other in a whisper which carries nevertheless, like adolescents whose voices are breaking. 'For sure, it's something new to them',

185

Anne thinks, resignation forms part of her weariness. And in a futile way: 'At their age'.

But the other Anne, more disenchanted:

It's not a matter of age. You tear yourself away, or somebody tears him or herself away from you, this is something you have known since childhood. You were asleep in a bedroom, the shutters half-open upon a green and tender afternoon which appeared to be without treachery, and when you wake up the Presences have disappeared, you stay lost in labyrinths of hunger and cold, and the feeding-bottle – any old feeding-bottle – which your mouth at last discovers after the cry is only the repressed sob of perfect non-existence. And later, how many public parks, stations, tunnels where this Person, who was there and who is no longer there, is caught away. 'A tooth', Anne thinks. 'Like pulling out a tooth', and the pain is so violent that it anaesthetizes itself of its own accord, and what remains? Nothing except to burrow into your own body, your own sleep, your dreams of restoration in which all the Presences, always, are standing there, luminous and warm, infinitely enfolding.

But however much Anne now studies the faces of the two boys in front of her: nothing about them denotes that they have known what it is to break away, on the contrary, while Jean-Louis is joking about a dead cat by the roadside you could believe that they have always had death in them as a natural thing. As for Jean-Louis, who is a countryman, it is possible. It is sufficient to recall what they are like with their animals, how they are fond of them with their death already written into them since the first day of their life, and their affection (assuming that is what it is) never overflows that exact frontier of animals-that-are-to-die. Anne envies them, envies Jean-Louis and perhaps also Fred, who knows, for having that extra skin. At the same time, she is well aware, she has feelings of hatred for them.

'Hang on', Jean-Louis says, 'I'm turning!'

Their futility, she thinks, exasperated. This smile of Jean-Louis in the driving mirror. 'He doesn't *know* anything', Anne thinks, and this time some unexpected tears come to her eyes, she takes out her handkerchief angrily, and at once Jean-Louis in the mirror:

'Is anything wrong?'

'No, not at all', Anne says, and she starts laughing. Stupidly. So *childish*, she sees herself, with this mouth trembling in the middle of a smile and tears running down her face, and Jean-Louis, precisely then, from the exact centre of her own hate, plays that trick which he knows, 'Oh yes, he knows', Anne thinks hatefully, and the two, very evidently reassured by her normality, are at once all attention, brotherly and protective, and sorry all the same:

'You'll see, it will be all right', Fred says. 'You'll get by.'

'Don't you worry', says Jean-Louis.

And suddenly, as if to a baby:

186

'We'll set you up in your little house, you'll see.'

If I had a child. If now, along with the cases, the furniture, the saucepans, I were taking *in addition* one. If I had done that. And if I. Not even a cat. Not the smallest living thing. Myself? Nothing, practically nothing, only this enormous, over-loose envelope that I can't fill. The dense, glutinous liquid in the ears which keep on ringing. Even walking is not steady. *Over there* those empty rooms which ought to disappear, and *behind* Jerome who is not there. *Who was never there*, Anne thinks, and again hatred. And straight away, the other Anne who knows Jerome's language:

'Whose fault is it, eh! Who wanted it? Eh!'

I am unjust, she knows. But there you are: envy, the need to be unjust. A perfect wax effigy of a man, she thinks (to be sure, perfect!), serious-minded, who does not make mistakes, who knows, who has faith, who walks straight forward, a wax effigy of a man all linearity, disconnected, breathless, a real Giacometti – but the moment you want to strike, to implant the arrow in the figure's heart, pity drowns you, drowns you entirely, and the arrow comes back upon itself, destructive and devastating. To be unjust: this time, just this time, to see only the linearity, the atrocious unpitying rectitude, and unkindly plant your arrow in the wax. It is easier to kill than to abandon. I shall never avoid drowning, never. But now, this step that I am taking: a step for myself. For myself alone. Already one too many. As in the past: 'a mouthful for Daddy, a mouthful for Mummy', but today a mouthful for Anne. 'A monster of egoism.' And all that solitude left around the skeleton of Jerome-Giacometti?

'Mind the cat, Jean-Louis. If you please.'

And Jean-Louis laughs, relieved.

'Don't worry, I know how to drive.'

He knows how to drive. He knows. At last, this glimmer of irony in the act of drowning: a slow fish passes by, without fins, but he does not *know* this, that is why he swims without.

'Don't worry', says Fred, his voice high-pitched all at once.

'No', says Anne.

They both laugh. Then all three.

So relieved, the two in front, that their faces rise up like bubbles in the cab of the van.

'Have you heard the latest story that is going round about the people of Fribourg?'

'Bastards', Anne says.

They laugh. They move about on the seats in front. 'Once. . .' Fred starts. They are still laughing. Except for Anne. This village they are arriving at, almost a hamlet, and it is here that she is going to live. For years, Anne thinks. I shall cross the bridge, then take the little road, every day. She can't believe it: this

187

picture-book. And in her head the throbbing noise starts up again; eyes shut, not to see, to go straight ahead. But she does look, divided perfectly into two, and sees herself looking. This splitting in two, *a legitimate act of self-defence.*

'To the right, after the wall', Anne says.

Italian

Giovanni Orelli   translated by Raffaella Ferrari and June Salmons

From *L'anno della valanga*

There had been no movement on the great mountain overhanging our village. We had reports from a plane flying over the valley that there was an avalanche high up beyond the wood above the village, but this one had not moved. In the middle of the night, however, an avalanche had swept down on to a group of houses and another had crashed angrily down near Nostengo, the rush of air breaking all the windows of the houses. Even we heard this one in the distance, it woke us all up with a start. Instinctively we began to run, all of us, men, women and children, just as we were, in our night clothes, through the narrow streets which weave up and down the village. The wind kept blowing the snow sideways, lashing our faces. We ran, heads bent low, instinctively seeking the shelter of the church.

Even the sanctuary lamp had been blown out, but Numa had an acetylene lamp, and he shouted to us to go to his house, which was the safest in the village – what were we doing there, kneeling on the ground? Giuseppe's wife Maria, who was in the middle of the church shouted to him to leave her there to die, but then she too began to run when she saw us all, every single one of us, run out, leaving the door wide open: the wind would blow the snow right up to the altar. When we reached Numa's house we noticed that some people were missing, and so a few of us went back to call out to those still outside in the raging blizzard. It was so bad you could hardly breathe; we shouted, our voices suffocated by the wind: we went to look for them and in front of the open door of the church there we found Naldo's girl Verena. How could we have forgotten her like that? She stood, as if playing with a doll, but she had no doll. But when she saw me in front of her, she opened her mouth as wide as she could, but she could neither shout nor cry, just like little girls hold their breath and frighten their mothers to death. I was just as terrified as any mother, as if she were a child of mine. I seized her roughly and shook her, frightened she would die there and then, still holding her breath. I was so relieved I was suddenly aware of the snow which seemed to burn under my feet when she started to cry as if she would never stop, so that I felt like covering her with kisses. She had her small plump arms around my neck, calling out in the midst of her tears 'Mommy, Mommy' as we stood on the path between two high banks of snow, in the swirling smoke of wind and snow. When we reached the door of Numa's house, we almost tripped over Assunta,

188

who seemed to be crawling on her knees like a frightened mouse.

In the light of the acetylene lamp our shadows were very tall, reaching the ceiling. We all looked around counting how many we were, everyone looking to see if their own families were safely there.

The last to arrive was Norma, who came carrying on her back, as a man would do, her old semi-paralyzed mother-in-law. Even in the glare of the acetylene lamp the old lady wasn't ashamed of crying without restraint, like a child, and she kept on saying 'she's a saint, a real saint'. Norma sat down, folded her hands on her lap, with a look on her face as if to say 'Well, well, at last I seem to have done something right', but she remained silent. No one was missing. We felt we ought to recite the Rosary three times. Santa's eyes were still full of fear. I thought 'It isn't even Friday, and she's only ever seen out of the house on Fridays'. No one felt sleepy any more, and in any case, before long the men had to go back to see to the animals in their sheds. Rachelina said she would go and put on a pan of coffee.

When dawn came, later than usual, we went out to see what things were like. The whole village, although it was hidden under snow drifts was nevertheless still there, safe and sound. The sky was pale grey, you could even see the snow-covered mountain; and it had stopped snowing. Over the phone the news came of the incredible depth of the avalanche which had descended on the other village. Many people were caught in their sleep. Fausto the postman had lost his wife and little girl, while he escaped unharmed, – he had found himself safe and sound in his bed, while the rest of his house had been swept away. 'It was just after midnight', he said, 'and the wife, who had some kind of premonition or fear, I don't know, asked me if it wouldn't be better to bring the little girl into our bed. I said yes, so she went towards the little one's bed, and was already holding the child in her arms when everything went blank. I heard something like a very loud clap of thunder which shattered all the windows, and I felt as if hundreds of snow-balls were hitting me. Instinctively I hid under the blankets. When it was over, I called and called. . .' He was weeping while he told his story. They will find them clinging to each other under the snow.

More news came confirming or correcting details of the first. The avalanche which hit the village was not 30 but 35 metres deep. And how many died? At present, said the policeman gravely, there are no official figures yet on the disaster. But no one who didn't actually see it would believe . . . it came down over the big wall crushing a row of houses. Had it bounded over once more it would have destroyed another row of houses causing a hundred deaths.

Avalanches usually came hurtling down from the same height, starting from about 1800 metres up. I pictured the isobars on maps. Our mountain, the most terrifying of all, rises to far above the 1800 metres curve, and yet it had not moved. It must have been the cold which had saved us that night. A hundred metres further up, at that height, the temperature is lower, maybe by just one degree, and the snow hadn't given way, but had clung to the slopes. On our 1800 metre line there are larches and the larches had done the trick, they had blocked the snow there while elsewhere it had come crashing down.

'It's not your theory which has saved us but our holy wood. . .'

'It's got nothing to do with woods, holy or otherwise; if the avalanche had begun at the top of the mountain it would have taken the wood with it, and I still maintain that it's a matter of temperature. I'm telling you that one degree more or less makes all the difference.'

'What's all this rubbish about degrees of frost – don't try that one on me . . . I wasn't born yesterday. I know every inch of that mountain and I'm telling you it's the wood that did it.'

So we remained uncertain if we owed our lives to one degree more of frost, to the holy wood or to Providence, as the women maintained, and they always have the last word.

Meanwhile we looked at her – our mountain – which, were it not for the mist would be towering above us. Then after a long silence Numa took out his watch from his waistcoat pocket and asked, in a loud voice, if it was slow or not.

Later (it was already night) they told us the names of those who had been buried beneath the avalanche. Bodies of mothers, husbands, of strong men, of young boys, of young girls.

On the avalanche, hard, firm, soiled with earth, torn tree trunks and broken branches, people were weeping for their dead. The rescue team were digging vertical shafts to reach down to the houses buried in the snow. By the light of their lamps they consulted maps, took measurements. They had the whole place mapped out centimetre by centimetre, they knew precisely where to dig through the layers of compacted snow to reach the crushed kitchen, the child's bed. If only they could find uncrushed bodies which had only lacked air, bodies in which the heart had passed from sleep to death as if from an incurable mortal weariness.

But even bad news is like winter, you soon get used to it. If there is talk of deaths, we all want to know at once how many, five here, nine there. The excitement of the night and the different excitement of the following morning (as if death were satisfied for the moment and would leave us in peace, at least for a while) we took ourselves off to the inn; we drank wine and grappa. Someone said the usual kind of thing – life is a lottery, and someone else, one who had no head for drink, said that had he known he would have carried his wife right into the path of the avalanche; and he laughed at this more than anyone. Our number is not up yet, but in other villages their number has come up, in this game the one who loses wins (and they aren't even relatives of ours, possibly one or two but only distant relations).

We drank wine even over lunch; the women talked about Our Lady who had really given us a sign that we were under her protection. Let them say whatever they like.

We hardly stopped to drink a mouthful of coffee so that we could return to the inn. They are depressing, these women with their black scarves on their heads. Someone brought out a mouth-organ, it was months since we had had any music. We started to sing and dance, we men together, arms linked over our broad shoulders, swaying this way then that, beating time with our nailed boots, happy to be dancing like bears.

Plinio Martini

From *Aunt Domenica's Funeral*   translated and adapted by
                                                  Raffaella Ferrari and June Salmons

Now the pinewood coffin of Aunt Domenica, white in the sun, was being swallowed by the open doors of the church. Marco saw it through the wide circle of the confraternity, with the priest officiating in great solemnity. *Tunc acceptabis sacrificium iustitiae, oblationes et holocausta.* In the incense-filled half-light beneath the arch of the nave, while Marco was still outside lost in memories, the chanting no longer drifted away in the outside air, full of the roar of the streams swollen by the thaw, as they plunged into the gorges, but gained strength and vigour. It was a choir of peasant voices, used to finding their individual and collective short cuts through the ancient Gregorian chant as if it had been a maze of mountain tracks. Aunt Domenica was lying so still in the coffin, black stockinged feet pointing forward, her minute body clothed in black, Rosary wound round her hands, her pale face asleep and on her head the kerchief she used to wear to Mass. Borne on the shoulders of four nephews, Aunt Domenica was now being engulfed in that chant and in that dim light, which she would have recognized at once, were she able to remember that she had been alive. But now she entered for different incensings, different prayers, during which she would be taken into the presence of God, His angels *offerentes eam in conspectu Altissimi, eam*, that is, the fair pure soul of His handmaiden now called by the solemn Latin name of *Dominica*. During her life on this poor earth, so full of petty acts of great malice which hurt even the purest of heart, she was usually known as 'Aunt pious ejaculation' because of her habit, during the Religious Instruction classes, of teaching and exhorting her pupils to recite those short prayers such as 'Sweet Heart of Jesus we implore make us lovely more and more.' And what did 'make us lovely' mean? These pious ejaculations, Aunt Domenica explained, and rightly so, thought Marco, came from the Latin *iaculare* (or *iaculari*?) to throw. Anyway, they are like arrows sent speeding to the heart of Jesus, the Madonna and the saints, to obtain the grace so necessary for our daily needs, and if that grace were not forthcoming, so be it, the pious ejaculation is, in any case, bound up with its own goodly bundle of indulgences. These, in the words of the theologians, mean 'the remission of the temporal

191

punishment owing to God for sins committed after Baptism, and which had already been forgiven. These indulgences were granted, not as part of the Sacrament of Penance, but by Lawful Authority, applying the Treasury of the Church, to the faithful who fulfil the required conditions'. Aunt Domenica could not only recite by heart the definition, but she explained each one of these esoteric words at great length so that each of her pupils could fully understand their meaning. It was therefore a good thing to recite these prayers on every conceivable occasion – it cost so little to say them. When you stop at a shrine along a mountain path so that angelic hands would frighten and drive away any snakes; when you go into the cattle shed to see to the cow to avoid being clumsy and upsetting the pail of fresh milk, or when you start to sow a field in order that the potatoes will grow well even if the sowing has been done when the moon is on the wane; again, when you begin to reap even the little hay on a rough mountain meadow, and it doesn't matter if it's only half a basketful (but even if you pray, it wouldn't have any more time to grow, the usual impertinent child found in every class would remark: be quiet, be quiet, she would say, we'll soon finish the catechism class, and then, if you are good, I'll tell you a little story. This long awaited story was almost always about a dead man who returned to life to bear witness to the bliss or the terror of life after death. Now she knew all about it herself).

Purified seventy years earlier by the waters of Baptism, Aunt Domenica had gone out of that same church to face her life as an industrious ant. Just one of the many in the anthill, always busy in the meadows and woods, gathering hay, chestnuts, potatoes, turnips, wood and straw, collecting, piling up and taking away to put into lofts, cellars and haylofts, with no other thought in her mind than her holy fear of God and the need to work incessantly, to making ends meet. Marco remembered her at Sonlerto, a tiny figure, on her thin legs and shod in large felt boots, which seemed to make her waddle as she went striding along the many paths which led from the hamlet to the open country and the surrounding woods: she led the way, followed by Aunt Maria, her younger sister, who also waddled along, poor dear, then came Marco. All three carried basket, rake or scythe on their shoulders, according to the work to be done that day. Now she lay still, as if saying that nothing matters in this world except being alive.

Marco's father used to send him to Sonlerto every summer to help his two aunts with the haymaking (grandfather, over eighty years old, would sit on the terrace mending baskets and rakes, or making new ones). And it was at Sonlerto that he had met Giovanna. It was the year when Hitler's madness came to its tragic end and all Europe listened, hardly believing, as the war ended on the islands of the Pacific.

It frightened Marco to think that nearly twenty years had passed since then, eighteen that summer, to be precise. A long time in the life of a man, yet only a short time in the life of the valley, if you thought of the changes which had taken place. If they were beginning to alter the face of the village and the way of life of the people, Sonlerto was still two and a half hours walk away along the mule track whose stones, because of the passage of men and animals, were worn smoother than the pebbles in the river: setting out along that track meant moving back in time towards an ancient world beyond history, where life was still governed by the rising and setting of the sun, and men's labour was not paid in coin. News of great events, eagerly awaited by millions of human beings, reached here days late, and had little impact, as if they lacked reality and importance, serving only for the gossiping of Uncle Clement, who every so often received a parcel of old newspapers; back there you were part of the immutable cycles of the seasons, and clouds were more important than news of war and peace, because rain might fall on the fields piled high with hay.

Not that Marco, who was only just sixteen, was able to appreciate the peace of Sonlerto and the religious meditations of Aunt Domenica, who among the humble people of that land had found her rightful place as a kind of deaconess, watching carefully over the salvation of others. He would have preferred to spend his holidays in the village where it would have been easier to find the company of people of his own age; in Sonlerto in summer there were only old folk, women and children, in all about seventy people, perhaps less, because the men and boys over fourteen years of age were all away, either in the mountains or working down in the village. So Marco, too old to play with the children, was not yet old enough to be accepted by the only two young men of the hamlet, and remained, alone and miserable, lost in vain dreams of love, as are, or rather were, most boys of his age. He had brought with him for rainy days a school edition of Leopardi's poetry, with a commentary by Biondolillo, and he would read, sighing deeply, of phantom Silvias or Nerinas; in the same way he re-read in an anthology of Latin poets *Passer, deliciae meae puellae*, imagining a Romantic Catullus dreaming of his chaste Lesbia, lover of sparrows.

The sound of a very different kind of Latin, the *Dies irae*, woke Marco from his reveries with a start. The priest gave a fierce warning look to the restless group of altar boys and then solemnly seated himself near the lectern. Only then did the congregation sit down, but Giovanna waited a few minutes before sitting like the rest and finding herself on the other side of the central aisle, a few benches in front of Marco, turned to glance at him. This time Marco returned her look, his gaze lingering on her breasts and hips until she sat down, *Teste David cum Sibylla*, and fortunately they were the only two who knew and remembered what he now recalled with desire, there before the coffin of his poor Aunt Domenica, who all those years ago had played no small role in the love affair between the two young people; and who knows how much pain it had caused her?

193

News of Giovanna's arrival had been announced, one evening in the square, after the recitation of the Rosary, by Leonilde, with all the self-importance of a gossip telling such unusual news to her surprised and somewhat jealous friends: a girl from Locarno was coming to help her, a girl called Giovanna, fifteen years old, the only child of an accountant who had married a distant relation of hers, and the girl was at a convent school. From Locarno. Who knows how dull she would find Sonlerto? In Locarno they had tarmac roads, while we only had cows. And stones. That girl would return home at once. How clever she must be if she attended a convent school. And what a beautiful name, Giovanna, a truly Christian name, we would never have dreamt of giving it to our girls, always Angela, Mariangela, Anna and Maria. But things were changing, Alma, Nives, Stella, Mara. What names! 'Is she pretty?' Marco asked suddenly. And as Leonilde, obviously worried about answering with an uncertain and hesitant 'yes' waited a moment, she was interrupted by the quick and ready answer of Aunt Domenica: 'Wait and see. Does she really have to be so pretty to keep you company? You must take people as they are.' But he had already associated that name with all his dreams, all his hopes, and his fervent prayers each night as he went to bed not to fall into temptation. For of course Aunt Domenica used to read out to Marco such heartfelt exhortations as these, though they were intended for women (to think that Marx and Freud were writing at the time!). 'Don't you feel every evening a kind of oppression at the thought of the sinister silence in which you'll shortly find yourself? Your bed is like a tomb, your sleep will cut you off from the world . . . the eyes of God are watching you. Doesn't all this frighten you?'

Desired and feared in this way, Giovanna arrived at Sonlerto, and Marco unexpectedly met her one day at noon, under the dark archway between two houses, where it was impossible for two people to pass without touching; he heard rather than saw her, was aware of the perfume of the scented soap she used, an unusual thing in those days; he saw against the light her slim figure dressed in an unusually short skirt – obviously she had grown since last summer. You must be Giovanna. You must be Marco. They went out into the light, she standing a step higher so he could see what she looked like, her brown legs, the striped skirt of faded rose, a short-sleeved blouse which seemed to him supremely elegant, though almost certainly it had been brought to Sonlerto like the rest of her wardrobe because it was old. No one can say when two young people meet each other, how long are the moments during which their eyes meet and they measure each other, in an anguish of mutual shyness which will never come again. Neither could Marco remember what they said to each other as he took her back to Leonilde's house, where he stayed to listen respectfully to her chatterings and her silences, the rest of the world forgotten, until Aunt Domenica arrived saying 'But Marco, what about our hay?'

The haymaking, in fact, went on with that resolute industry which the mountain peasants had to exert at harvest time. Although the meadow land around the hamlet was vast and crossed by a hundred paths branching out and merging again, which became less and less visible as you went further from the hamlet, and finally disappeared in the woods, the differing times when the hay was ready to be cut forced the peasants to work on neighbouring meadows at the same times. Therefore you were likely to see them all grouped together mowing in the same area. Something that pleased Marco very much at that time. All his thoughts and dreams were centred on Giovanna – Giovanna in the green countryside of Sonlerto, that vast and varied land, divided by little walls, lines of flowering ash trees, grassy hillocks or banks as we called them, with hazels and other shrubs, and the wood all around, so that you couldn't make out if the wood stretched its leafy branches into the meadow or the fields were invading the dark secrets of the wood, creating in it small glades, invitations to dreams of pastoral love. Marco never stopped inventing ways and means of meeting her, helped not only by the naivety of his aunts and the varied contours of the land itself, but also by the girl's own keenness to find out where he was and so appear to him in the least expected places. This was something which Marco did not know and couldn't even suspect. In his restless longing he would tear off the petals of daisies – 'She loves me, she loves me not'. He was doing this during one of their meetings and ended up with the disappointing 'She loves me not', when the girl laughed merrily and said 'But of course she loves you!', and it was then they kissed for the first time, lips touching lips behind a benevolent hazel tree.

He had seen her another time sitting on one of those great boulders found in the valley, which had been covered with a layer of earth during the old times of dire poverty, so that it became a tiny field yielding a few handfuls of hay, almost always burned by the sun. Giovanna was up there and she called out to him to wait for her to come down, she wouldn't be a moment, and she did come down, slowly, and he was able to gaze at her from below, seeing her thighs and even that strip of white which only just hid the ultimate, inconfessable object of his desires – may God forgive me this sin already recognized and now becoming closer and more disturbing – until the girl came down alongside him. Then they put down their baskets and joined their no longer hesitant lips, their bodies trembling, a sin not only of thought, but of words and deeds. What sighs and shared eagerness were there for the fulfilment of their desire, especially for him, with the girl there in the flesh beside him.

Sonlerto had its own little square of ancient grey stones, inhabited by lizards and covered with lichens and moss. It was no larger than the drawing-room of a well-to-do house; enclosed by the chapel with its belltower beside it: by Uncle Clement's house, an ancient three-storied building, now used as a barn, inexplicable in its height and fortress-like appearance, in its windows like archers' loopholes. Alongside this, completing the quadrangle stood an almost prehistoric cowshed, separated from Aunt Domenica's house by a narrow lane.

Three other lanes opened out into the square and were joined to the little roads which led to other houses and to the fields in such a way that anyone walking, even blindfold, in the seemingly haphazard web of paths, lanes, arches and narrow alleyways which formed the hamlet's network of roads, would sooner or later, and without realizing it, end up there. Between the chapel and the belltower beside it, from the hidden door of the room used by the priest on his visits to the hamlet, was a stairway at an angle, which led down to a courtyard, a smaller square just three steps higher than the square itself, which was roughly paved with cobblestones: a second stairway also at an angle, led down from Uncle Clement's house, and a third went from the fortress, so that the square became a miniature amphitheatre on whose steps all the inhabitants could sit.

This happened every night, except that the small children with a last sign of the cross on their foreheads had been put into their cots on mattresses stuffed with beech leaves. At dusk the Rosary bell rang, giving the awaited signal, indicating that it was time to stop work, and calling the handful of inhabitants to the chapel for night prayers. In the chapel, as in the other houses of the hamlet, there was no electric light, and two wax candles burned, candles which gave little light, but whose smell pervaded the immense peace of that place. Usually it was Aunt Domenica, that saintly soul, who began the recitation of the Rosary, a right which was implicitly conferred upon her because of the religious instruction she gave the children: that is, unless some impertinent girl got in first to get it over more quickly. The fact was that as well as the Rosary, which she recited with devout care, Aunt Domenica would always add a whole series of other prayers: an *Our Father, Hail Mary and Glory be* for a good harvest, for the sick, for those far away, for the dying, for the souls in Purgatory, for sinners, for our benefactors, for those who had harmed us, in reparation for those who blasphemed and for those who commit sins of the flesh, prayers that the young might remain virtuous, – on and on. Then, in her thin, shrill voice she would intone:

> *Mary, throned above*
> *In the starry city*
> *Cast us in thy pity*
> *But one look of love.*
> *If our sorrows sore*
> *Fail to touch thy mind*
> *Then we are resigned*
> *Shouldst thou look no more.*

Marco, recalling to mind the two verses vaguely reminiscent of Metastasio's poetry, remembered having understood only much later that it was the pity which the Madonna was required to feel which explained the 'But one look' of the first verse. And with these memories in his heart he turned his eyes to the coffin where the admirer of this and other hymns no longer heard anything, not even the *Dies irae*, and he offered her a sad and loving posthumous tribute: *Tantus labor non sit cassus* – the work of Aunt Domenica of course.

The singing over (that of the two verses of the hymn, not of the *Dies irae* which having begun in a resounding tone fitting for such a great text, was now being sung in a noticeably less solemn way and would end in a final rushed mumble), the people of Sonlerto went out into the square, whose stones in the approaching twilight were gradually losing the heat they had absorbed during the daytime. This was the best time of the day, a time of rest and of the comforting nearness of other people, the well deserved and long awaited pleasure of leaning one's body against the stone, seeking contentedly the most comfortable position, savouring the warmth of the stones, a pleasure more exquisite and intimate because of the cool air which came down from the smoking mouth of the glacier high above. The talk, except in very special circumstances, consisted of monotonous remarks about the hay, the weather, or rather the precarious balance and complicated links between the weather and the peasants' work: cooler weather would have been welcome in Sonlerto but not higher up: they pondered on the future, remembering proverbs as old as Methuselah, and they would quote the almanac found in everyone's house, which tried to predict the weather of the year and give advice to the peasants on the right time for sowing and reaping: but in the end everything was entrusted to Providence, with the usual resignation of the poor, and given the seal of approval of Aunt Domenica. But the talk could also be about the war, discussed as if it were something unreal, about emigration, remembering people who could still have been with them, but instead were lost beyond the seas, who knows where.

Giovanna and Marco would sit together in silence in a corner, a right they had been given on the first evening, kindly granted by the pious women because they were of the same age and both at grammar schools. Taking advantage of the dark they held hands in a silent dialogue of hand claspings, sighs and Marco's tentative caressing of her knees and his attempts to go further; her gentle denials, followed by tacit permission to regain lost ground. . . Marco was already resigned to think of himself as in a permanent state of mortal sin, and despaired of ever being able to find himself repenting with 'perfect contrition' which means 'the greatest of sorrow, because mortal sin is the greatest of evils', of his intense desire to commit mortal sin, to possess Giovanna. That same desire which, after eighteen years, he experienced with the same intensity as he watched her stand up for the Preface of the Mass. No one, looking at her, could believe that she too had chosen to dress in black, her face enclosed in the suffocating wimple, covered by the austere and forbidding veil of the Sisters of Menzingen. Everyone stood up, unwillingly, thought Marco as he glanced at his watch, but then the church resounded with a *Vere dignum et iustum est* sung as in solemn Mass, and the pattern of the three notes of the Gregorian chant

197

brought back to him the echoing walls of ancient monasteries and faith in all its purity: notwithstanding war and famine, the prejudices and fears which guide the hand of the oppressors and bend the oppressed into submission, notwithstanding death here present in the remains of Thy servant Domenica, it is very meet and right that we should at all times and in all places give thanks unto Thee, O Lord, Holy Father, Almighty, Everlasting God, together with Thy Angels and Archangels, for the gift of life ever renewed. But the Sanctus was lifeless, weak and hurried. The sun had remained outside, and Giovanna, when she knelt down this time, didn't turn round. . .

Giovanni Bonalumi

From *Chestnut Trees*   translated and adapted by
                                        Raffaella Ferrari and June Salmons

When you think of it, it's odd how a person can die leaving so little behind, sometimes only a name. Who is likely to think of Rosaria now, who will remember her? Perhaps her mother, although she had banished her from her heart; or Karl about whom I know absolutely nothing, except that now, perhaps more than ever, he has to watch out for those who keep him on a leash and can ruin him at a moment's notice.

Karl can have had no reason to kill Rosaria. If he did it, I'll bet they made him do it. Rosaria was not the gossiping type. But you know what life is like. She might have dropped some compromising remark, and they didn't think twice about it.

But I'm only guessing. It's more likely that Rosaria, coming to her senses, had kicked them all out. Blackmailing them, of course. What I can remember of Rosaria doesn't really help to make things clearer. These memories are too ordinary and naive, all more or less centred around her possessions, her house.

What's the point of thinking about it? All those discussions, for instance, on what she should call the house. In the end she decided on *Chestnut Trees*, because, as she explained, chestnuts are rather special trees, a kind of symbol – she must have learnt that at school – they are typical of all or most of the Ticino. Except that in the grounds of the villa there were only two chestnut trees, both pretty old and decrepit. Obviously that name, which meant nothing to me, fascinated her. In the same way she loved those cups and tankards painted in the colours of our flag which, seen like that in a row, are an eyesore. Karl had had a flagpole put up in a corner of the garden, but then he had never bothered to fly even a rag from it.

She used to complain about this every now and then. 'Next summer', she said, 'I'll see to it myself'. But then with all that coming and going of people in the house, time went by and nothing was done about it.

'Why on earth are you so keen about it?' I once asked her.

198

We were standing up there last year, towards the end of October, and the vines already like a tangle of dead twigs: the evening air was as soft as silk. She pointed towards the islands.

'On that piece of land over there as far as Ronco, how many of those villas do you think belong to local people?'

'Only a few I'd imagine.'

'You're right, hardly any. Now perhaps you understand what I mean.' I wanted to reply that a flag changes nothing, but I was loath to spoil such a perfect evening arguing about it.

I remember her satisfaction when one day she told me that someone had painted a slogan in very large letters on a wall in Orselina, not far from the cemetery: GIVE TICINO BACK TO THE TICINESI. It was during the time when a small group of people from Ascona had launched a kind of 'Liberation front'. 'Liberation from what? It's utter nonsense. The people I know', I told her, 'if there's anything they regret it's having sold too soon, or occasionally, too late. Then there are a lot of people who are annoyed because they have nothing left to sell. The others, the majority, and I count myself among them, just look on. Not that they are less disgusting than the rest',

'Why disgusting? You know I don't like it when you talk like that. If my friends heard you saying such things they would do everything they could to stop me inviting you here.'

'They'll find out soon enough, don't you worry!' I'd let that slip out because, as the saying goes, I have a big mouth. It was also a bit of boasting, to show off. But don't worry, I'm not the type to go looking for trouble with strangers, German or not. If a man behaves like a human being, that's good enough for me, and that's that. I couldn't stomach those people. Yet I'd been careful not to offend them, especially because associating with them, or so I fancied, might turn out to my advantage.

For them I was 'the painter', that is, a mildly eccentric type, maybe even with a bit of talent. Anyway this seemed to be the opinion of one of that crowd, a certain von Schultern, whom they called the Baron. He said that if I'd been a bit more crafty I would have made a very good naif painter.

'But if I were that', I said once, but just like that, without malice, 'how would it go with being a naif?'

He burst out laughing, that big mouth of his open so you could have counted every single gold tooth in it.

I am sure I could have palmed off at least a couple of paintings onto him, and certainly not for the starvation price which is all I get from my usual customers in the square.

They also called me 'the expert'; they called me 'their guide' when I took them to some open-air restaurant in the country where, with any luck, you can still eat trout fresh from the river.

199

However, I'd never set foot in their houses. Verboten. Just once they'd invited me to a place belonging to an acquaintance of theirs, a beautiful house called *Albatros*. The owner was already pretty tight and was swanning around from one group to the other, grabbing hold of the arms of the lovely ladies who didn't bat an eyelid. There were at least fifty people there, and the champagne was flowing. They spoke German mingled with English and Swiss German. There were even some people speaking our dialect. Lawyers, business men from Ascona and Locarno.

They say that nine times out of ten you can recognize a painter by the way he dresses. You could tell what those people did for a living by looking at their faces. There was something fox-like about them, they were always on their guard. They bowed to the ladies, kissed their hands in a manner which was at the same time attentive and so fatuous that you couldn't bear to look. Then I heard a name being mentioned. That name meant something to me as if I'd seen it in a newspaper headline. Sardoni. A man was picking his way through the crowd and I knew immediately that it was him, the guest I'd seen that night at Rosaria's, whom everyone, from the moment he'd entered the room, had called by his pet name Pupo. Just Pupo. This Pupo, I remember, while shaking hands had looked me up and down as if he were inspecting a chair. Without a smile or a word. Then, during the course of the evening, I suddenly realized that it was all a sham. Every time he took a sip from his glass, every time he moved away from a little group, he threw a glance in my direction, then looked away immediately as soon as I made a move towards him. Maybe you are just imagining things, I said to myself. You don't like the man. So what? Finally as I moved among the various groups of people, I found myself behind him.

The man seemed to make an effort to swallow a last word in German, then started to speak English. As he hadn't even turned round this was probably a coincidence too, but I felt he was enjoying it – as if he'd left me behind, just like a Jaguar overtaking a Mini, but he didn't know that I have an odd gift for the English language. I can guess the meaning even of the most difficult words. And while he lorded it over that crowd – that's important too, circumstances and the like, when you are discussing something – while he held forth about weapons, and in the same breath about Trieste, I could see in my mind's eye lorries and wagons on their way to that port, crammed full with machine-guns and bazookas.

It's true that the greatest bastards are those you least suspect: local folk, your own townspeople. I knew little or nothing of Sardoni: only that he'd been suspected of arms dealing at the time of Chombe, that he was filthy rich. Things I'd read in the papers but which hadn't meant anything to me at the time. One thing was certain now though: that he disliked me even more than I disliked him; that at his first sight of me he must have thought 'the sooner I get rid of this chap the better'.

So I decided to mention him to Rosaria, and she shrugged her shoulders and was annoyed, although she pretended it was all a big joke. 'All I know', she said 'is that he is all right, an army officer, a lawyer, a respectable person. If the papers talk about him, it's nothing but jealousy'. This happened in August last year, a few weeks before my last visit to *Chestnut Trees*. One evening there were more people there than usual, von Schultern, Sardoni and the rest of that crowd, and the conversation had turned to the last war. I was listening absentmindedly and a bit sorry because von Schultern, only a minute before, had mentioned my work in front of everybody, and I was hoping the conversation would develop in that direction. . . Just then someone had fished out a Wehrmacht cross from his coat pocket and had swung it in mid-air, dangling from a piece of ribbon. God knows why.

'Heil', some of them shouted. I had got the impression that more or less all of them had spent the war behind the lines, in the occupation zones. Now, one after the other, they told of their adventures, quite calmly, just like people who know they are evoking memories that, after so many years, sound like pure fiction. Then one, who until then hadn't said a word, and was sitting slightly apart from the rest, intervened to say that it was sickening to waste time over useless memories when only two days ago the German television had spent two hours on a rat, a traitor like General Stauffenberg. 'Richtig gesagt', many of them cried out. And immediately, like a drum roll, 'Eine Schweinerei!'

Everyone had suddenly become very excited.

'Television in Europe is all in the hands of the Reds', continued the man who had started it all, 'even the little stations like yours, eh Pupo?'

Sardoni made a gesture of resignation. 'You're telling me! It's disgusting. But let them get on with it. One day they'll get what they deserve, just as they have in other places.'

I was keeping my head down, as if to hide; I didn't want to be dragged into the discussion, but the voice of the self-styled judge got me by calling my name. 'And you, what do you think about all this?'

'Me?' I muttered, talking at random, as if someone had stolen my tongue. 'Me, I never watch television'.

They sniggered.

'Self-possessed as usual, our dear painter!' The voice this time belonged to Sardoni. It sounded rather sharp, more and more annoyed.

'Speaking among friends, among people who understand each other at a glance, I am sorry to admit that to be quite frank I find all this dodging of issues like a bad smell under my nose.'

'I get the message', I said to myself while he was talking. 'If it's my head you're after, you can have it.'

I felt very calm, but suddenly terribly tired, incapable of uttering anything, not even a single appropriate word.

I looked at Rosaria. She was staring at me, but I knew she wasn't seeing me at all.

'Television. . .', someone started to say. And immediately it was as if that flow of words turned into something concrete, like bricks or planks, behind which I could hide. All I had to do now was wait for a suitable moment to leave.

'What have you got to lose?' I said to myself. And then I remembered von Schultern's money, that half-promise he'd let fall. 'What do I care about money?' I said to myself. But I was still sorry that I wouldn't be seeing him again. Von Schultern could have been very helpful in my career. I was sorry for Rosaria too. After all I was her guest, and Sardoni's slap in the face was partly directed at her too. Ah well, there were two of us to take the blow. Unless . . . at the other end of the room Rosaria had given the signal, and the greedy ones were already trooping towards the buffet. If I really wanted to go, that was the moment. But I had to do it slowly with a certain style, so that no-one would think I'd been forced to leave.

I spent December and part of January in Provence, in a caravan belonging to some painter friends of mine. There, on the edge of the Camargue, we only heard the news on the radio. I learned of the outrage of Piazza Fontana and a whole series of terrorist attacks in Palermo.

We expected a revolution at any moment, and my friends said that after all we were nothing but parasites, sitting there painting, when just a few hundred miles away there were people plotting a terrorist coup d'état.

It was there, a stone's throw from the sea, that I finished my painting. Rosaria had turned out less well than in the original drawing, stiffer perhaps, but all in all, considering it was my first oil portrait, I felt I could almost be pleased with myself.

'It's good', said my friends. They added: 'What a crazy idea, wasting time on a portrait, in a place like this, where the light is so wonderful, has a charm, that back in Switzerland you couldn't begin to imagine what it was like.' I just made up some story to the effect that the painting had to be finished by the time I returned; that it was virtually commissioned.

Back home I started to put together a good stock of drawings, little views ready for my open-air show, as the season was approaching. Every now and then, during that humdrum work of copying from the same model, my thoughts went back to the villa at Contra. The last time I'd been there, a few days after I'd got back, the house had looked empty. There was snow on the vineyard slope and, by the gate which opened onto the garden, there were recent footprints. I went all the way round the hedge, and at one point I saw a man shovelling away the snow to clear a passage near the wood. Suddenly the man thrust the shovel into a pile of snow and lit a cigarette. He turned round just enough for me to recognize him as the gardener. Now I could go. But then it occurred to me to glance at the name printed under the door bell, to see if by any chance they'd changed it. In fact, instead of Miraglia, there was a German name, something like Helfensburg.

I was none the wiser really. Because the name Karl, even supposing this was his name, didn't appear at all, not even the initial. Bastards!, I felt like shouting; lousy bastards! And away I went. The last thing I saw, as I turned round, I remember, was the flagpole, slightly crooked at the top, as if bent by the wind.

'Why do you keep thinking about it?', I said to myself over and over again. No one can do anything about it, and you least of all. They are like tanks, like steam-rollers, they destroy everything wherever they go, not a blade of grass survives. You just think about your work, think about the money you need to buy canvasses, frames and all that. Luckily the weather kept fine, and the warm air encouraged people to go out. So that this time I didn't have to wait until Easter to set up my open-air studio.

First, however, I had to get rid of a whole lot of small paintings, hundreds of drawings. For once Maurilio and Pietrini were still busy with their own work and I was by myself. The first two days, a Saturday and Sunday, I sold a fantastic number of works. Then, one morning, at the beginning of Holy Week, towards eleven o'clock, a chap came along, tall and rather elderly, complete with walking-stick and hat; he looked for a long time at all my stuff, and finally, in flawless German, he said to me: 'Someone has recommended you to me. Of course, I presume for something different from this kind of thing. Why are you hiding it? Bring it along, tomorrow or the day after. And then, if I am interested, I have a little gallery, we could discuss it. . .'

I thought immediately of von Schultern; he must have put in a good word for me. So I was tempted. So the following morning, it was Tuesday, I took a few of my paintings down to the square, five or six, the ones I liked best, and among them my portrait of Rosaria. Not that I was that eager to part with them, but I was interested, very interested to know who that distinguished, scholarly-looking gentleman was.

I waited all day, not at all worried. Feeling somewhat disappointed but in the end a little tired, sick of seeing those people making a bee-line for those things which you could tell at a glance were quite different, not at all the mass-produced stuff.

'He'll come tomorrow', I said to myself. In the meantime I had to take precautions, to let people know, put a little label saying 'sold' on each of those special works. The following morning, I noticed at once that this precaution saved me a lot of explanations.

Midday struck, and there was still no trace of the German with the walking-stick. Suddenly it crossed my mind that it could have been a practical joke; what a fool I'd been to fall for it. And yet I still hoped: I went on like this until five o'clock, when lifting my eyes from my display I saw on the other side of the square, under the arcade, a few shops which had already put on their lights.

Then I suddenly felt sick of the whole thing – all I'd managed to sell all that day was a couple of small pictures – I clapped my hands to let people know I was packing up. There were still quite a few people nosing about, and at that very moment a girl came towards me, tall, jet-black hair and eyes, wearing a long dress to her feet that made her look a bit like an Indian. The girl bent down to look and squatted in front of it.

I started picking up my bits and pieces, and every time I went near her I felt a growing urge to talk to her. 'Do you like it?', I wanted to ask, or something like that. But she had turned round and smiled, her gaze on someone who was standing motionless, a little way off. The man touched the brim of his hat and then he came towards me with an air of assurance, so nonchalant that I suddenly froze, unable to utter a word.

'What did I tell you? This is the real stuff. Congratulations!' And putting a hand on the girl's shoulders: 'This is my niece, you saw how she spotted it straight away?'

The girl muttered something like 'wunderschön' and stood up. I felt her eyes looking at mine; there was a glint in them – a kind of sly wink.

'If you agree, to start with' – the man was facing me, leaning on his cane – 'I'd like to buy the oil portrait and a couple of drawings. After that we'll see. Now it's up to you to tell me what you want for it.'

'About the drawings' – I could hardly speak, my voice was hoarse – 'that's fine, no problem. The portrait. I should have told you at once. I'm sorry, but it's not for sale.'

'Why ever not! I can understand your problem, but if you'll allow me . . . what about two thousand?'

I managed to pull myself together and blurt out, 'No, you must understand, it's not a question of money'.

'If I offered you three thousand, including the drawings.'

'I'm sorry. . .'

'I'm even sorrier and my niece most of all. If you are willing to part with the portrait, naturally I won't stop at two drawings. Please think about it. A chance like this. . .' As he was speaking, he pulled out his wallet and fumbled about in it, obviously put out by my refusal, and pulled out a card. 'This is my telephone number. Get in touch. You can't lose anything by doing that. . .'

No sooner had those two left – she turned round two or three times with a searching look I won't forget for a while – I could have kicked myself. Three thousand francs down the drain. And for what? A whim. What an idiot I'd been!

But as I was picking up the last few paintings and lifted up the portrait of Rosaria from the ground, I suddenly felt different. Elated, like a man who's won a bet. What bet I couldn't have said. But it was an elation that filled me, and that was enough to make me feel I'd done the right thing. Rosaria was coming back home with me. And she, if thoughts can travel through the dark, would have been pleased.

Something was still puzzling me. A silly thing perhaps, but it niggled at me. I couldn't get it out of my mind. So, as soon as I reached home, I rang Irene, a distant cousin of mine who worked in the telephone exchange in Bellinzona.

'Look, Irene', I said to her, 'see if you can trace whose number this is'.

'Is that all?', she said. 'If I find it, will you give me one of your drawings?'

Irene is wonderfully efficient. She called me back at eleven o'clock on the dot at the Bar Gambrinus. 'Is that you, scatterbrain? The number is that of a certain Karl Helfensburg, business representative. Address, a house called *Chestnut Trees*. Got it? Berto, is anything wrong? What's going on? Berto, come on, say something. Why don't you answer?'

Cla Biert — Rhaeto-Romansh

Before the Fruit Is Ripe   translated by John B. Avery

The forest of Cimbrian pines stood silent.

The August sun with its sultry heat sent ripeness coursing through the spiky branches; the sap brimmed over in the cones and the needles dripped with liquid resin.

Heavens, how heady it all smelled!

They had come from over yonder, apparently, from the far slope where the Alpherd had his hut. Not that they could be said to have slipped away stealthily, this boy and girl. No, they were old enough.

But they were not the right age!

They stopped beside the giant pine. They did not speak. They did not say a single word. Their shoe-soles sank into the moss, and the red needles patterned the ground like a costly carpet. That dry branch, now, which poked into them . . . it was just like a sting and seemed to say: 'Not a sound! This is a place where you do as you're told!'

Not a breath of wind.

If even the ants had made a skittering sound . . . but they did not, they too were walking barefoot. Everything walked barefoot in this spot.

Only deep inside the hard folds of the rumpled bark was there something which revealed its presence and would tolerate no interference from anyone outside. That was why the wood stood silent.

And these two also were cowed into silence, for there was a constant and soundless outpouring of this force deep within, which penetrated them through and through.

The whole process was so immense as to escape human hearing.

They had both sunk down into the moss.

The girl pointed across to the scar left by avalanches. The new, young fir-trees were standing close together. They sprang out of the turf or from under boulders and twisted and raised their hardened, crooked plumes. For them the avalanche held no fears. They bowed their curved backs, they yielded and laughed to themselves. But once the steep slopes high above had shrugged off their burden, once the green went climbing up the mountainside, then they, too, lifted their heads and held up to the light their flowers which shed a golden mist, as though they were so many candlesticks. The boy took her hand and lightly caressed it with his fingertips. He sank his fingers into her black hair and gazed at her. His lips were thirsty, thirsty for her.

The great pines, however, which overshadowed them were mounting guard. Now and again their cone-laden heads nodded heavily. They understood the quiet answer breathed back from all around, the calm of immense maturity. They said to themselves: those rocky cliffs over there where there is a constant battle with the sun . . . they are stark naked and have to submit to gloating, brazen looks. But we are different, we are expectant. Then they would bow to one another and say: 'This is an important matter, this fact that we are expectant! We are proud of it!' Countless hopes, testimonies and promises went whispering away through the trees.

The girl was still looking up at the tree-tops, listening to what they were saying. She could understand them.

The old and dishevelled pines raised their crooked fingers and wagged them in warning at the young saplings: 'You there, not so fast!'

And the young trees made no answer, because they were filled with awe when their elders brandished their stiff limbs:

'Woe betide any of you who isn't quiet while your mothers are expectant! Have a care, anyone who is cheeky!'

Not even a bird made a sound. No one dared.

That was why she turned to the boy and said pleadingly:

'Darling, we mustn't. We must wait; just as the trees have waited which are now proud to be expectant.'

But he did not believe all this and had not heard what the trees were saying. All he saw was her face and the black eyebrows above her eyes and also those cheeks which made him want to eat them.

And then he gazed away at the sunbeams as they played amid the branches and enjoyed twining themselves about the bluish stems. They cast fantastic shadows on the stony ground: animals stirred there, ha! and men smoking huge pipes, and even old women waving their arms, and in among these, great black, slithering snakes and multi-headed dragons with razor-sharp crests. Oh! how they must be laughing, those sunbeams! And when the clouds came by, they were away in a flash and their patterns vanished; just like the sharp little shadows, cast by the girl's eyelashes on her eyes, those eyes which glowed like black, sunkissed cherries. Then suddenly, back they came again and went on with their game. Those sunbeams were at their merriest when the wind came and moved all the twigs. At such times, they would go wild with delight and have fun even with the stiff old trees, which could not help a slight dancing of their stiffened limbs.

The sunbeams said: 'Ah, we have seen what it is to be young and the wind has even heard, but the old are deaf.' Then they darted down and played in her dark hair, slid over her face and bare arms and set her eyes aglow. The boy felt them streaming right through him, making his blood pound through his veins and leaving him faint with thirst.

Oh, how they were laughing again, those sunbeams, now that he had suddenly slipped an arm round her. Hey! how they ran and danced with glee! Come on, nearer, nearer, still nearer! We'll colour her lips red and her teeth white as marble, till they shine, till they cannot help but bite into her lips, till the blood flows.

★

But then, this girl who had understood the language of the trees glanced up at some cones ripening right on the tip of the topmost branch. No, no, they would have no cause to grieve, not those.

'What are you looking at?' he asked.

She pointed upwards.

'Do you want me to get them for you, then, those four at the top, eh?'

She shook her head but he had meanwhile stood up and now said: 'I'll climb to the very top and throw them down for you, wait and see if I don't, but then you mustn't cry any more, eh?'

This particular pine was unkempt, tousled by wind and storm, and with splintered stumps of bough where lightning had struck it. Near the base, it patiently bore a misshapen bough which jutted out and up, like a child which had lost its way. This branched into withered shoots which jutted up sideways. From a distance it looked for all the world like the giant antler of some stag.

She hid her face in her hands: 'No, don't go! They're still unripe, we cannot eat them.'

And she looked up fearfully, up to where the forking branches separated and tapered upwards, up to those clusters of twigs. There the four cones hung out into space, swaying menacingly: 'Woe to anyone who risks coming right up here!'

'Don't go, you'll be dashed to pieces! The pine doesn't want you to, can't you hear?'

He could not hear.

The roots, like well fed serpents, writhed out from the trunk and snaked down round the stones. He tried to get a grip on the bole, which was hard and gnarled like a rock and so stout that four men could not have encompassed it. His fingertips sank into the bark, dragged away slivers and scored it like knife-cuts till the resin ran. He lost his hold and fell to the ground. His eyes shot hatred and fury at the tree and fire at her. Like a cat, he dug his nails into the bark, flattened his face against the trunk, twisted up and up, little by little, and reached out his hand towards the first branch.

'Come back,' she begged, 'can't you hear what the forest is saying?' 'Wicked thief . . . thief.' The echo came from back up the valley, as though from a great distance: 'thief'. Forbidding and uncanny.

Then clouds came scurrying over the mountain, the sun disappeared, dark shadows swooped over the landscape, black patches moved and glided over the crests only to make way for others even larger, even heavier, which blotted out the colours as they advanced up the valley. But the boy climbed on from branch to branch, from one foothold to the next. When he arrived up where the branches divided, the clusters of twigs grew more densely and he found it harder to keep going. With one hand he forced a way through, but the springy twigs lashed his face again and again. Under his feet, he could feel that the branches no longer supported him safely. They were growing whippy. The bark was wafer-thin and the sap made everything as slippery as a piece of glass.

He slipped! but quickly grabbed a branch and steadied himself. A moment's hesitation and he would have fallen without a chance. He was gasping and had to pause to recover.

Down below him and seemingly very far away, he could see the girl through the twigs, lying on her back in the moss with her hands under her head. And didn't she seem to be amused by that impudent breeze which filled her skirt and made it flutter and lift? There was a smile on her face. She didn't even try to stop it. She enjoyed the wind and let it stroke her bare legs. One innocent hand moved across her blouse and bared her breast. She let the sun kiss this rose-tinted dawn. Then she tossed back her head and her arms.

High above, he gave a powerful heave, the twigs parted and he squeezed up and through, taking no notice of the rents the branches were tearing in trousers and shirt. Just twice his own height now and he would have made it!

The top began to sway to and fro. With each tug he gave, the twigs shook to the very tip and so did the four pine-cones hanging out at the end. The girl no longer dared to look up, because the wind was rising now, at first gently and then more fiercely with sudden squalls. Through the whole forest there ran a weird sound which grew ever louder and turned into a wild, straining roar. The trees started to heel over to one side or another and the topmost plumes whistled in the wind. To the girl it seemed that the trees were growing feverish, calling for help, weeping for one another, scowling and making strange threats against this black-hearted thief perched high atop one of their number. Indeed, he was even at that moment stretching out his hand to the twig with the four cones on it, but the tree-top bent, the branches writhed and whirled. Gusts of wind hurled him to and fro. The whole tree fought in self-defence, waiting only for the right moment to heave this enemy down off its back in its terrible rage. Even the black clouds reaching out above the crags were heavy with menace as they heaped and gathered above the main valley.

The steep, grassy slopes grew dark, the bad weather was already on this side of the mountains and the cliffs showed black in the rain; distant thunder rumbled across the sky, and the storm poured down out of the side-valleys.

Now!

Now his hand closed round the cones!

A flash in the distance; the lightning had just struck high on the mountain-ridge. With a sharp tug, he snapped the cones one after another off the twig. Dammit! They stuck to his hand as though they would never let go, as though they intended to grow on it.

Thump, thump, thump. The cones fell through the branches, landed with a thud on the grass, rolled over a root and came to rest.

Dead.

In the sky, all hell was let loose. Anyone would have thought the rock-faces were splitting and shattering into a thousand pieces. The forest was a raging sea: through the tree-tops which looked ready to crash in headlong ruin, the disaster maddened wind shrieked like a host of barbarians rushing into battle. Now the pelting rain rolled over their hillock and the whole valley sank into darkness. Heavy raindrops beat down on his back and up from below rose the smell of moist earth, wet bark and newly cut wood. High above, the lightning's glare lit up the bare crags to be followed by another crash and rumble. The entire mountain seemed ready to hurl itself down on him.

He felt as though he were being squeezed from all sides, squeezed so that he could hardly breathe, as though steel clamps were gripping his chest. The wet branches were slippery and treacherous but he moved with assurance and his sturdy arms did not fail him. If only he could shut out those voices wailing and crying through the woods.

As soon as he set foot safely back on the ground, he saw her crying, the poor thing, huddled pitifully under the branches of a great pine. He gathered up the cones and ducked in beside her.

They said nothing.

They just listened to the rain sheeting down outside their shelter.

A feeling of grief oppressed them.

The pine-needles wept.

They looked at the cones. The boy wanted to open one. With his fingernail he tried to push in under the scales and lift them, but it was still green and full of resin.

She said: 'Don't try, they're not ripe!'

They felt cold.

They stood huddled together.

She put her arm round him. He bit into the cone. The sap squirted out. But it was bitter, sour enough to turn the eyeballs over.

★

Crack!

Fire!

A smell of sulphur!

The sting of smoke in the nostrils.

The lightning had struck, and right beside them.

Something was burning.

They were too stunned to move, terror blazed in their eyes.

Then they leapt out from under the tree. A pine had caught fire at no great distance. A breathtaking crash of thunder followed instantly. The sky and the earth reeled. The flames were hungrily at work, even round about the tree. Like molten metal, resin ran in streams of fire down the trunk and out along the roots. Higher up, the twigs were crackling, and blazing branches swished down through the air like fiery brooms.

However, as luck would have it, the rain was now cascading out of the sky. Amidst hisses and fierce explosions, the whole tree became enshrouded in steam and smoke. Only down near the ground and close in to the trunk were there a couple of branches still burning.

The girl darted back, picked up the pine-cones and returned to where the boy stood near the fire.

Then they threw them one at a time into the heart of the glow. The cones turned yellow, then brown. The scales, softened by the heat, grew loose and opened out to reveal underneath the white and unripe kernels. Then the fire made the scales lift and curl up.

Sss! how the heat made them hiss, like so many snake's tongues!

The heart of the fire turned grey but the four cones went on glowing; red spheres, gradually devoured by the heat.

They grew transparent, like four crystal balls purified in the flames. Then they crumbled. At last they were only four black and smoking coals.

When the wind fanned them, there was still a brief glow, like a dying sigh. Then it was all over. Just charcoal and falling rain, black and grey.

The two of them were soaked to the skin. How good it felt . . . that cool, running water, as though it were washing them clean and lifting away the burden which so weighed them down.

Their breath came easier.

What fine, clean air!

The rain stopped.

They walked down the hill.

The mists were lifting. Overhead, the clouds raced by.

Then, little by little, a window opened to the sky and the tentative sun sent two bright and tremulous rays up into the valley.

Two souls, they seemed, going in search of the light.

Gion Deplazes

From *Bitter Lips*   Translated by John B. Avery

A really humourless sort he seemed to be, this Meltger. No sooner had they finished their afternoon tea than there he was, back at work again. His father, Toni, was the wiser man in that respect. He was more easy-going and enjoyed it if he could sometimes stop to have a chat; not about people, he never gossiped about people, but rather about gentian-roots or other natural curiosities, or about old customs and tales from the past. Like a bubbling spring, he was, ever ready to leap forth as soon as anyone was ready to listen. Meltger, on the other hand, thought of nothing but his work, roots, roots and more roots . . . and he slaved away stubbornly at his digging, as though doomed to dig till Judgement Day.

By now evening was coming and he'd been a good long while up on that rocky outcrop, hacking and digging away without a moment's rest. 'Poor Margrit,' she thought, 'if she one day finds herself tied to that fellow who can't think of anything but digging,' and her weariness increased as the shadows of the tall fir-trees grew longer.

At long last, he rose to his feet and started down towards them with a large bush in his hands. Or was it a root, after all? To judge from the leaves, it looked as though it should, or could be one. But it was not very likely. While still at some distance, his whole face broke into a laugh:

'Senza, what do you think of this? I've never seen one like it.'

'It looks almost like a tree,' said Senza admiringly, 'like one of those strange, foreign trees I once saw somewhere in a picture Bible . . . a palm, or a pine or something.' Her weariness was temporarily forgotten.

'But if we strip off some of those leaves, put a string round it and drag it along behind us, it'll look more like a huge snake.' It really was an enormous root. It had grown right under a slab of rock and was all of seven foot long and as thick as a man's ankle; not a skinny man either. A root like this was a rare find.

Meltger stood right in front of Senza with the root in his hands. He looked as though he'd been turned into stone, or as if he'd changed into the 'wild man of the woods' with his 'pine-tree' in his hand. Suddenly, he spoke. There was a tremble in his voice.

'Senza, I dug this root for you. You were kind enough to come digging roots with us,' and he held it out to her. But, at the same moment, he too came nearer, placed a hand on her shoulder and kissed her on the lips.

At first she was stunned, so taken aback that she didn't know what she was doing and could find nothing to say. All she could feel were his lips . . . and the

211

root, caught between them and squashing her breast so that she could hardly breathe.

Their lips parted, and the root fell to the ground between their feet, but they were both oblivious to it just then. 'Meltger, how bitter your lips are!'

It was more complete surprise than anything else that made Senza say these words. Meltger, too, was lost for words. He stared at the girl, gazing long and hard into the eyes in front of his and then looking up and over her head at the Vigliuz Glacier. Then he murmured:

'I think it must be fate.'

'And what about Margrit who gave you the carnation?' she interrupted. 'What would she say, if she had seen us?' She was gradually getting over her first surprise.

'Senza! Now whose lips are bitter?' he answered.

'Look, I didn't mean it like that,' she said, 'you mustn't be annoyed. But, your lips really do taste bitter . . . it's the roots. . .'

'I understand. I see you know what they're like. And that wasn't the first kiss you've ever given, or been given. . .'

Senza blushed to the roots of her hair.

'Not one of them was given willingly, not one!'

In the meantime, Meltger had picked up the root and was holding it out to her a second time. 'Do you want it? You can keep it if you like.'

'I'd love to, Meltger.' She took the huge root from him with obvious pleasure. Her eyes ran caressingly along its whole length.

Meltger risked returning to the attack: 'But I want something in return, and not something I have to steal.'

'A root, do you mean?' laughed Senza.

Seeing her flashing eyes, Meltger slipped his arm round the girl and pulled her close to him.

'No, a kiss, but I don't want to have to take it like a thief,' he whispered.

Then Senza raised her bright-red lips for the first, brief and willing kiss. Once more, though, she tasted the bitterness of the root-digger's lips and, while they crushed her own, her thoughts flew again to his answer: 'I think it must be fate.'

212

BIOGRAPHICAL NOTES

Etienne Barilier, born 1947, studied at Lausanne, taking his doctorate there with a thesis on Albert Camus. *Prague* (1979) is one of the eight novels he published in the 1970's. It takes the form of letters addressed to a young Swiss who is spending some time in Prague during the summer of 1968. Etienne Barilier has also written literary and musical criticism.

Peter Bichsel, born 1935 at Lucerne. His first collection of short stories appeared in 1964 and was translated into English by Michael Hamburger as *And Really Frau Blum Would Very Much Like to Meet the Milkman* (1968). A further collection of 'prose miniatures', *Stories for Children* appeared in English in 1971. *Jahreszeiten* (1967) is a prose narrative.

Cla Biert, born 1920 at Scuol, died 1981. He studied at Zürich and Geneva, was a schoolmaster until 1976, and president of the Society of Rhaeto-Romansh Authors 1967-71. He wrote mainly narrative prose, including collections of short stories. A volume of stories, *Only a Game*, appeared in English in 1963, translated by Alan Brown.

S. Corinna Bille, born 1912 at Lausanne, died 1981. She was married to Maurice Chappaz, and lived principally in Valais. She wrote mostly narrative prose, including the volumes of short stories *La fraise noire* (1968), *Juliette éternelle* (1971), *Cent petites histoires cruelles* (1973), *La demoiselle sauvage* (1974). *Les invités de Moscou*, a novel, appeared in 1977.

Silvio Blatter, born 1946 at Bremgarten, studied at Zürich. His first published volume was *Brände kommen unerwartet* (1968). Among his subsequent writings of narrative prose are the volume of short stories centring upon industrial production *Schaltfehler* (1972) and the novels *Mary Long* (1973) and *Zunehmendes Heimweh* (1978).

Giovanni Bonalumi, born 1920 at Muralto, studied at Freiburg, professor of Italian at Basle University. His novel *Gli ostaggi* appeared in 1954. 'Chestnut Trees' appeared in the collection *Pane e Coltrello* (1975).

Georges Borgeaud, born 1914 at Lausanne, educated at the Collège d'Aubonne and the Collège de Saint-Maurice, has lived a long time in Paris. His third novel *Le voyage à l'étranger* (1974) centres mainly upon the experiences of a young Swiss as tutor in a wealthy Belgian family during a period in the 1930's.

Nicolas Bouvier, born at Geneva, studied at Geneva. A professional photographer, he began publishing in 1963. He has written about Japan and the Far East. *Le poisson-scorpion* (1981) recounts experiences and impressions formed in Ceylon.

Rainer Brambach, born 1917 in Basle, died there in 1983, worked as stonemason and gardener. His first collection of poems *Tagwerk* appeared in 1959. *Wahrnehmungen* (1961) and *Für sechs Tassen Kaffee* (1972) are volumes of prose pieces. Other volumes of poetry include *Marco Polos Koffer* (jointly with Jürg Federspiel, 1968), *Ich fand keinen Namen dafür* (1969) and a volume of collected poems, *Wirf eine Münze auf* (1977).

Beat Brechbühl, born 1939 at Oppligen, Bern. He has published poetry and prose, and has brought out collections of verse since 1962 at regular intervals; *Traumhämmer. Gedichte aus zehn Jahren* (1977) is a selection from some of these volumes of verse.

Hermann Burger, born 1942 at Menziken. He studied at Zürich, and has been active as a member of staff at the Eidgenössische Technische Hochschule there and as a journalist. The volume of stories *Bork* appeared in 1970. *Diabelli* (three stories) was published in 1979. *Ein Mann aus Wörtern* (1983) is a collection of essays containing literary criticism and the recounting of personal experiences.

Erika Burkart, born 1922 at Aarau. Married to Ernst Halter. Her first collection of poetry, *Der dunkle Vogel*, appeared in 1953, and has been followed by a number of further volumes, including *Die Transparenz der Scherben* (1973), *Das Licht im Kahlschlag* (1977) and *Die Freiheit der Nacht* (1981). There have been two novels, *Moräne* (1970) and *Der Weg zu den Schafen* (1979). *Rufweite* (1975) is a collection of short prose pieces.

Theo Candinas, born 1929 at Surrein/Sumvitg. Studied at Fribourg, Paris and Perugia. Schoolmaster. Has been president of the Society of Rhaeto–Romansh Authors. Author of poetry and of short stories, he has been publishing since 1950.

Angelo Casè, born 1936 in Locarno. Schoolmaster. He began publishing in 1960, and is a lyrical poet and author of children's books.

Maurice Chappaz, born 1916 at Martigny. Married to S. Corinna Bille. He began publishing in 1944. *Portrait des Valaisans* (1965) is a collection of stories with an emphasis on local regional ways in Canton Valais. The volume *Un homme qui vivait couché sur un banc* (1966) contains an autobiographical account. *La haute route* (1974) evokes the high mountains early in the year. *A rire et à mourir* (1983) is a sequence of poetry and some prose.

Jacques Chessex, born 1934 at Payerne. Studied at Fribourg and Lausanne. Schoolmaster. He began publishing in 1957. The story *La confession du pasteur*

214

Bourg appeared in 1967. The author became more widely known after the publication of the novel *L'ogre* (1973). *Le séjour des morts* (1977) is a collection of 30 short stories. He is well known as a lyrical poet as well as a writer of prose.

Anne Cuneo, born 1936 in Paris, spent her early childhood in Milan, and after the death of her father in 1944 and the consequent break-up of her family, she came to Switzerland, where her mother was working, in 1947. *Le temps des loups blancs* (1982) is an autobiographical account of the author's adolescent years, spent mainly in Lausanne. After studying at Lausanne and Florence, she began to publish in 1967, becoming a writer of prose narrative, poetry and scripts for radio and television.

Flurin Darms, born 1918 at Flond, studied theology at Zürich and became a Protestant minister of religion. He has been known as a lyrical poet from 1960 onwards, and he has also written short stories. He has translated a range of literary works into Rhaeto-Romansh.

Gion Deplazes, born 1918 at Surrein/Sumvitg, studied at Zürich and Fribourg. Schoolmaster. Since 1951 he has been publishing novels and shorter prose work, verse and radio-plays. The tale *Levzas petras* was first published in 1960.

Walter Matthias Diggelmann, born 1927 at Zürich, died 1979. His first novel, *Mit F-51 überfällig*, appeared in 1954. The 1960's were a decade of great productivity in the author's story-writing, with such novels as *Die Hinterlassenschaft* (1965) and *Die Vergnügungsfahrt* (1969). The collection of short stories, *Reise durch Transdanubien*, appeared in 1974, and the novel *Der Reiche stirbt* in 1977.

Friedrich Dürrenmatt, born 1921 at Konolfingen, studied in Bern and Zürich, and began his career as a dramatist with *Es steht geschrieben* (1946) and as a prose-writer with *Die Stadt* (1946). Among his best known plays are *Der Besuch der alten Dame* (1956) and *Die Physiker* (1962). He has also written on dramatic theory. The volume *Stoffe I-III* (1981) contains an interweaving of autobiographical material with imaginative writing.

Ernst Eggimann, born 1936 in Bern. Studied in Bern. Schoolmaster at Langnau in the Emmental. Author of short stories, verse, drama and essays; he began publishing in 1963. The stories *Vor dem jüngsten Jahr* appeared in 1969; *Die Landschaft des Schülers* was published in 1973.

Albert Ehrismann, born 1908 at Zürich. From 1930 onwards, when he published his first volume of verse, he has continued to write lyrical poetry, frequently emphasizing public issues and a local Swiss environment. Among his later collections of poetry are *Gedichte des Pessimisten und Moralisten Albert Ehrismann* (1972), *Mich wundert, dass ich fröhlich bin* (1973), *Später Aonen später* (1975), *Inseln sind keine Luftgespinste* (1977) and *Schmelzwasser* (1978).

Remo Fasani, born 1922 at Mesocco. Studied at Zürich and Florence. Lecturer in

Italian literature at Neuchâtel University. He began publishing in 1945. Literary critic and poet. *Qui e ora* (1971) and *Senso dell'esilio/Crrme del vivere/Un altro segno* (1974) are collections of poetry.

Dieter Fringeli, born 1942 at Basle. Studied at Basle and Fribourg. Literary editor of the *Basler Zeitung*. His first volume of lyrical poetry appeared in 1965. He has written in particular about German-Swiss literature of the twentieth century in *Dichter im Abseits* (1974) and *Von Spitteler zu Muschg* (1975). *Mach keini Schprüch* (1981) is an anthology of Swiss-German dialect poetry of the twentieth century.

Max Frisch, born 1911 in Zürich. Studied in Zürich, firstly German literature, then architecture. He began publishing in the 1930's. His best known novels are perhaps *Stiller* (1954), *Homo Faber* (1957) and *Mein Name sei Gantenbein* (1964). Among his later prose writings are *Montauk* (1975) and *Der Mensch erscheint im Holozän* (1980). The drama *Santa Cruz* (1944) led the way to a succession of plays, such as *Andorra* (1961) and *Biografie* (1967). The volume *Tagebuch 1946-1949* appeared in 1950, *Tagebuch 1966-1971* in 1972.

Raffael Ganz, born 1923 in St. Margarethen. From 1945 he had long periods of residence abroad, including North Africa and America. *Orangentraum* (1961) and *Abend der Alligatoren* (1962) are collections of short stories. Further volumes of prose are *Im Zementgarten* (1971) and *Sandkorn im Wind* (1980).

Louis Gaulis, born in London 1932, died in Lebanon 1978. After studying at Geneva, he became a playwright and man of letters and of the theatre. In 1972 he began work for the International Committee of the Red Cross; in this capacity he visited Bangladesh, Vietnam and Cyprus. *Zig-Zag Street*, a novel about Cyprus and Cypriots, was written in 1976.

Vahé Godel, born in Geneva 1931 (his father was Swiss, his mother Armenian). Schoolmaster. His first collection of poetry appeared in 1954. *Poussières* and *Voies d'eau* appeared in 1977. He has also written essays and has translated from the Armenian.

Eugen Gomringer, born at Cachuela Esperanza, Brazil, in 1925. Studied at Bern. Professor of Aesthetics at the Staatliche Kunstakademie, Düsseldorf. His first verse *konstellationen* appeared in 1953. Verse and theoretical writing are included in *worte sind schatten* (1969). The author has edited the anthology *Konkrete Poesie* (Reclam, Stuttgart, 1972).

Kurt Guggenheim, born in Zürich, 1896. His first novel appeared in 1935. In addition to novels and short stories, he has written essays, plays and scripts for radio and film, and worked on translations. *Der Friede des Herzens* (1956) is a novel. *Nachher* (1974) is a collection of short stories.

Alexander Xaver Gwerder, born in Thalwil in 1923, committed suicide at Arles (France) in 1952. Offset-copyist. He published during his lifetime the collection of poems *Blauer Eisenhut* (1951). *Dämmerklee* (1955) is a posthumously published volume.

Georges Haldas, born in Geneva in 1918, with a Greek father and a Swiss mother. Studied at Geneva. He began publishing in 1942, and is author of lyrical poetry, of essays and of television scripts, and a translator. His first volume of notes, comments and aphorisms appeared as *L'Etat de Poésie. Carnets 1973* in 1977. A second volume, *L'Etat de Poésie. Carnets 1979*, was published in 1982.

Philippe Jaccottet, born in Moudon in 1925. Studied at Lausanne. He has written lyrical poetry (*Poésie 1946-1967*, 1971), prose fiction (the novel *L'Obscurité*, 1961), and essays and short stories (*Eléments d'un songe*, 1961). He has been a translator of work by Musil among others.

Roger-Louis Junod, born in Corgémont in 1923; his father has been described as a 'mechanic-inventor'. Studied at Neuchâtel. Schoolmaster and literary critic. *Les enfants du roi Marc* (1980) is his third novel. He has also written for radio. Manfred Gsteiger has described Junod as standing 'in a tradition of West-Swiss-Protestant introspection'.

Jürg Laederach, born in Basle in 1945. Studied at Zürich and Basle. His first publication *Einfall der Dämmerung* (1974), a collection of stories and sketches, was expanded in a subsequent edition as *Nach Einfall der Dämmerung* (1982). His second novel *Das ganze Leben* (1900) has been described (by Harald Hartung) as an 'extremely artificial book', but one that 'leaves behind a strong impression of authenticity'.

Monique Laederach, born in 1938 in Les Brenets, studied at Neuchâtel. Schoolmistress. From 1970 onwards she has been publishing, beginning with lyrical poetry; the collection *La partition* appeared in 1982. Her large-scale novel *La femme séparée* (1982) is an account of a young woman's life in the period following her decision to leave her husband.

Gertrud Leutenegger, born 1948 in Schwyz. Studied dramatic art in Zürich. Her first novel *Vorabend* appeared in 1975. The novel *Ninive* was published in 1977.

Hugo Loetscher, born in 1929 in Zürich. Studied politics, sociology and economic history. Has travelled extensively, in particular in South America. He has worked in journalism, including radio and television. *Wunderwelt* (1983) is 'a Brazilian encounter'. *Die Kranzflechterin* (1964), *Noah* (1967) and *Der Immune* (1975) are novels with an emphasis on social comment. The author examines the role of Switzerland in the world in *How Many Languages Does a Man Need?* (1982).

Kurt Marti, born 1921 in Bern. Studied theology at Bern and Basle. Protestant pastor in Bern. His poetry is often trenchant and direct, with frequent reference to topical themes (*Republikanische Gedichte* (1959), *leichenreden* (1969), *abendland*

(1980)); some of his verse uses dialect (*Rosa Loui* (1967), *Undereinisch* (1973)). His prose includes essays, sermons, sketches and short stories (for instance, *Wohnen zeitaus* (1965) and *Bürgerliche Geschichten* (1982)).

Plinio Martini, born 1923 at Cavergno, died 1979. Schoolmaster. He began writing poetry in 1951. His novel *Il fondo del sacco* (1970) centres mainly upon the protagonist's decision as a young man to emigrate from Switzerland to America.

Grytzko Mascioni, born 1936 at Brusio. Head of programmes of 'spettacolo RTSI'. Began publishing poetry in 1968. The collection *I passeri di Horkheimer* appeared in 1969.

Gerhard Meier, born 1917 at Niederbipp. Spent 33 years as worker, designer and technical director in a lamp factory. *Der andere Tag* (1974) and *Papierrosen* (1976) are collections of prose sketches. *Toteninsel* (1979) and *Borodino* (1982) are novels in which family memories and artistic-cultural associations are interwoven with impressions of the moment.

Herbert Meier, born 1928 in Solothurn. Studied at Basle, Vienna and Fribourg. Dramatist, novelist, poet and critic. The collection of poetry *Siebengestirn* appeared in 1956 and *Sequenzen* in 1969. *Ende September* (1959), *Verwandtschaften* (1963) and *Stiefelchen* (1970) are novels; *Anatomische Geschichten* (1973) is a volume of short stories. His plays include *Stauffer-Bern* (1975) and *Bräker* (1978).

Jacques Mercanton, born 1910 in Lausanne. Studied at Lausanne, Paris and Dresden. University professor, critic and author of novels and stories. *Celui qui doit venir* (1956) has a priest as central figure. *De peur que vienne l'oubli* (1962) is a novel of personal relations. *La Sibylle* (1967) is a collection of stories with an Italian setting.

E. Y. Meyer, born 1946 in Liestal, studied philosophy and German literature, qualified as a primary schoolteacher. *Ein Reisender in Sachen Umsturz* (1972) and *Eine entfernte Ähnlichkeit* (1975) are collections of short stories. *In Trubschachen* (1973) is a novel of a visit to the Emmental in midwinter. *Die Rückfahrt* (1977) describes the convalescence and re-orientation of someone recovering from a bad car accident.

Jean-Pierre Monnier, born in 1921 at Saint-Imier. Studied at Neuchâtel. Schoolmaster. He began publishing in 1953. *La clarté de la nuit* (1956) is a novel centring upon the activities and concerns of a Protestant pastor in a rural area. *L'arbre un jour* (1971) concerns a group of forestry workers in the Jura.

Adolf Muschg, born 1934 in Zürich. Studied at Zürich, held teaching posts in Japan, Göttingen and the United States, and since 1970 he has been professor at the Eidgenössische Technische Hochschule, Zürich. Among his novels are *Im Sommer des Hasen* (1965), *Gegenzauber* (1967) and *Albissers Grund* (1974).

Fremdkörper (1968), *Entfernte Bekannte* (1976) and *Leib und Leben* (1982) are collections of short stories. He is also a dramatist (for instance, *Die Aufgeregten von Goethe* (1971) and literary critic (*Gottfried Keller* (1977)).

Alberto Nessi, born 1940 in Mendrisio. Studied at Fribourg. Schoolmaster. He has written poetry, radio plays and children's books. The collection of poems *Ai margini* appeared in 1975.

Paul Nizon, born 1929 in Bern. Studied history of art. *Die gleitenden Plätze* (1959) is a volume of prose pieces. The prose narrative *Canto* appeared in 1963, *Im Hause enden die Geschichten* in 1971, *Untertauchen. Protokoll einer Reise* in 1972, and *Stolz* in 1975. *Diskurs in der Enge* (1970) examines problems of artists in their relationship with society, in the Swiss context.

Giorgio Orelli, born 1921 in Airolo. Studied at Fribourg, Schoolmaster. He began publishing poetry in 1944; the collection *Nel cerchio familiare* appeared in 1960. The collection of short stories *Un giorno della vita* was also published in 1960.

Giovanni Orelli, born 1928 in Bedretto. Studied in Zürich and Milan. Schoolmaster and educationalist. His principal literary works are the novels *L'anno della valanga* (1965) and *La festa del ringraziamento* (1972).

Andri Peer, born 1921 in Sent. Studied in Zürich and Paris. Schoolmaster in Winterthur, member of staff at Zürich University in Rhaeto-Romansh language and literature. He first published poetry in 1946; the collection *Sgrafits* (with Urs Oberlin) appeared in 1959, *Il chomp sulvadi* in 1975. *Erzählungen* (1968) and *Jener Nachmittag in Poschiavo* (1974) are volumes of short stories. Dramatist, writer of radio-plays and documentaries, literary critic.

Anne Perrier (pseudonym of Anne Hutter), born 1922 in Lausanne. Began with lyrical poetry in 1952 (*Selon la nuit*) and has published verse at regular intervals since then, for example *Le petit pré* (1960), *Feu les oiseaux* (1975) and *Le livre d'Ophélie* (1979). The collection *Poésie 1960-1979* appeared in 1982.

Alice Rivaz (pseudonym of Alice Golay), born 1901 in Rovray. Studied at Lausanne conservatoire. An author of novels and short stories, whose first prose work appeared in 1940. A relationship between mother and daughter forms the main theme of the novel *Jette ton pain* (1979). The collection of stories *De mémoire et d'oubli* appeared in 1973.

Werner Schmidli, born 1939 in Basle. Author of novels, short stories and radio and television plays. *Meinetwegen soll es doch schneien* (1967) and *Das Schattenhaus* (1968) are novels of closely observed family life in an urban setting. *Fundplätze* (1974) and *Ganz gewöhnliche Tage* (1981) are also novels. *Der Junge und die toten Fische* (1966) and *Der alte Mann, das Bier, die Uhr* (1968) are collections of short stories.

Hansjörg Schneider, born 1938 in Aarau. Studied at Basle. He worked for a time as an assistant director and as an actor in the Basle theatres. Has had extensive periods abroad, e.g. in Paris, the United States and Mexico. He has written stage-plays (e.g. *Sennentuntschi* (1972)) and plays for radio and television. His novel *Lieber Leo* appeared in 1980.

Tristan Solier (pseudonym of Paul-Albert Cuttat), born 1918 in Porrentruy. Studied at Bern, Basle, Lausanne and Geneva. He published his first collection of poems, *Portulans baroques*, in 1968. He has been concerned with the publication of writings by those who, like himself, identified themselves with the culture of the Bernese Jura.

Hendri Spescha, born 1928 in Trun. Studied at Fribourg and Zürich. Schoolmaster in Domat-Ems. Secretary of the Ligia Romontscha (Rhaeto-Romansh League) in Chur. Editor of periodicals for young people. Contributor to radio and television. Author of prose narrative and of verse, he began publishing in 1953.

Jörg Steiner, born 1930 in Biel. Schoolmaster. *Der schwarze Kasten* (1965) and *Als es noch Grenzen gab* (1976) are collections of verse. *Strafarbeit* (1962), *Ein Messer für den ehrlichen Finder* (1966) and *Das Netz zerreissen* (1982) are novels. The collection of short stories *Auf dem Berge Sinai sitzt der Schneider Kikriki* appeared in 1969.

Urs-Martin Strub, born 1910 in Olten. Studied medicine at seven universities. Was medical superintendent at the psychiatric hospital Kilchberg, 1947-69. His first collection of verse appeared in 1930. The sequence *Wandelsterne* was published in 1955.

Pierre-Alain Tâche, born 1940 in Lausanne. Studied law at Lausanne. Professional lawyer. Began publishing poetry in 1962. The volume *La traversée* appeared in 1974, *L'élève du matin* in 1978.

Raymond Tschumi, born 1924 in Saint-Imier. Studied at Geneva. Taught in Great Britain and the United States. On the staff of the Economic High School, Sankt Gallen. Has published literary criticism and essays, in English as well as French (e.g. *A Philosophy of Literature*, London, 1961). A first collection of poetry appeared in 1950; *Grange du veilleur* was published in 1981.

Walter Vogt, born 1927 in Zürich. Studied medicine; psychiatrist. *Husten* (1965) and *Melancholie* (1967) are collections of stories. Novels centring upon medical themes are *Wüthrich (1966)* and *Der Wiesbadener Kongress* (1972).

Alexandre Voisard, born 1930 in Porrentruy. Bookseller. Began publishing poetry in 1954. The collection *Liberté à l'aube* appeared in 1967; the edition of 1978 is augmented by further poems. He has identified himself with the separatist movement in the Bernese Jura.

Silja Walter, born 1919 in Rickenbach. In 1948 she became Sr. Maria Hedwig O.S.B. Began publishing poetry in 1944; the volume *Gesammelte Gedichte* appeared in 1972. Has also written narrative prose (e.g. *Der Fisch und Bar Abbas*, 1967, and *Abteien aus Glas*, 1972) and plays (e.g. *Der Turm der Salome. Monodrama*, 1976).

Urs Widmer, born 1938 in Basle. Studied in Basle and Montpellier. Publisher's reader, literary critic, author. Among his prose works are the tale *Die Amsel im Regen im Garten* (1971), the novel *Die Forschungsreise* (1974), and the collection of stories and other short pieces *Vom Fenster meines Hauses aus* (1977). He is a writer of radio-plays.

Heinrich Wiesner, born 1925 in Zeglingen. Schoolmaster. He began publishing in 1951. *Lakonische Zeilen* (1965) and *Lapidare Geschichten* (1967) are volumes of largely aphoristic prose. *Schauplätze* (1969) contains autobiographical material.

Gertrud Wilker, born 1924 in Solothurn. Studied German literature, psychology and history of art. She began publishing in 1957. Her novels include *Elegie auf die Zukunft* (1966), re-issued as *Wolfsschatten* in 1980, *Jota* (1973) and *Nachleben* (1980).

Werner Zemp, born 1906 in Zürich, died 1959. Studied in Zürich and Munich, taking his doctorate in Zürich with a thesis on Mörike. He devoted his literary activity to lyrical poetry and criticism. A posthumous collection of his writings is the volume *Das lyrische Werk. Aufsätze. Briefe*, ed. Verena Haefeli, 1967.

SELECT BIBLIOGRAPHY

Egon Ammann and Eugen Faes (eds.), *Literatur aus der Schweiz. Texte und Materialien*, Suhrkamp Verlag, Zürich, 1978.

Dieter Bachmann (ed.), *Fortschreiben. 98 Autoren der deutschen Schweiz*, Artemis Verlag, Zürich and Munich, 1978.

Reto R. Bezzola (ed.), *The Curly-Horned Cow. Anthology of Swiss-Romansh Literature*, Peter Owen, London, 1971.

Nicolas Bouvier and others (eds.), *Almanach du Groupe d'Olten*, L'Age d'Homme, Lausanne, 1973.

Jeanlouis Cornuz (ed.), *Texte/Les Romands. Prosa junger Autoren der Westschweiz*, Benziger Verlag, Einsiedeln, Zürich and Cologne, 1965.

Dieter Fringeli (ed.), *Gut zum Druck. Literatur der deutschen Schweiz seit 1964*, Artemis Verlag, Zürich and Munich, 1972.

Dieter Fringeli (ed.), *Mach keini Schprüch. Mundart-Lyrik des 20. Jahrhunderts*, Ammann Verlag, Zürich, 1981.

Frank Geerk (ed.), *Lyrik aus der Schweiz*, Benziger Verlag, Zürich and Cologne, 1974.

D. B. Gregor, *Romontsch Language and Literature. The Sursilvan Raeto-Romance of Switzerland*, The Oleander Press, Cambridge, 1982.

Bernd Jentsch (ed.), *Schweizer Lyrik des zwanzigsten Jahrhunderts. Gedichte aus 4 Sprachregionen*, Buchclub Ex Libris, Zürich, 1979 (Benziger Verlag, Zürich and Cologne, 1977).

Jochen Jung (ed.), *Ich hab im Traum die SCHWEIZ gesehn. 35 Schriftsteller aus der Schweiz schreiben über ihr Land*, Residenz Verlag, Salzburg and Vienna, 1980.

Hugo Leber (ed.), *Texte. Prosa junger Schweizer Autoren*, Benziger Verlag, Einsiedeln, Zürich and Cologne, 1964.

Bruno Mariacher, Friedrich Witz and others (eds.), *Bestand und Versuch. Schweizer Schrifttum der Gegenwart. Lettres suisses d'aujourd'hui. Lettere elvetiche d'oggi. Vuschs svizras da nos temp*, Artemis Verlag, Zürich and Stuttgart, 1964.

Alex Natan (ed.), *Swiss Men of Letters. Twelve Literary Essays*, Oswald Wolff, London, 1970.

'Quarta Lingua' (ed.), *Rumantscheia. Eine Anthologie rätoromanischer Schriftsteller der Gegenwart*, Artemis Verlag, Zürich and Munich, 1979.

Max A. Schwendimann, *Gegenwartsdichtung der Westschweiz, Zwölf Autorenporträts mit Textproben*. Benteli Verlag, Bern, 1972.

Zürcher Seminar für Literaturkritik mit Werner Weber (eds.), *Belege. Gedichte aus der deutschsprachigen Schweiz seit 1900*, Artemis Verlag, Zürich and Munich, 1978.

Werner Bucher and Georges Ammann (eds.), *Schweizer Schriftsteller im Gespräch*, 2 vols., Reinhardt Verlag, Basle, 1970 and 1971.

Dieter Fringeli, *Von Spitteler zu Muschg. Literatur der deutschen Schweiz seit 1900*, Reinhardt Verlag, Basle, 1975.

Manfred Gsteiger (ed.), *Die zeitgenössischen Literaturen der Schweiz* (Kindlers Literaturgeschichte der Gegenwart. Autoren, Werke, Themen, Tendenzen seit 1945), Kindler Verlag, Zürich and Munich, 1974.

Hugo Loetscher, *How Many Languages Does Man Need?*, The Graduate School and University Center, City University of New York, New York, 1982.

Kurt Marti, *Die Schweiz und ihre Schriftsteller – die Schriftsteller und ihre Schweiz*, EVZ – Verlag, Zürich, 1966.

Karl Schmid, *Unbehagen im Kleinstaat*, Artemis Verlag, Zürich and Munich, 1963.

Schweizerischer Schriftsteller-Verband (Société des écrivains, Società degli scrittori, Uniun svizra da scriptuors) (ed.), *Schweiz (Suisse, Svizzera, Svizra)* (*Schriftsteller der Gegenwart, Ecrivains d'aujourd'hui, Scrittori d'oggi, Scripturs da nos dis*), Buchverlag Verbandsdruckerei, Bern, 1978.

ACKNOWLEDGMENTS

Particular thanks are due to authors and publishers who kindly granted permission to reproduce in translation extracts from their works:

Etienne Barilier, from *Prague*, © 1979, Editions l'Age d'Homme, Lausanne.

Peter Bichsel, 'The earth is round', from *Kindergeschichten*, © 1969, Luchterhand Verlag, Neuwied and Berlin (translated by Michael Hamburger, in *Stories for Children*, © 1971, Calder and Boyars, London).

Cla Biert, 'Before the fruit is ripe', from *Amuras*, © 1956, Chasa Paterna, Lavin.

S. Corinna Bille, 'Café des voyageurs', from *La fraise noire*, © 1968, La guilde du livre, Lausanne.

Silvio Blatter, 'The stranger' and 'A family story', from *Brände kommen unerwartet*, © 1970, Die Regenbogen-Reihe, Zürich.

Giovanni Bonalumi, from 'Chestnut Trees', in *Pane e Coltello*, ©, 1975, Armando Dadò, Locarno.

Georges Borgeaud, from *Le voyage à l'étranger*, © 1970, Bertil Galland, Vevey.

Nicolas Bouvier, 'A depression from the Kuriles', from *Ecriture 12*, © 1976, Bertil Galland, Vevey.

Rainer Brambach, 'Weariness', 'Caution is indicated', from *Tagwerk*, © 1959, Fretz & Wasmuth, Zürich; 'Men alone in the world', from *Ich fand keinen Namen dafür*, © 1969, Diogenes Verlag, Zürich.

Beat Brechbühl, 'Simple mirror' and 'Being ill', from *Traumhämmer. Gedichte aus zehn Jahren*, © 1977, Benziger Verlag, Cologne and Zürich.

Hermann Burger, 'The happiest day of your life', from *Bork. Prosastücke*, © 1970, Artemis Verlag, Zürich and Stuttgart.

Erika Burkart, 'Family ballad', from *Die Transparenz der Scherben*, © 1973, Benziger Verlag, Cologne and Zürich (This translation first appeared in *International Poetry Review*, vol. II, 1976, Greensboro, USA).

Theo Candinas, 'Vision of childhood' and 'Cold' (translated by H. M. Barnes, in *The Curly-Horned Cow. An Anthology of Swiss-Romansh Literature*, ed. Reto R. Bezzola, © 1971, Peter Owen, London).

Angelo Casè, 'The same movement', from *Le precarie certezze*, © 1976, Edizioni Cenobio, Varese-Lugano.

Maurice Chappaz, 'The obscure saints. Villages sold for an apple, bought back by a heart', from *Portraits des Valaisans*, © 1965, Le livre du mois, Lausanne.

Jacques Chessex, 'Dylan Thomas's Mirror', from *Le séjour des morts. Nouvelles*, © 1977, Editions Grasset & Fasquelle, Paris.

Anne Cuneo, from *Le temps des loups blancs*, © 1982, Bertil Galland, Vevey.

Flurin Darms, 'Peak' (translated by W. W. Kibler, in *The Curly-Horned Cow. An Anthology of Swiss-Romansh Literature*, ed. Reto R. Bezzola, © 1971, Peter Owen, London); 'All I have is my mother-tongue' (translated by John B. Avery).

Gion Deplazes, from *Levzas Petras*, © 1960, Romania (translated by John B. Avery).

Walter Matthias Diggelmann, 'The self-induced accident', from *Reise durch Transdanubien*, © 1974, Benziger Verlag, Cologne and Zürich.

Friedrich Dürrenmatt, from *Stoffe I-III*, © 1981, Diogenes Verlag, Zürich.

Ernst Eggimann, 'Before the last year', from *Vor dem jüngsten Jahr. Erzählungen*, © 1969, Verlag der Arche, Zürich.

Albert Ehrismann, 'Earth's Children', 'But the earth, the earth, the earth, the earth. . .', from *Mich wundert, dass ich fröhlich bin*, © 1973, Werner Classen Verlag, Zürich.

Remo Fasani, 'Ode', © 1974, from *Senso dell'esilio. Orme del vivere. Un altro segno*, Edizioni Pantarei, Lugano. 'Giovanni Giacometti', © 1971, from *Qui e ora*, Edizioni Pantarei, Lugano.

Dieter Fringeli, 'Slight change' and 'Fear', from *Zwischen den Orten*, © 1965, Verlag Jeger-Moll, Breitenbach; 'Morning post 11.7.74', from *Durchaus*, © 1975, Eremiten-Presse, Düsseldorf.

Max Frisch, 'Sketch', from *Tagebuch 1966-1971*, © 1976, Suhrkamp Verlag, Frankfurt (translated by Geoffrey Skelton, in *Sketchbook 1966-1971*, © Harcourt Brace Yovanovich, New York).

Raffael Ganz, 'If you don't shout, you'll leave empty-handed', from *Sandkorn im Wind. Erzählungen*, © 1980, Orell Füssli Verlag, Zürich (translated by Don S. Stephens in *Dimension*, vol. X, © 1977, Austin, Texas).

Louis Gaulis, from *Zig-Zag Street*, © 1979, Editions Fontainemore/Journal de Genève, Geneva.

Vahé Godel, 'I pass through a forest', 'I pass over a river', 'Where are you?', 'As you go up the river', from *Ecriture 19*, © 1982, Lausanne.

Eugen Gomringer, 'cars and cars', 'americans', 'butterfly' 'ireland', 'roads 68' (written originally in English), from *worte sind schatten, die konstellationen 1951-1968*, © 1969, Rowohlt Verlag, Reinbek.

Kurt Guggenheim, 'Switzerland, province?' from *Fortschreiben*, ed. Dieter Bachmann, © 1977, Artemis Verlag, Zürich and Munich.

Alexander Xaver Gwerder, 'Lines for Rheila', from *Dämmerklee. Nachgelassene Gedichte*, © 1955, Verlag der Arche, Zürich.

Georges Haldas, from *L'état de poésie. Carnets 1979*, © 1981, Editions L'Age d'Homme, Lausanne.

Philippe Jaccottet, 'The night is a great city', 'Interior' and 'The office of the poet' and 'Letter of June the 26th.', from *Poésie 1946-67*, © 1971, Editions Gallimard, Paris.

Roger-Louis Junod, from *Les enfants du roi Marc*, © 1980, Editions Bertil Galland, Vevey.

Jürg Laederach, 'I and crime', from *Nach Einfall der Dämmerung*, © 1982, Suhrkamp Verlag, Frankfurt.

Monique Laederach, from *La femme séparée*, © 1982, Editions de l'Aire, Lausanne.

Gertrud Leutenegger, from *Ninive*, © 1977, Suhrkamp Verlag, Frankfurt.

Hugo Loetscher, from *How many languages does a man need?* (ed. Tamara S. Evans, © 1982, City University of New York, New York (passage translated by Peter Spycher)).

Kurt Marti, 'the lord our god' and 'she did not make much of a stir', from *leichenreden*, © 1969, Luchterhand Verlag, Neuwied and Berlin.

Plinio Martini, from *Delle streghe e d'altro*, © 1979, Armando Dadò Editore, Locarno.

Grytzko Mascioni, 'The Spring of Life' and 'Whitsun in Lugano' from *I passeri di Horkheimer*, © 1978, Libreria Editrice Cavour, Milan.

Gerhard Meier, 'As if they were asked to judge', 'At the time of the gentle lights' and 'It is raining in my village', from *Papierrosen. Gesammelte Prosaskizzen*, © 1976, Zytglogge Verlag, Gümligen (Bern).

Herbert Meier, 'The time of woods that have turned', 'Paths one afternoon', 'Eyes', from *Sequenzen*, © 1969, Benziger Verlag, Zürich (translated by Ian Hilton).

Jacques Mercanton, 'Except his face', from *Oeuvres complètes – Tome 1. Récits et Nouvelles*, © 1980, Editions de l'Aire, Lausanne.

E. Y. Meyer, 'Island story', from *Ein Reisender in Sachen Umsturz*, © 1972, Suhrkamp Verlag, Frankfurt.

Jean-Pierre Monnier, from *La clarté de la nuit*, © 1956, Le livre du mois, Lausanne.

Adolf Muschg, 'Distant acquaintances', from *Entfernte Bekannte. Erzählungen*, © 1976, Suhrkamp Verlag, Frankfurt.

Alberto Nessi, 'It is a fortune', from *Ai margini*, © 1975, Collana di Lugano, Lugano.

Paul Nizon, from *Diskurs in der Enge*, © 1973, Benzig er Verlag, Zürich and Cologne.

Giorgio Orelli, 'For a friend about to be married' and 'In the family circle', from *Nel cerchio familiare*, © 1960, Scheiwiller, Milan (translated by Lynne Lawner. This translation first appeared in *Chelsea Eleven*, New York, 1962), 'March strophe', 'Second TV program (or conflicting program)' and 'Sinopie', from *Sinopie*, © 1977, Mondadori, Milan (translated by LV. This translation first appeared in *Italian Poetry Today: Currents and Trends*, ed. Ruth Feldmann and Brian Swann, © 1979, New River Press, St. Paul, Minnesota.)

Giovanni Orelli, from *L'anno della valanga*, in *La festa del ringraziamento. L'anno della valanga*, © 1972, Arnoldo Mondadori Editore, Milan.

Andri Peer, 'The Föhn-wind' and 'On looking at paintings by Paul Klee', from *Il chomp sulvadi*, © 1975, Andri Peer, Winterthur (translated by John B. Avery).

Anne Perrier, 'This last song', 'Somewhere else perhaps', 'The flowers' and 'Cheerless flutes', from *Le livre d'Ophélie*, © 1979, Editions Payot, Lausanne.

Alice Rivaz, 'The pushchair', from *De Mémoire et d'Oubli. Récits*, © 1973, L'Aire Coopérative Rencontre, Lausanne.

Werner Schmidli, 'I know how things have to look in a house', from *Junge Schweizer erzählen. Kurzgeschichten junger Schweizer Autoren*, © 1971, Schweizer Verlagshaus, Zürich.

Hansjörg Schneider, from *Lieber Leo*, © 1980, Benziger Verlag, Zürich and Cologne.

Tristan Solier (pseudonym of Paul-Albert Cuttat), 'Origin', 'Trinity' and 'Day of Ashes', from *Portulans baroques*, © 1968, Edition des Malvoisins, Porrentruy.

Hendri Spescha, 'Two sonnets' (translated by H. M. Barnes, in *The Curly-Horned Cow. An Anthology of Swiss-Romansh Literature*, ed. Reto R. Bezzola, © 1971, Peter Owen, London.)

Jörg Steiner, 'At school the children hear a story. . .', from *Der schwarze Kasten. Spielregeln*, © 1965, Walter Verlag, Olten and Freiburg i. Br.; 'When there were still frontiers' and 'Report of a man who was not deported', from *Als es noch Steine gab*, © 1976, Suhrkamp Verlag, Frankfurt.

Urs-Martin Strub, 'Neptune', from *Die Wandelsterne. Prosadichtungen*, © 1955, Kiepenheuer & Witsch Verlag, Cologne and Berlin.